BRITISH SUPERLINERS OF THE SIXTIES

An unusual view of the Meridian Room of *Canberra*
taken from beneath the spiral stairs. (Stewart Bale, courtesy
of P & O Group)

PHILIP S DAWSON

BRITISH SUPERLINERS OF THE SIXTIES

A Design Appreciation of the
Oriana, Canberra and QE2

Foreword by Sir Hugh Casson

CONWAY
MARITIME PRESS

To Mary M Dawson in memoriam

© Philip S Dawson 1990

First published in Great Britain 1990 by
Conway Maritime Press Ltd,
24 Bride Lane, Fleet Street,
London EC4Y 8DR

British Library Cataloguing in Publication Data
Dawson, Philip S.
  British Superliners of the Sixties.
  1. Great Britain. Passenger Transport. Shipping. Liners,
  history
  I. Title
  387.2'43

ISBN 0 85177 542 X

Designed by Tony Hart
Typeset by Inforum Typesetting, Portsmouth
Printed and bound in Great Britain by Butler & Tanner Ltd, Frome

CONTENTS

		Foreword by Sir Hugh Casson	vi
		Introduction	1
Chapter	I	The 20/20 Ship	4
	II	The Design Process	14
	III	A Third Queen	23
	IV	Why and Wherefore Machinery Aft?	40
	V	Simple Forms, Clean Surfaces, Clear Colours	61
	VI	From Grand Hotel to Modern Resort	79
	VII	A Dual-Role Flagship	89
	VIII	The Most Exciting Thing Since Apollo 1	112
	IX	In Their Wake	130
Appendix	A	Technical Specifications of Principal Ships	144
	B	Register of Other Ships	146
	C	Canberra Route Analysis	149
		Acknowledgements	150
		Bibliography	151
		Index	153

FOREWORD

THIS is a fascinating book, analytical, authoritative and affectionate. The author knows his subject from stem to stern and has been in love with liners all his life. His heroines this time are three great passenger ships, *Oriana*, *Canberra* and *Queen Elizabeth 2*, each a showcase of advanced ideas in naval architecture and interior design. All of them were designed and built in the UK around thirty years ago. Their influence has been worldwide. Two fo them are still successfully at work.

What was the secret of this success? Nothing new about the answer to that one at least, for the recipe and the process is always the same. A well researched brief, flexible and far-sighted enough to invite alternative solutions. A design concept (or concepts) devised to meet the programme. The testing and balancing of the concepts against each other and the development of the preferred solution on the drawing board or in the laboratory. The last and quickest of all, the execution of the final choice. It may take about five years to build a ship but probably even longer to decide what sort of ship to build, and what makes this problem even harder is the quickening pace of change in technology and passenger travel, habits to which response must be constantly and immediately made while designing and building are in progress.

It is throughout a gripping story and, like all tales of bold human achievement, a moving one. What makes it different from the normal run of huge dams, adventurous bridges or even space travel is the fact that the finished product has somehow been transformed not only into a work of art, fashioned, it would seem, by one creative mind, but endowed also in some way with its own recognisable personality. It is this quality that makes every ship unique. Not many people feel that way about jumbo jets. Most of us seem to treat trains like litter bins and cars like old shoes. Ships always seem to inspire respect and to attract affection and loyalty. Their stately indifference to our admiration, their inbuilt mystery, the slow rhythm of their arrival or departure, the way they hum comfortably to themselves as you walk past them on the dockside are all qualities that help to make every ship not just a vehicle but more like a magic, movable island waiting each time to be explored anew.

Philip Dawson is an experienced traveller in the shipping world but this story has obviously been for him a voyage of discovery that he has much enjoyed and he succeeds in sharing his enjoyment with us, and I am sure there will be many readers of his book for many years to come.

HUGH CASSON
London, May 1989

INTRODUCTION

When the Peninsular & Oriental Steam Navigation Company's (P & O) *Canberra* made her debut in 1961 she was widely proclaimed as 'the ship which shapes the future'. She was clearly a decade ahead of her time in such things as her machinery located aft, her graceful exterior profile, crisp modern interior design, and numerous other technical and engineering innovations. Her entry into service had been preceded barely six months earlier by another outstanding British liner, *Oriana*. Although less publicised at the time, the design of the earlier Orient Line ship is in its own right no less advanced and innovative. However, many of *Oriana*'s features were of a generally more technical significance, having to do with her lightweight construction. In fulfilment of their creators' vision, both *Oriana* and *Canberra* have effectively shaped the way in which modern passenger ships are designed and built.

Both ships have had a powerful influence in shaping Cunard's *Queen Elizabeth 2*, the third British superliner of the decade. Structurally, she bears a considerable measure of *Oriana*'s design approach, while she has strong architectural links with *Canberra*. The new Cunard flagship emerged eight years later with her own innovations, mainly in the realm of passenger facilities, interior layout and design. She was, for instance, one of the first ships to have proper conference facilities and to make specific provision for professional entertainment. Her greatest influence lies in the overall sense of modern luxury and elegance which has set the pace for much of the cruise industry.

All three superliners owe a great deal of their individuality to circumstances of the era in which they were planned and built. The sentiment behind 'the ship which shapes the future' ran much deeper than mere publicity hype, for if passenger shipping was to survive in the future then it had to change as a matter of survival. It echoed P & O's firm conviction that the time had come to take the lead in moving forward, out of the twilight of traditional line passages, into a dawning new era of leisure and holiday travel by sea.

At the same time Cunard was grappling with the realities of replacing their famed Queens in the face of an uncertain future on the North Atlantic run. The planning process, which began as early as 1951, evolved through various stages from Q3, as a near-direct replacement, to the altogether new Q4, eventually launched as *Queen Elizabeth 2*.

These ships had the good fortune to be created at a time of great worldwide design awareness. The Modern Movement of twentieth century architecture was then at one of its high points. Names like Frank Lloyd Wright, Mies Van der Rohe, Walter Gropius and Alvar Aalto were widely known to the general public.

Products of superb industrial design from sources such as Germany's Braun and Italy's Olivetti had made their way into the ordinary home and workplace. To whatever degree such design awareness may have influenced *Oriana*, *Canberra* and *Queen Elizabeth 2*, it also served to make the whole world aware of these outstanding ships.

They were lucky enough also to be built before the advent of present day marketing strategies, which tend to impose a bland Las Vegas or International style stereotype on the entire travel industry. It is unlikely that later concerns for company and fleet 'images' would embrace the degree of freedom accorded the designers of *Oriana*, *Canberra* and *Queen Elizabeth 2*.

These ships were, however, not necessarily the first to introduce many of the design innovations for which they are best known. For instance, the accolade 'first modern passenger ship with engines aft' rightfully belongs to the little French ferry *El Djezair*, a ship which predates *Canberra* by nearly a decade. Similarly, ships of the 1930s such as *Orion* and *Orcades* were credited with introducing outstanding modern shipboard interior design, rendered by professional architects.

The first manifestation of a new idea does not always inspire others to adopt and refine it, no matter how good it is. New ideas tend to be born into conceptual purity, either as experiments or in response to some particular need. Often it is a later contrivance of the original brainchild, objectively compromised and rationalised at the hands of others than its inventor, which becomes the ultimate success.

Canberra's designers realised the potential of *El Djezair*'s machinery layout in overcoming the problem of both greater speed and passenger capacity, using a far more refined hull form. Ultimately, it was the overall impression of *Canberra*'s profile and layout which left a lasting impression of a successful design with engines aft, while *El Djezair* has been all but forgotten.

Queen Elizabeth 2's architectural design achieved worldwide acclaim, not only on its own merit, but also because of a rare flurry of interest in passenger ship interior design on the part of the British architectural profession. They were concerned that the new Cunarder should demonstrate a significantly better standard of architectural and industrial design than her predecessors had done. The ambassadorial status of such a ship demanded that she compete with design standards of ships from other industrialised nations such as the United States, Italy and Scandinavia.

Others were soon to follow in the wake of *Canberra*'s success. Her influence was quite apparent in the profiles of several magnificent Italian liners built in the 1960s. More than twenty years later, many of the same basic design features are clearly recognisable in, for instance, *Royal Princess* and *Star Princess*. These and a number of their contemporaries are distinctly 'Canberrian' in character, with nested lifeboats, large open deck spaces topsides and in various aspects of their internal layout. Elements of her design are even to be found in the plans of ships still being dreamed about for the future.

Queen Elizabeth 2 soon became the prototype of the interior layout of a number of Scandinavian-built cruise ships in the early 1970s. The greatest likeness is in the arrangement of public rooms on the Royal Viking Line ships and in *Stella Solaris*, converted for Sun Line from the French liner *Cambodge*. Other features such as multilevel floors in lounges and perimeter circulation amongst public rooms have since become standard on today's cruise ships and ferries.

Since entering service, *Oriana*, *Canberra* and *Queen Elizabeth 2* have all experienced their share of troubles. There were mechanical failures and other mishaps which threatened public confidence in each ship. They were later hard pressed by the oil crises of the 1970s, which courted the possibility of their withdrawal from service altogether. They not only survived, but managed to become increasingly successful and popular.

In a historical sense, perhaps the greatest shortcoming of *Oriana* and *Canberra* was that neither served on the North Atlantic, and thus never got the recognition they deserved. It seems that this is the only ocean capable of according true greatness to its ships. It is *Queen Elizabeth 2* which is by far the best known of these ships.

This book does not endeavour to retell the history of shipping, the companies which own these liners or their builders, other than to establish the background of the ships themselves. This has all been adequately done elsewhere, as can be seen from the bibliography. Instead, this is a discussion of the three superliners in the context of those ships, and shoreside works of architecture and engineering which have influenced them. It attempts also to give some insight into the background of the people whose creativity shaped their structural and architectural design.

Apart from what was actually built, there were the ideas which, for one reason or another, were never realised. For instance, there were the futuristic funnels and a glass dome over the swimming pool which regrettably never materialised on *Canberra*. Likewise in *Queen Elizabeth 2*'s case, there were ideas which got no further than the drawing boards, but which deserve at least to be mentioned.

Now is the time to document these outstanding ships before they are long gone and forgotten. Two of them are still in service and the third remains with us, preserved as a static structure in Japan. Although they can be seen and appreciated first hand, the necessities of their service lives and commercial success have over the years changed their character. Consequently some of the conceptual purity of their original design has now been lost. It is always a matter of debate as to which of these changes have been for the better and which for the worse. Since many of these alterations were not made by the original designers, they are generally outside the scope of this book, which describes the superliners and their impact as built.

Chapter I

THE 20/20 SHIP

W HEN P & O's Chairman, Sir William Currie, addressed the spring meeting of the Royal Institution of Naval Architects in 1955, probably neither he nor anyone else realised that his two latest passenger liners would be the last of their type ever built. *Arcadia* and *Iberia*, which had been completed within the preceding year, were British tropical liners of essentially traditional design. Likewise Orient Line's latest *Oronsay* and *Orsova* were to be that company's final examples of this type of ship. Within two years Cunard's *Sylvania* was also to be the last of a long line of intermediate North Atlantic liners. The changing future of passenger shipping was then of great concern, though the ships themselves which would help bring about such change were yet to be visualised.

Sir William's subject on this occasion was, *Liners of the Past, Present and Future on Service East of Suez*. He dealt specifically with development in the preceding half century, using P & O's 1903 *Marmora* and 1954 *Arcadia* as examples from the past and present, before speculating on the twenty or so years to follow. His portrayal of this period of his own company's development gives an insight into the general background of shipping history against which such change would ultimately occur:

Fundamentally, the progress made in shipping over the past half-century is comparatively small in relation to many other industrial developments. The vast achievements and accomplishments of the aircraft industry; scientific research into nuclear physics; electronics and other modern sciences show great inroads into new fields. However, the task of the shipowner and shipbuilder are tackled with no less enthusiasm, although the basic requirements and conditions have not changed in essentials over the years. Seaworthiness, under which heading safety is covered, efficient and economic propulsion and passenger and crew comfort have ever been the primary requirements of a successful ship, the standards in each being steadily improved.

In each department of the ship, changes have been gradual rather than revolutionary. In the first stage of a new design, considerable knowledge obtained from the exhaustive towing tank and water tunnel experiments, together with gleanings from the aerodynamicist's harvest, have enabled more accurate predictions of ehp [effective horsepower] for required speed; hull form for maximum efficiency; and design of propeller for maximum thrust. To technical men engine efficiency and reliability owe everything. The design of the ship's structure itself shows a more knowledgeable approach to the problem by using the properties of plates and sections to best advantage. Modern trends in navigation have accounted for possibly the greatest advance in the mercantile field. As the principal earnings of a liner are obtained from the travelling public, it is axiomatic that there should be continuous improvements in the standard of accommodation and service and in amenities such as swimming baths, cinemas, airconditioning and the fitting of stabilisers.

The development of shipping has proved continuous in all parts of the complex structure.

Looking beyond the period to which Sir William had restricted his address, the history of shipping is a continuous evolutionary process. Progressing at a faster pace in some ages than in others, it has generally built on precedent, derived originally from the most basic principles of seaworthiness learned by the first men who assembled primitive rafts and barges. The fundamentals of more advanced shipbuilding concepts began to be applied as things became more sophisticated. This was done at first by trial and error, until the knowledge gained was organised into the precise technical and scientific disciplines of naval architecture and hydrodynamics, as they are known today. Greater commercial demand for merchant shipping has brought about gradual increase of carrying capacity and sailing speed through the ages, which in turn has demanded continual refinement to the shape of water craft.

Perhaps one of the earliest documented lessons in shipbuilding is to be found in the account of Noah's Ark told in the Old Testament. While its historical basis may be contested, the characteristics of this legendary biblical livestock carrier prove that ancient shipbuilding knowledge was absolutely sound. The ratios of the Ark's length to its beam and depth are considered to be fairly optimal – even according to modern shipbuilding practice. In his talk to the naval architects, Sir William pointed out that the ratios of *Arcadia*'s dimensions were in fact much closer to her Old Testament prototype than were those of the earlier P & O example, *Marmora*.

Prior to the Industrial Age, the development of ships and shipping was far more progressive than that of land based transport. Ashore, the first ox-drawn wheeled carts are believed to have been used around 15,000 BC, at about the time it is thought that the first Asian emigrants crossed the Bering Strait. The magnificent roads built by the Romans some fifteen millennia later were a feat of engineering vastly superior to the primitive vehicles still in use.

Ground transport progressed comparatively little, while the development of merchant shipping advanced steadily through the ages. The ancient Phoenicians were among the first to engage in peaceful ocean-going commercial enterprise. Their ships were a further development of the earlier Egyptian galleys used in raids on their homelands around 2740 BC. The Phoenicians ventured from what are now Syria, Lebanon and Israel as far afield as western Europe and Britain for exploration and trade. Later, the Greeks and Romans used larger and further refined sailing galleys for trade and the colonisation of their territories.

After the decline of the Roman Empire, and the generally quiet period of world history known as the Dark Ages, came the Viking ships of the Norsemen about AD 900. These sturdy ships differed from the Mediterranean galleys in that they were double ended, having a tall prow both fore and aft. One of their most notable features was that they were clinker-built. This means that their hull planks were overlapped, as opposed to being butt-joined, or carvel-built, as it is called. This technique provided the additional structural strength needed for these

North Atlantic vessels, which would carry the Vikings from Scandinavia and northern Europe to Iceland, Greenland and beyond.

The full-rigged sailing ship came into being later, during the Renaissance period of the fifteenth and sixteenth centuries. By then the single stern rudder and tiller replaced the oar-like side rudders of earlier ships. Temporary 'castles' erected aboard ships in the Crusades for combat purposes were adopted as permanent structures on merchant ships. The full-rigged ship was the key to vast European navigational exploits and territorial discoveries during this age of enlightenment. The development of this type of ship reached its zenith much later with the express tea clippers of the mid-nineteenth century. These remarkable ships represented a formidable final challenge to the emerging conquest by the steam ship.

It was not until the Machine Age brought the steam engine into practical reality that ground transport progressed from carts drawn by beasts of burden, first to the railways, and later to the 'horseless carriage'. The altogether new idea of railways started out in its infancy as a development founded in steam engineering. Conversely, the introduction of steam power aboard ship applied its advantages to an already advanced, sophisticated and well established mode of transport. Ships had in a sense already become 'mechanised' thousands of years earlier when men first learned to harness the power of the winds to propel them. The speeds achievable under sail were at first far greater than anything which could be coaxed out of early marine steam engines, not to mention the problems of fuelling and maintaining those cumbersome and coal hungry monstrosities. Yet despite these odds, the potential of steam was realised as a reliable source of power which was not dependent on the whim of the winds.

The earliest steamers were purpose-built river craft which used cumbersome machines derived from the primal Newcomen engine. One of the first of these to carry paying passengers on a regular route was operated in the United States by John Fitch. During 1790 he ran a scheduled steamboat service on the Delaware River, between Philadelphia and Trenton. Although this was discontinued after the summer of that year, it stands nonetheless as a significant milestone in the history of transport. It was not until thirty-five years later that the railway age was born in England, with the opening of the Stockton to Darlington line in 1825.

In the meantime steam ships took to the high seas, and inevitably

The transition in design philosophy from sail to steam is illustrated in these photos of *Umbria* and *Lucania*. Both are steamers, but *Umbria* has three masts and still carries a fully operational sailing rig. (Cunard, courtesy of Gordon Turner)

the first machine-powered crossings of the North Atlantic were undertaken. In 1819 the American ship *Savannah* crossed from her home port of the same name to Liverpool, although much of the trip was in fact made under sail. Three years later the British steamer *Rising Star* made the far longer voyage from England to Chile. This in turn was followed by the crossing of a Dutch ship, *Curaçao*, which made three round trips to the Dutch West Indies from 1827 to 1829.

In all of these cases the voyage could only partially be made under steam. None of the ships could carry enough coal to sustain continuous running of their engines over such distances. There was also the need for considerable upkeep of the machinery including frequent descaling of the seawater-fed boilers. It was not until 1833 when the Canadian built *Royal William* steamed from Nova Scotia to the Isle of Wight that the first Atlantic crossing was made under steam alone, although a number of stops still had to be made to descale the boiler.

The overall design of these early steamships was based on sound sailing ship practice, with steam engines fitted as auxiliary equipment. *Savannah*, which was originally intended for coastal service, was fitted with demountable paddle wheels which could be stowed on deck when not in use. Inevitably, refinements in hull form were introduced as the inherent sea-keeping characteristics of machine-powered ships became better understood. Generally speaking, these developments took the form of a more streamlined underwater shape which minimised heeling, thereby yielding a more consistent operation of the paddle wheels. The weight of boilers, engines and bunkers, and their layout, brought other special considerations to bear on the hull's structural design. For the first time, shipbuilders began to be plagued with the problems of engine-induced vibration – a menace which has persisted to some degree ever since.

A noteworthy corollary to these developments was that a number of early steamers which proved commercially unsuccessful ended up as successful sailing ships once their machinery had been removed.

Despite the relentless march of nineteenth-century engineering progress, it took time for the basic design of ships to change. Increases in size and tonnage were introduced gradually (with the one notable exception of Brunel's colossal *Great Eastern*). Deckhouses were eventually enlarged into superstructures. It was, however, not uncommon for steamers of considerable size and power still to be equipped with a complete and fully operational sailing rig until the end of the nine-

Lucania's absence of canvas, higher superstructure and dominating funnels introduced a balanced steam-packet profile which, in varying manifestations, remained for many years to follow. (Cunard, courtesy of Gordon Turner)

teenth century. Gradually the auxiliary role shifted from steam to canvas, until finally steam proved to be reliable enough for sails to be eliminated completely. The process of evolution does not discard the ways of the past lightly!

More significant perhaps than its engineering developments is the fact that the Machine Age fostered the development of fast modern communications. The industrialisation of the civilised world produced an ever increasing demand for dependable transfer of personnel and materials from place to place. People needed to travel more frequently and over greater distances for commerce, scientific endeavour and government. Raw materials had to be brought to the world's industrial centres and finished goods taken to its markets. Increased postal communication, and the government subsidies granted for carriage of the mails by steamship helped to establish some of the world's most prominent sea routes and the companies which operated them. Later on, the vast emigrant trade to the New Worlds of the Americas and Australia introduced cheap mass-market travel.

A key element in the commercial success of at least two notable British steamship companies was their securing of government postal contracts. A subsidy was granted to the Peninsular Steam Navigation Company in 1837 to carry mail to British possessions in the Mediterranean. After the unfortunate loss of their steamer, *Don Juan*, on the return leg of her first mail run to Gibraltar in 1837, the company opened an extended service in 1840 under a new contract. It operated from Falmouth to Gibraltar, Valletta and Alexandria with the paddle steamers *Great Liverpool* and *Oriental*. Another such arrangement was struck in 1840 with Samuel Cunard's British and North American Royal Mail Steam Packet Company to carry the mail from Liverpool to Halifax and Boston. A twice-monthly transatlantic mail service was inaugurated with his fleet of four paddle steamers, *Britannia*, *Arcadia*, *Caledonia* and *Columbia*.

The transfer of these duties from Admiralty ships to the merchantmen of these newly-formed companies gave tremendous impetus to the development of modern merchant shipping. Before the onslaught of mass emigration, it ensured these owners profitable voyages while the demand for passenger accommodation was still light. Both companies are still trading today; although under their now more familiar names, P & O and Cunard, respectively. However, postal subsidies to steamship companies have by now long been a thing of the past.

Competing interests were quick to follow in the wake of both companies' success, particularly on the North Atlantic. Britain's Inman and International Steamship Company and White Star Line, along with the European contenders, Norddeutscher Lloyd, Compagnie Générale Transatlantique and Holland America all were born within the next thirty-five years. Meanwhile, the short-lived Collins Line emerged as one of the first American contenders. The inevitable quest for superiority among these rivals served dramatically to quicken the pace of technical development.

Inman were particularly progressive. They succeeded commercially without the benefit of a postal contract or subsidy, proving the viability of well managed ships of superior design. Their first ship, *City of Glasgow*, was bought in 1850 after she was proven on three Atlantic crossings made on her builder's account. Apart from being one of the world's first propeller-driven liners, she was of quite remarkable internal layout. Her double-beam engines were on one side of the ship, balanced against the triple-reduction gearing on the opposite side. This compact asymmetrical arrangement provided increased revenue-earning space fore and aft for passengers and cargo. Although their later ships were of a more conventional engine layout, the line still continued to emphasise passenger accommodation and service.

City of Paris, completed in 1867, was the first steel ship on the North Atlantic. In 1888 Inman's later ship of the same name introduced twin-screw propulsion. Cunard countered with their own *Servia* of 1881 and the later twin-screw pair *Campania* and *Laconia* in the 1890s. Of course, they in turn brought along their own innovations.

Competition was less diversified on the Australian and Oriental routes. Here trade tended to be dominated by P & O and the younger Orient Line, which was founded in 1878. Operation of these much longer routes even made a certain degree of collaboration commercially expedient, particularly with regard to postal services. Orient Line was later bought by P & O in 1918 and eventually merged with them in 1960. Nonetheless, ships on these routes rode close in the wake of North Atlantic progress. Orient Line's *Austral* entered service as their first steel ship in 1881, followed by the twin-screw *Ophir* ten years later. P & O's ambitious four-ship Jubilee-class, *Victoria*, *Britannia*, *Oceana* and *Arcadia* arrived during the 1880s. Although twin-screw propulsion did not come to the P & O fleet until after the turn of the century, their ships were among the first to dispense completely with the auxiliary sailing rig.

It was during the latter decades of the nineteenth century that the modern passenger liner began to emerge as we know her today. This was taking place at about the same time the Canadian Pacific Railway's transcontinental line was opened and Gottlieb Daimler produced the first motor car in 1886.

What was beginning to catch the eye of the, perhaps machine-weary, industrialist steamship passenger was not so much the latest engineering marvels, but rather a new-found sense of home comfort, service and extravagance at sea. This went beyond the bare Cunard essentials of 'swift and regular passage' to provide at least the impression of hotel living. Astute owners quickly began to realise that these qualities were becoming as commercially important as the basics of safety and reliability.

In deep-sea steamers of the 1840s and 1850s, revenue earning accommodations tended to be confined to a single deck. Here passengers were berthed in rudimentary box-like little cabins which often flanked the only public room – the saloon. This space was the dining room-cum-everything-else. It too was sparsely furnished, usually with long tables and benches. A particular shipboard curiosity of this era was the movable bench backrests which could be swung either towards or away from the table, expediently converting the room from its mealtime role to its recreational uses. Food was served from a cook house topsides by way of the open deck. Passengers had to venture above for their ablutions and ritual daily promenades. There were no deck chairs, and gentlemen of the day stood unsheltered in the lee of the funnel to smoke their cigars.

The larger steel screw-propelled steamers of the 1860s and 1870s, had two, or maybe three, decks apportioned to passenger accommodations. They brought along some 'technical' creature comforts such as electric lighting, introduced aboard ship for the first time in 1879 on Inman's *City of Berlin*. The ship had a total of six Edison incandescent lamps in her saloon. Yet, apart from this, and perhaps the addition of a small ladies saloon, or marginally better lavatories, there was little concession to luxury.

Cabins were still without private toilet facilities, other than compactum-type washstands. These primitive fixtures consisted of a wash bowl which could be filled with cold seawater from a tank above it, and emptied into a second bucket below after use. Some of the later models used in First Class were enclosed in elegant cabinet-work which concealed the supply tank behind a mirror and the drainage receptacle within its pedestal. The basin itself was fixed to a drop leaf door, which when raised to empty the water from it, closed the cabinet and concealed its real domestic purpose.

Open promenades were still primarily working spaces which often provided the only means of getting from one part of the ship to another. A smoke was still taken topsides in the company of the ship's funnel.

Umbria and *Etruria* introduced the first signs of luxury and extravagance for their time to the Cunard Fleet in 1884. Following to some extent the earlier Inman and White Star examples, they initiated a steady progression in shipboard design and service leading ultimately to *Queen Elizabeth 2* in our own time.

Each ship had four passenger decks and a range of public rooms which included the dining room, music room, ladies' room and smoking room. Other facilities included a ladies' boudoir and a barber shop. In the dining room, there was an elaborate cupola extending up though the music room above, and the long 'flip back' benches were replaced by individual swivel chairs. The music room was equipped with both a piano and organ. There was electric light throughout the public rooms, though not yet in the cabins. Although meagre to say the least by today's standards, these amenities then represented the very last word in ocean going opulence.

At about the same time, Orient line was first to engage a noted professional architect, J J Stevenson, to design the interiors of their *Austral* and *Ormuz* in 1881 and 1886. Mr Stevenson's outstanding work here was a forerunner to the magnificent architectural interiors later rendered aboard ship by the renowned Mewès, Davis and Bischoff collaborative.

Cunard's *Umbria* and *Etruria* were followed a decade later by the larger twin-screw steamers *Campania* and *Lucania*. These were the first Cunarders to have period interiors, rendered in Elizabethan and Italian Renaissance styles. The suite of public rooms was expanded with the addition of a library and an elegant 'grand staircase'. Electric lighting was extended to the promenade decks and, for the first time, deck chairs were provided. What was most significant about these ships was that they started to foster an elegant and refined shipboard lifestyle which began to set the pace for ocean voyages of leisure as well as those of necessity. Passengers dressed in their finest for dinner and there was music in the air. Smoking room conversation and camaraderie flourished, and the ritualistic pastime of promenade deck strolling, dozing and socialising began to thrive.

These ships were also noteworthy as being the first Cunarders to dispense with sails altogether. The middle mast was eliminated, leaving the remaining two as kingposts fore and aft, bracketing the balanced profile of the two substantial funnels between them.

Cunard's *Caronia* and *Carmania*, which followed in 1905, each had a speed of around 20 knots and both were nearly 20,000 tons. They were also among the line's first ships built with straight and parallel sides along the middle body. The curvature of the clipper-type hull had given way to the parallel-sided steamship form. This became characteristic of all but the very fastest liners, where the curved middle-body geometry of the Yourkevitch-type hull form ultimately prevailed.

Carmania was distinguished as being the company's first turbine-powered liner, qualifying her to some extent as the prototype of the famous *Lusitania* and *Mauretania* completed two years later. Both ships were otherwise nearly identical. They were among the first to feature a large dominant superstructure in the absence of the sailing paraphernalia of earlier liners. Each had a completely enclosed shelter deck with two full bridge decks above it. This gave a solid appearance and balanced profile typical of the later *Aquitania* and eventually of the first two Queens.

The layout of passenger accommodations and public rooms began

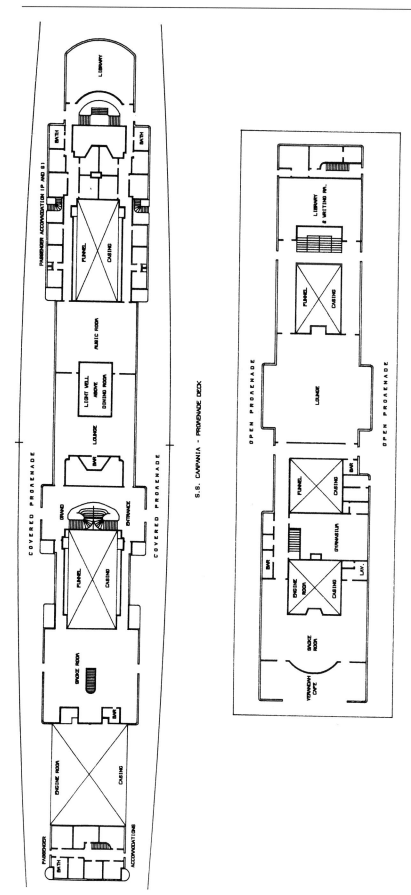

S.S. CAMPANIA - PROMENADE DECK

S.S. FRANCONIA - "A" DECK

Outline plans of the principal public rooms in *Campania* and *Franconia*. While the familiar pattern of smoking room aft, lounge amidships, library and other smaller rooms forward had already emerged in *Campania*, it had become substantially refined by the time *Franconia* was built only a few years later. Note that the aftmost of the two cabin blocks in the *Campania* plan was accessible only via the open deck or from below. In *Franconia* the entire deck was allocated to public rooms except for the Captain's quarters fully forward. She was also the first Cunarder to introduce a gymnasium and to feature a veranda café. The public rooms were located higher up on the later ship, in her superstructure, rather than along the weather deck as in - *Campania*. The *Franconia*-style plan remained virtually standard on Cunard's liners until the debut of *Queen Elizabeth 2* in 1969. (Author's drawing) with these ships to evolve into the virtually standard Cunard plan. The sequence of public rooms on the upper bridge deck set the general pattern for many years to come, with the smoking room aft, main lounge amidships and smaller rooms forward. These were interspersed with blocks of passenger cabins between the main lounge and smoking room, and further forward on the same deck. On *Franconia*, completed in 1911, the suite of First Class public rooms was enlarged and extended to occupy the entire Promenade Deck for the first time. This type of layout was closely followed in *Aquitania*, *Queen Mary*, *Queen Elizabeth* and countless intermediate liners. Likewise the lower deck arrangement of First and Second Class dining saloons fore and aft of a central galley remained constant. With a few notable exceptions these were consistent features of worldwide passenger ship design until the 1960s.

Perhaps the most significant feature of the 'Pretty Sisters', as *Caronia* and *Carmania* were called, was their relationship of speed and size. This 20/20 combination of 20,000 tons and 20 knots speed has characterised the largest class of passenger ships built ever since. The greatest North Atlantic greyhounds were always augmented by several 'intermediates' of this type.

Many lines such as Norwegian America, Swedish American, Royal Mail and Matson operated with passenger fleets which seldom exceeded this size and speed. The modern cruise industry originated with a number of fine ships of these characteristics built during the 1970s. Those of greater size and speed have, until recently, been the exceptions to the general rule.

Development of the Australian and Orient trades differs in that 20,000-ton ships appeared later, and there was a general progression to still greater tonnages. P & O's *Mooltan* and *Maloja* of 1923 along with Orient Line's second *Orama* of 1924 were first in this class. In the late 1940s both lines progressed to ships of nearly 30,000 tons on the way to the debut in the early 1960s of the faster and still larger *Oriana* and *Canberra*. Thus Sir William Currie's comparisons between *Marmora* and *Arcadia* were more dramatic than would have been a comparison with, for example, *Carmania* and *Sylvania*, representing as they do the same period of North Atlantic history.

The fact that the speed and size of *Caronia* and *Carmania* have been the standard for so long would indicate that passenger liners had reached a plateau of perfection at the turn of the century. This occurred at a time when the railways were still in their formative years and automobiles were very much in their infancy. Aviation was still a dream yet to be realised.

Progress over the next fifty years was more in the line of refinement of what had already been accomplished rather than the introduction of anything radically new or different. Among the greatest technical breakthroughs were the transition from coal to oil fuel in the early 1920s, the gradual adoption of diesel propulsion on some liners, and the introduction of fin stabilisers in the late 1940s. Passenger accommodations and amenities were steadily upgraded with the addition of cinemas, swimming pools, lifts, more lounges and bars; staterooms (cabins no longer) were vastly improved during the 1950s, the majority of which by then were provided with private en suite toilet facilities.

From an engineering viewpoint the added passenger comfort made the ship considerably more complex. Natural ventilation was gradually replaced by full airconditioning. The simple steam hot presses and stockpots of turn-of-the-century ships' galleys gave way to modern electric ranges, food-slicers, cold rooms of various temperatures, dishwashing machines, icecream machines and ice makers. Fully equipped hospitals, print shops, photographic laboratories and broadcasting systems all had to be provided and maintained. One of the biggest technical changes which had taken place was the dramatic increase in auxiliary electrical power needed on liners of the 1950s such as *Arcadia* and *Iberia*.

By the time Sir William Currie delivered his address, aviation had come of age, and the DeHavilland Comet airliner was beginning to infringe on the ocean liner's domain. This aircraft inaugurated BOAC's first commercial jet passenger service, between London and Johannesburg, on 2 May 1952. Non-stop transatlantic jet schedules commenced later, on 30 September 1958. Air fares were then higher than the cost of a Tourist Class ticket on one of the major liners of the day plying the same route. However, the Comets, along with the later Boeing 707s and Douglas DC8s reduced the London to New York flying time from thirteen to six hours. They were also much quieter, more comfortable and were scheduled more frequently than the DC7s and Constellations which they replaced. The later introduction of the Boeing 747 Jumbo Jet, at about the time of *Queen Elizabeth 2*'s debut, brought with it the modern age of cheap mass air travel at well below the new Cunarder's minimum fare.

As Sir William Currie spoke of the future of passenger shipping, he expressed the opinion that the jet aircraft would never usurp the passenger ship's existence. While the demise of the traditional liner services in the years which followed looked as though it would prove him wrong, the transition of passenger shipping to cruising has ultimately shown his prophecy to be correct. However, airline competition was by no means the only factor to be considered.

New contenders were also to be found at sea level, as a number of neophyte lines have come into being since the late 1940s. Among these were Home Lines (taken over in 1988, first by Holland America, and later by Carnival Cruises), Sitmar (now part of the P & O group), Chandris and Costa. Later came the challenge of the Soviet Union's huge passenger fleet. Lines such as P & O, Orient and Cunard would also have to find ways to sustain their livelihood against changing travel patterns and lifestyles, as well as the decline in emigration and various traditional colonial trades.

P & O and Orient were already looking to the Pacific Rim for new opportunities. The granting of independence to India and Ceylon (now Sri Lanka) in 1947 and 1948 had curtailed these nations' dependency on the services of both lines. Increased Australian trade with Japan, North America, Indonesia and China helped form the basis of new Pacific routes opened up in the early 1950s. Apart from trade and commerce, the Pacific was seen as a vast untapped reservoir of tourism and leisure travel.

A number of shipping lines were beginning to visualise themselves as not only being in the transport field, but also in the resort and leisure business. This sort of thinking would play a vital role in realising Cunard's plans for a successor to their great Queens, *Mary* and *Elizabeth*. These companies would have to be able to attract a new clientele away from the alternative of shoreside resorts. Ultimately this clientele would not so much have to be drawn away from the alternative of jet travel, but rather by way of it from anywhere in the world to their floating resort.

The two decades which followed were among the most progressive ever throughout the entire history of shipping. Supertankers and bulk carriers, containerisation of dry cargoes, and the development of roll-on/roll-off ships and short-sea car ferry services were all products of this era. *Oriana*, *Canberra* and *Queen Elizabeth 2* were pivotal elements in changing passenger shipping even more radically than container ships and supertankers had changed the cargo world.

Chapter II

THE DESIGN PROCESS

IT is often said of ships that they are the biggest man-made things which move. More significant, though, is the fact that the modern ocean-going passenger liner or cruise ship is about the most comprehensive microcosm of human civilisation yet to be produced by mankind. For at least the duration of her voyages, the universality of the ship and her communities of passengers and crew potentially transcends that of most towns ashore.

A totally selfcontained environment encompassing virtually all facets of daily life is encapsulated aboard the liner. There are the working facilities needed by the men and women who navigate her, keep her various services and amenities going and look after the well being of her community. She is also equipped to provide her human complement with the full and sophisticated lifestyle which they expect ashore. There may be sufficient fuel aboard to take her half way around the world and enough provisions to last for three months. She generates her own electricity and fresh water, and is equipped with incinerators and a completely selfcontained sewage treatment plant.

A ship only has brief periodic contact with the outside human world at her terminal ports and other destinations. Once everyone has embarked and the umbilical gangways, mooring lines, fresh water hoses and telephone cables are severed, she is completely alone, underway in her own element, which is at times inhospitable to her and quite alien to some of those aboard. Be it an express North Atlantic crossing or a more sedate tropical island circuit, the liner or cruise ship is isolated on the high seas for periods of anywhere from twelve hours to a week or more. Her only outside contact is through the invisible electronic medium of radio.

During these long periods alone, the ship must also be able to handle any type of emergency without outside help. Surface vehicles can be stopped virtually at will if necessary. Even an airliner will at worst only have to remain airborne for a matter of hours before it can land. If something goes wrong at sea, it may be days before outside help can be reached. The large liner thus has to cope with a variety of situations. These may include medical emergencies, policing and fire fighting.

A ship is subject to safety requirements which generally exceed those governing other forms of transport. She is required by internationally agreed conventions to respond to heavy structural damage in a very precise manner. A ship is also unique as the only type of vehicle to carry smaller replicas of herself as safety equipment. Lifeboats for all persons must be provided for escape when all else fails.

The ability to survive a collision or fire, launch lifeboats in such an emergency or to cope with various other perils are only a part of what has to be considered in creating the intricate infrastructure of a tremendously complex man-made organism. There are the considerations of hull form and strength. The planning of her accommodations and human services has to be closely integrated with her operational and technical design as a means of transport.

The main machinery which provides the primary source of power and movement requires a variety of supporting pieces of equipment including various pumps and filters. Stabilisers and transverse thrust units have to be fitted in as well. Storage tanks are needed for fuel, lubricating oil, ballast and fresh water. Auxiliary services including electrical power, fresh water, ventilation, airconditioning, refrigeration, sewage treatment and incineration of domestic and engine waste are necessary. Water standpipes, and foam and inert gas firefighting facilities have to be provided throughout the ship. In addition to the navigation, communications and control electronics, wiring for telephones, radio/TV, loudspeakers and alarms adds to the arterial network of technical services which penetrate every conceivable part of the ship.

The planning of crew and passenger spaces is always subordinate to the ship's primary function as an ocean-going vehicle. The prescribed number of passengers must be accommodated within her structural envelope, limited by the operating dynamics of the hull and superstructure. Crew and passengers must be housed as two separate communities. Each is entirely selfcontained and revolves about the other with little social contact. Both will be served by the same galleys, laundries and domestic stores, to which direct access must be provided. Separate, and discrete, access routes are needed to connect the crew quarters with the various working parts of the ship, without intrusion into the passenger spaces. All crew and passengers must also have direct and unrestricted access to the emergency muster stations and to the lifeboats. If the passengers are to be segregated into classes, these complexities of the interior layout are compounded by two or more orders of magnitude. Each class has to be provided with separate access to its own cabins, public rooms and deck spaces without coming in contact with the other.

The overall conceptual design of a ship may well be born within one person's mind. However, its detailed development and realisation is a colossal enterprise of creativity involving various scientific and technical disciplines as well as important commercial and logistical considerations. The completed ship emerges as a product of the combined knowledge, skills and experience both of her owners' and builders' design departments. The process may well also involve the participation of other specialists in structural design, engineering, architecture and interior decoration.

The key roles of the owner and builder were explained in a paper on passenger ship design, which was read in London at the October 1962 meeting of the Royal Institution of Naval Architects. This was jointly written by three members of the Vickers Armstrong technical department, presenting their view of the whole process:

We are aware that our functions and responsibilities as members of a shipbuilding and marine engine building technical team are automatically limited in scope and that our part in the design process for any passenger ship must necessarily be second to the part played by the owners' design team. There is always in the design stage of any merchant ship a heavy responsibility carried by the owner in balancing the functions which the ship is intended to perform against the amount of capital to be invested. In no class of merchant ship is this responsibility more involved or more onerous than for the large passenger liner. For it is the owner who has to determine the number of passengers, the standard of accommodation, the extent of public rooms and open spaces, the passage speed and fuelling range; he alone can carry out the necessary research into potential and actual passenger traffic volume, the optimising of schedules, and the economic assessment of bunkering programmes. The builder of a passenger liner realises his limited knowledge and limited responsibility in these matters, and, if he is wise, will content himself with the perfection of those aspects of the design which he can guarantee and which require from him the knowledge and data which only his experience can provide... [These are] divided into the three principal classifications of hydrodynamics, machinery, and strength and stability.

The authors went on to explain that variations from standard or conventional practice in any aspect of the design sometimes had to be accommodated to best serve the special needs of the owner:

Experience shows that on many occasions departure from the optimum in weight and cost must be accepted in order to achieve the required layout of passenger accommodations, public rooms, and open deck spaces. It is entirely a matter for the owners in these cases to balance the many factors involved, but the builders remain with the duty of providing in any event the cheapest and most efficient hull and machinery to suit the owners' choice of arrangement.

The process of designing a ship usually begins with the owners' brief, which defines in broad commercial terms what kind of tonnage is needed. It specifies the routes to be served and voyage durations, the number of passengers to be carried and the type of accommodations and service to be provided for them. It also covers other concerns such as whether or not revenue cargoes and mails are to be carried, and perhaps, contingencies for off season services. Whether she is to be a modest coastal ferry or a great liner of unprecedented size, speed and capacity, the new ship has to turn a profit for her owners as the smallest, slowest and most economical movable asset able to do the job in question.

Passenger ships are seldom built merely as direct replacements of older tonnage, which may have become worn out and unable to serve any longer. Planning often begins while the ships to be eventually replaced are still very much in their prime. Changes in ship design and engineering, trading patterns, competition and shoreside lifestyles since the existing fleet was built may well have brought about the decision to build in the first place. If not, such developments at least have to be taken into account. With a life expectancy of anywhere from twenty-five to thirty-five years, a ship also has to be planned with a view to the future. The important decisions which the owners must make at this early stage often involve considerable technical and financial risk. The choices which they are faced with are apt to be based to some extent on new routes and services, as well perhaps as untried structural design, engineering and layout of the ship herself.

P & O's planning of Canberra, for instance, involved maintaining the company's 20,000-passenger-per-year capacity on its traditional UK/Australia route, with the addition of a new onwards transpacific service to Honolulu, Vancouver and San Francisco. The longer route had to be covered without greatly prolonging the interval between sailings. The proposed tonnage was also to be suitable for cruising in the off season. This gave P & O the choice of replacing their two existing 28,000-ton liners either with three new ones of similar size and speed or with two larger and faster ships of about 40,000 tons.

A decision to build the bigger ships would involve a far greater capital cost and building time for each. The higher speeds would allow the three major legs of the voyage, London–Port Said, Suez–Colombo and Colombo–Fremantle, to be shortened in duration by twenty-four hours each in either direction. However, meeting the power and speed requirements of the 40,000-ton ship would be dependent on new developments in engineering and structural design which were then unproven at sea. Also to be considered were the improved port facilities needed by larger ships and the fact that these vessels would be unable to enter some of the smaller ports along the way.

The advantages of greater speed and reduced overall staffing levels offered by the large-ship alternative were considered to outweigh the opposing factors by a wide margin. The impending merger of the Orient Line with P & O and the amalgamation of their liner services were also deciding factors. Each line would build a single ship which it would operate in tandem with the other. Although *Oriana* was independently planned, built and financed by Orient Line, she was intended to be *Canberra*'s running mate from the outset, long before the two lines merged.

Once the basic commercial decisions have been made, the owners' technical department can begin to determine the speed and overall dimensions of the ethereal ship envisaged by their executives. This starts with a detailed analysis of the route, based on the time allowed in the schedule to cover each leg and various other limitations imposed by its waterways, port facilities and navigating conditions. If the route is a familiar one, the owners already have the best source of information, drawn from experience with their existing fleet. Planning new routes, or the inclusion of new ports in existing ones, requires considerable research, including market studies and on site reconnaissance of port and shoreside support facilities.

The route that *Oriana* and *Canberra* were designed for is extremely long and complex, reaching three-quarters of the way around the globe and encompassing most of its inhabitable latitudes. The first part of the voyage must allow for the ship to arrive at Port Said early in the morning to join a canal convoy for passage to Suez. Late arrival here could result in a costly twelve hour wait for the next convoy. After passage of the canal, a ten hour stop is made at Aden for bunkering.

Early morning arrivals are important at terminal ports, to coincide with the beginning of the stevedoring shifts. If the ship arrives late, her operators are usually required to pay for the entire shift. Should overtime work then be required, this is of course surcharged. If an evening arrival is inevitable, then the ship will normally remain in port overnight, with stevedoring and other commercial operations beginning the following morning. On the homeward voyage Naples was substituted for the outward European call at Marseilles to avoid an evening arrival at the French port. At other stops such as Colombo and Honolulu, where sightseeing is a major attraction, an early morning arrival is also best. These stop-overs are important too in relieving the fatigue of long periods at sea both for passengers and crew.

Allowances have to be made for weather conditions in determining the service speeds for each leg of the voyage. There has to be sufficient reserve speed to make up for lost time due to winter storms in the Bay of Biscay and for the seasonal monsoons in the Indian Ocean.

The overall dimensions of a large ship are more likely to be limited by practical considerations of the berthing facilities of the various ports which she is to use than by the scientific principles of naval architecture. Draught is the most critical dimension, which in this case was restricted by the depth in the Suez Canal and the harbour at Aden. The maximum length and beam were also limited to allow passage of the Panama Canal. Although not on the original route, this was considered important to the ships' auxiliary cruising role.

Like *Oriana* and *Canberra*, the much larger *Queen Elizabeth 2* was subject to many of the same physical limitations. In her cruising role, she too would sail through the Panama and Suez Canals, bunker at Aden and call at many of the same ports around the world. Her designers also had to contend with the special considerations of the express North Atlantic run, which as Cunard chairman, Lord Mancroft put it, 'attracts the headlines, the gossip, and for a few months in the year the passengers'.

Apart from its immense prestige, this route alone imposes the heaviest demands for speed and structural stamina. Most ocean-going ships are basically capable of making Atlantic crossings, But sustained regular service demands, among other things, exceptional strength, stability and a considerable margin of reserve power to make up for lost headway due to storms, fog and ice.

Although Cunard's traditional transatlantic service may appear to be quite mundane compared with *Canberra*'s exotic services to the Orient and Pacific, it nonetheless came under close scrutiny in the planning of *Queen Elizabeth 2*. Study of this route showed that, based on a planned service speed of 28.5 knots, a saving of one hour by shortening the route itself could permit a reduction in average speed of 0.25 knots over the entire voyage. The line investigated the possibility of substituting Le Havre for Cherbourg, thereby realising a theoretical two-hour saving, consequent speed reduction of 0.5 knots and a substantial saving in fuel costs.

This type of background research helps to establish a new ship's maximum service speed, along with her power requirements and overall dimensions. The next step is to produce a preliminary design of an actual ship as a basis for inviting shipyard tenders to build her. The plan is essentially a general outline of the proposed ship. It shows her overall shape, the number of decks and the type and location of the funnel. The masts, rigging, lifeboats, major pieces of deck equipment, various hatches, shell doors and other accesses are accurately illustrated in their correct locations. However the many structural and aesthetic details which will give the ship her own identity and unique character are still to be worked out.

The ship's internal spaces have at this stage been allocated in general terms for crew and passenger accommodations, public rooms, services, stores, and cargo. The plan reflects the basic decisions which have been made as to the type of machinery to be installed and its arrangement on board. The capacities of the various tanks needed for fuel oil, ballast, fresh water and so on have been calculated and space allocated for them too. Detailed planning of all these spaces will be done in collaboration with the yard after the building contract has been signed. It is on the basis of this nameless and faceless paper ship and the accompanying written specifications which describe the owners' expectations of her, both in technical and commercial terms, that the various yards will submit their tenders to build her.

The yard that ends up finally being awarded the building contract is likely to have as much responsibility for her design as it does for her actual construction. As partners with the owners in evolving the final detailed design, the builders usually assume the key role in the specialties of hull form and structural strength. Unless the contract specifies a so-called class-building of an already proven absolutely standard design (such as the SD14 cargo ship), it is bound to involve substantial research and development, particularly in the area of hull form. Even today, when passenger ship construction at many leading yards has become very much more systematised, each new passenger ship contract still tends to be a tailor-made job.

Hull design is derived to a great extent from the science of hydrodynamics. This involves determining the optimum underwater dimensions and form of the hull itself, along with the location and shape of appendages such as propeller shaft bossings, rudders and bilge keels which will yield the ship's expected performance. In the design of a large liner or cruise vessel, however, these theoretical values are likely to be compromised somewhat to meet the owners' requirements of optimum stability and maximum internal capacity as well as ample dry and secure outside deck space.

Structural strength and stability of the hull, and of the entire ship, are as important as the considerations of her hydrodynamics and performance. The weight of the machinery amounts to a major portion of the overall displacement of a passenger ship. Its location and distribution, along with the continuously variable masses of fuel and other consumables will greatly influence the way the ship responds to the natural movements of the sea.

The North Atlantic provides the ultimate test of any vessel's structural integrity. Its prolonged periods of appalling weather and adverse navigating conditions are without parallel. The ship must be able to withstand the bending and twisting forces inflicted by 12m-high waves measuring some 150m from crest to crest. Under these conditions the ship is constantly pounded by thousands of tons of churning seawater meeting her head on at speeds in excess of 40 knots. Numerous gales are apt to produce winds in excess of 60 knots. Given that the side area of a liner such as *Canberra* or *Queen Elizabeth 2* is in fact two-thirds to three-quarters above the water, the extent of these pressures alone can be colossal.

The longitudinal strength and stability calculations must account for the inherent buoyancy of the hull form and the distribution of weight. If, for instance, the machinery is to be located aft as in *Canberra*, additional strengthening will probably be needed to compensate for the distribution of its weight and that of fuel and ballast at the opposite ends of the hull. It has to be considered whether to use lightweight alloys in building the superstructure, and whether or not it is to be built as an integral strengthening element of the entire ship, as it is in *Oriana* and *Queen Elizabeth 2*.

Transverse stability calculations must also be made to determine the hull characteristics which best resist any possibility of the ship capsizing or being overturned. It is the transverse case which is most critical since the beam is smaller than the longitudinal dimension, and thus more susceptible to being thrown out of balance. Much of this work is concerned with the specific performance of the hull under damaged conditions. It involves such things as determining the optimum centres of buoyancy and gravity in addition to detailed planning of its internal subdivision into watertight compartments. Generally, should any two adjacent compartments be flooded through collision or other mishap, passenger ships must be able to remain afloat and regain a virtually level trim.

Transverse stability in passenger ships requires considerable subjective judgement from the standpoint of human comfort. The amplitude and period of side-to-side rolling are to some extent under the naval architect's control within the bounds of acceptable stability. In the theoretically safest conditions, the vessel will tend to be a 'stiff' or 'snappy' roller, with an unacceptably short period and sharp reversals of motion. This effect can be diminished by raising the centre of gravity, which results in a gentler or more 'tender' rolling motion. While these conditions are desirable, the designers must ensure that sufficient safety margins are still retained. This is especially important for sustained service on long deep-sea routes such as the North Atlantic.

Oriana, *Canberra* and *Queen Elizabeth 2* each required special design consideration since they were among the first ships of their type.

Canberra in particular is unique as being the first really large express liner with a service speed in excess of 27 knots to be built with engines aft. Her building contract was awarded to Harland & Wolff, who already had the experience of building the aft-engined Shaw Savill liner, *Southern Cross*. However, the much bigger and faster P & O ship demanded a great deal of design work on the builders' part. Extensive testing of the hull was carried out at the St Albans towing tank of the National Physical Laboratory before the hull form was finalised. Detailed calculations of the vibration characteristics of the ship's electric propulsion motors, shafts and propellers were made by the mathematics division of Thomson-Houston, who were responsible for the design of her machinery.

Oriana and *Queen Elizabeth 2* are each unique in their own right in regard to their emphasis of lightweight construction. This was particularly important in the case of *Queen Elizabeth 2*, a twin-screw ship of greater versatility which was expected to replace her much larger quadruple-screw predecessors with no apparent compromise of luxury and prestige. The process of designing *Queen Elizabeth 2* differed from that of the other two ships because consultant designers were engaged at a very early stage to work with the owners on the detailed structural calculations and design. When the building contract was later signed with John Brown Shipbuilders, details such as the precise placement of watertight bulkheads, structural webs and supporting stanchions had already been finalised. Nonetheless, the builders were still faced with a formidable design task.

The special considerations for weight economy and space saving demanded an enormous amount of advanced planning. Much of the cabling, plumbing and other fitting work, traditionally left to the devices of individual yard workers on-site, was carefully planned ahead of time. In many instances entire assemblies were constructed ashore and installed aboard already completed. It is significant that the supership of the jet age demanded from her builders planning and construction techniques borrowed from the aircraft industry. Even the shaping of plates around some of the complex superstructure curves resembled aircraft construction, albeit with metals of ten times the thickness.

As the structural design is finalised and building is commenced, the owners in particular can turn their attention to interior architectural planning and decoration. The ship's ultimate commercial success will depend largely on this aspect of her design. Passengers are not consigned to one vessel or another as are containers and bulk cargoes – they are absolutely free to choose those ships which appeal to them, and to avoid those which do not. The choice of the right design approach, and the professionals who will execute it, is every bit as important as the primary decisions regarding structural design and machinery.

Some of the most outstanding results have been achieved by engaging professional architects and designers with notable shoreside experience. The land-based architect or designer is apt to be a comparative newcomer to the special considerations of ship design. He or she must be able to adapt quickly to this environment and to work with the owners, builders and other specialists in the ship design and building field.

Ships' interior design demands much more than merely replicating working restaurant and hotel designs from ashore within a steel hull. First, the designer's work will be subject to a vast range of regulations and conventions dealing with safety of life at sea and fire prevention. These are far more comprehensive and detailed than almost any building codes in existence ashore. Passenger ships operating out of American ports are now generally required to meet the standards of 'Class A Fire Prevention'. This is literally a philosophy of prevention rather than cure. It specifies that there can be nothing which will burn in the accommodations (except for the passengers themselves and their luggage).

Many smaller details of the design and fitting out of a ship are also subject to strict regulation. For example, stairways and companionways of more than one metre in width must, under British Department of Transport regulation, be fitted with centre handrails. The interior layout has to be planned to meet the need for speedy evacuation of the ship in an emergency.

Apart from the myriad hard-and-fast regulations there are other equally important matters of sound ship design practice to be considered. The interior designer is obliged to take up the naval architect's cause of minimising excessive weight and energy usage aboard ship. The benefit of an expensive lightweight aluminium superstructure to the ship's stability could well be upset by an interior designer who would unwittingly line the walls and floors of upper deck lounges with marble slabs and then laden these spaces with great chunks of heavy period furniture!

Above all is the fact that a ship is primarily a means of transport, and as such is subject to almost continuous motion throughout her life. Everything that goes aboard will, in the course of its everyday existence, be subjected to structural stresses, the likes of which are never encountered ashore. This requires special attention to the way in which various fittings will respond to sudden and even quite violent reversals of stress. Certain fittings must be rigidly fixed in place. Others need to be movable yet secure enough to stay put during a North Atlantic gale, either by virtue of their weight distribution or through the use of nonslip surfaces. Great attention to detail in matters of finishing is essential. Innocent enough ashore, a square corner or edge can be harmful to anyone thrown against it by the sudden and unexpected movement of the ship in heavy seas. Rounded edges, flush surfaces, recessed fittings and nonslip deck coverings are all significant details of safety and security aboard ship. In short, every part of the ship, no matter how large or small, must be 'ship-shape'.

For the land-based professional architect the ship is by her very nature a completely different medium to work with. She presents a unique sense of substance and scale which is unlike any building. This phenomenon was noted by M Mèwes's partner, Arthur Davis, in an article he published in the *Architectural Review* in 1914, at the time he was completing *Aquitania*'s interiors:

> The question of relative scale is of paramount importance. It is a well recognised axiom that no matter how large the size of a room to be dealt with on a ship may be, the scale appears somehow much smaller than a room of the same dimensions on land. The probable explanation of this is that the absence of heavy constructional piers, deep window and door recesses, etc, tends to diminish the monumental character. Hence, heavy or incongruous ornament looks oddly out of place when applied to the comparatively light construction of a ship.

Although this effect is perhaps less dramatic in a modern ship's interior design, which relies less often on replicating building architecture, it is nonetheless something that the designer still needs to be conscious of.

For the accomplished architect the special considerations of ship design work, detailed and exacting as they are, represent but a specific facet of a profession which demands versatility and attention to detail as matters of education and everyday experience. For example, when Sir Hugh Casson was commissioned to co-ordinate the interior design of *Canberra*, he was at the time involved in a diversity of projects ashore. These differed as much in scale and function from each other as they did from *Canberra*. They included modern multifunction university buildings at Cambridge and the restoration of the partially destroyed Holland House in London, with its integration into a modern youth hostel scheme.

From start to finish the process of designing and building a major passenger ship may take anywhere from three to five, or more, years. During that time there is much which can change. New materials, building techniques and equipment may be developed. Market trends and the public's travelling habits and leisure activities may change. The process has to be flexible enough to anticipate and, where warranted, quickly integrate modifications. When the ship is finally commissioned and her first passengers board her she must be completely up to date. The possibility of further modification during her career is a reality which must be foreseen.

In this regard it is noteworthy that the original building contract for *Southern Cross* signed with Harland & Wolff was based on a traditional design, with her engines in the centre of the ship. Later, during the course of *Queen Elizabeth 2*'s construction her accommodations were changed from the sacrosanct Cunard three-class structure to an open-class plan with minimal segregation in North Atlantic service only. At the same time her designers took the opportunity to rationalise the layout of the entire ship.

When changes do have to be made, it is perhaps the builders who have the most at stake, as it is they who have made the hard and fast commitments as to the building price and completion date. Sometimes these commitments stand, at other times they must be renegotiated. During *Queen Elizabeth 2*'s building, the yard's position was succinctly expressed to her design co-ordinator, James Gardner, by John Brown's managing director, John Rannie:

> Directly we lay yon keel there's gold draining away like sand in an hourglass, and there'll be no stopping it, not till she has wet her backside. I won't be saying you're not welcome, but anything you do that holds back that day costs in money. You understand, man?

No matter if the ship is late to 'wet her backside' or not, there comes the day when she must finally pass out of the hands of those who have visualised, designed and created her. By that time she has belonged to them almost exclusively for several years and has become a major part of their daily lives. To bid farewell as the owners accept delivery of the completed vessel can be sad or even traumatic. The feeling is perhaps somewhat akin to that which an artist may experience upon selling his best painting. In an article entitled 'A Ship is An Island', published in the June 1969 issue of the *Architectural Review*, Sir Hugh Casson gives an impression of what it is like to experience the critical last stages of a ship's completion:

> Foresight, sensitivity, persistence, experience, tolerance, creative skill fused into a sense of creative responsibility that, certainly in the last few months, is almost emotional in intensity, these are the qualities needed by those who at all levels, ranging from director down to the youngest apprentice in the yard, must together battle their way through the compromise and misjudgments, the financial cuts and changes in policy, the material shortages and late deliveries, that beset a project of this size and complexity. Nobody who has visited the yard in the last few weeks of completion could fail to sniff this air of urgency and personal commitment. Nobody leaves this battlefield without the scars. Everybody realises that if anybody bleeds it must never be the ship. They must nurse her and cherish her as well as build her, for once she is completed [sic] she is theirs no longer.

Chapter III

A THIRD QUEEN

THE present Cunard flagship, *Queen Elizabeth 2*, is in fact the fourth 'Queen-class' liner to be designed for the line's prestigious North Atlantic service, although only the third actually to be built. The Cunarder which never materialised was designated as a Queen merely by the company code name, Q3 (third Cunard Queen). She only made it as far as her preliminary contract design stage before she foundered on the drawing boards. Her place was to some degree effectively taken at the end of 1960 by another great British liner *Oriana*.

The name, *Oriana*, originally was bestowed upon the Tudor queen, Elizabeth I, by the poets and writers of her day. This sentiment was inspired by such works as the *Amadis of Gaul*, a popular romantic legend of the time, and Edmund Spenser's allegory of the *Fairie Queene*, *Gloriana*. Orient Line chose the name for their greatest-ever liner, thus identifying her with the new Elizabethan era of the present monarch, Queen Elizabeth II. She is so far the only passenger ship to have used this name, which coincidentally fitted in well with Orient's Or-nomenclature – *Orion, Orcades, Oronsay, Orsova* and so on. The background of this name seems the more charming now in the cruise-ship age of trite contrivances such as *Royal Caribbean Sun* and *Ocean Queen*.

Oriana as completed in the Orient Line's livery with corn-coloured hull, white superstructure and buff funnel. This was short lived as she was soon repainted with a white hull upon the merger of the P & O and Orient Line fleets. (P & O, courtesy of the National Maritime Museum, Greenwich)

Quite apart from her unique name, *Oriana* represents an important historical and technical link with the fourth queen, *Queen Elizabeth 2*. As one of the world's first really large and fast twin-screw liners, *Oriana* introduced a number of noteworthy innovations which were both the key to her own success and to further developments realised in the later Cunard Queen. Her large-scale use of aluminium and advanced weight economy were of particular significance. She also introduced a diversity of other detailed refinements, harvested from Orient Line's long association with Vickers Armstrong and from the eminent career of the owners' chief naval architect, Charles F Morris. In this regard she represented the culmination of the total knowledge and experience amassed by her designers, owners and builders throughout their respective careers. For all three, *Oriana* was their last great passenger liner.

Oriana and her near-sister, *Canberra*, were both designed for the same route, and with consideration for auxiliary cruising roles. They shared similar overall dimensions, passenger capacities and service speeds. These were the first ships in the 40,000- to 45,000-ton range to be built in the United Kingdom since *Empress of Britain* was completed in 1931.

Empress of Britain, along with the earlier *Olympic*, *Aquitania*, and the slightly larger German *Imperator* class, were in essence larger manifestations of the 20/20 Edwardian deep-sea liner format of 20,000 tons and 20 knots. These ships too were of modest speed and of fairly conventional steam packet design. Refinements in hull form and engineering aimed at achieving higher speeds were first introduced in the late 1920s and early 1930s on the larger 50,000-ton German sister-ships *Bremen* and *Europa*, and on Italy's *Rex* and *Conte di Savoia*.

The design criteria for *Oriana* and *Canberra* called for optimum overall dimensions similar to those of *Empress of Britain*. However, the higher speed would come closer to that of the considerably larger *Conte di Savoia*, but without her additional size, and in turn its demand for still greater motive power. The capacities of *Oriana* and *Canberra* were established at about 2,000 passengers each, similar to *Olympic*'s figures. At the same time, the uniformly high standards of modern accommodations, services and facilities to be provided were to be more akin to *Empress of Britain*'s then superlative facilities for about half these numbers.

These modern sister ships would be radically different from the earlier 40,000-tonners. They were the first twin-screw British liners in this

The second queen, Cunard's *Queen Elizabeth*, had four expansion joints dividing her huge superstructure into five structurally isolated parts. Her classic profile presented a more clean-lined appearance than that of the earlier *Queen Mary*, thanks to free-standing funnels which required no guy lines and to the absence of a forward well deck. (Skyfotos Ltd)

class. *Olympic* had been powered by a three-screw hybrid turbine and compound engine installation. *Empress of Britain*, along with her larger German and Italian contemporaries, were each of quadruple-screw turbine design. *Oriana* and *Canberra* are powered by modern compact and exceedingly powerful machinery. Lightweight aluminium alloys were used as never before in place of the old and comparatively diminutive steel superstructures of the earlier ships to provide the internal volume needed for accommodations without compromise to the important concerns of maintaining a minimum draught. Countless other smaller innovations were also necessary to turn the original conceptual visualisation of these ships into practical reality.

At first glance *Oriana* and *Canberra* have some visual similarity, with their long slender hulls, nested lifeboats and uniform funnel colours. Internally, there are layout features and some special equipment which are also common to both ships. However, beyond this they are remarkably dissimilar. Not only were they built for different owners and by separate shipyards, but each is the product of divergent concepts and philosophies. *Oriana*'s design stresses a particularly refined approach to lightweight construction and integrity of her steel and aluminium structures, while that of *Canberra* emphasises the unique advantages of a design with machinery located fully aft.

The designing of *Oriana* began in 1954, while the Line's then latest ship, *Orsova*, was still completing her maiden voyage. Orient Line teamed up with Vickers Armstrong (Shipbuilding) Ltd as design consultants to make preliminary investigations towards eventual replacement of their two older ships, *Otranto* and *Orontes*, and the future joint P & O/Orient programme then already foreseen for the 1960s. Once the concept of the new 40,000-tonner had been agreed to, and the optimum overall specifications of her hull and machinery were established, attention was focused on her structural design. The most important factors underlying the entire aspect of *Oriana*'s design were the need to minimise structural weight, and consequently the ship's draught, and to obtain maximum efficiency of the hull.

Although *Oriana* is of a conventional structural arrangement with her machinery amidships, her hull is, nonetheless, of a highly refined form. Its final shape was determined by extensive model tank testing carried out at the Vickers Armstrong test tank in St Albans during early 1957. The accuracy of these experiments was verified by also using a model of an existing ship, *Orsova*, whose actual performance was

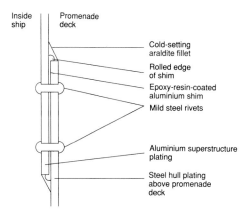

A section showing the bimetallic joint which is located just above the promenade deck. A simplified version of this, without the aluminium shim, was later used in *Queen Elizabeth 2*. (Author's drawing)

This dockside view of *Oriana* shows the tidy appearance of her superstructure overhang which is enclosed within an out-turn of the hull plating. (Author's photo)

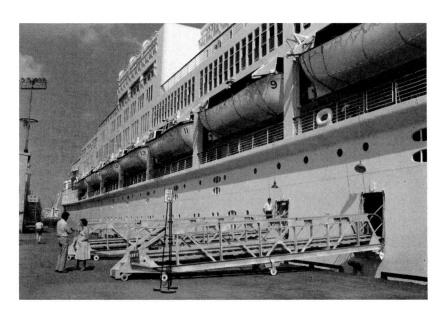

known and could be checked against the experiment results. Since *Oriana* was to be of a completely welded hull construction, this comparison was particularly valuable as *Orsova* was the first British passenger ship of this type. Elimination of the plate overlaps and flanges needed for riveting, and of the thousands of steel rivets themselves, amounted to a reduction of several hundred tons deadweight. Apart from this, the skin resistance of the smooth welded hull was reduced through the absence of the plate butt-ends and rivet heads.

Vickers Armstrong, who were awarded the building contract for *Oriana*, were particularly advanced in this regard, at a time when riveted construction was still prevalent in British merchant shipbuilding. In *Oriana*'s case, the saving of weight was estimated to be between 300 and 400 tons.

Oriana's large aluminium superstructure and its structural integration with the hull offered by far the greatest potential for weight economy. The saving of weight was given very high priority, not only in the ship's structural design itself, but also in consideration of all equipment and fittings which were to go aboard her. This advantage could all too easily have been severely compromised through the use of heavy deck coverings, deck machinery, airconditioning plants and interior furnishings, particularly on the upper decks. In other words, since the cost of the 1100 tons of aluminium alloys used was about three times that of the steel it replaced, it had to do a great deal more to earn its keep!

A precedent had already been set for aluminium superstructures on passenger ships with the well-known examples of *United States* and *Bergensfjord*, completed in 1952 and 1956 respectively. Of these, Norwegian America Line's British-built *Bergensfjord* was the first to have an aluminium superstructure of welded construction; that of the earlier American record breaker was riveted, and consequently of heavier construction.

The amount of aluminium alloy which went into the construction of *Oriana* amounted to about two-and-a-half times the 410 tons used in the earlier Norwegian ship. Most significantly though, *Oriana*'s aluminium structures were integrated as a strengthening element of the ship as a whole. This became possible due to the greater elasticity of the alloys used, which can absorb higher stresses than the more rigid properties of steel would allow. It meant that the expansion joints necessary in steel construction could be eliminated, thus giving the superstructure far greater potential strength.

Royal Rotterdam Lloyd's *Willem Ruys*, which predated *Oriana* by thirteen years, was notable for her nested lifeboats, carried in a two-deck recess low in the superstructure. (Skyfotos Ltd)

This was a significant technical advance over traditional shipbuilding practice, where a steel superstructure was merely a deadweight load supported on top of the hull. As bigger ships were built, it became necessary to separate their much larger deck houses into structurally isolated sections by means of vertical expansion joints. These allowed the three or four sections of the superstructure to move independently of each other as the hull responded to various stresses.

Apart from the normal forces of bending and twisting which the sea inflicts upon a ship while she is underway, other severe stresses can also be brought to bear when safely in port, while bunkering or handling cargo. The superstructure is particularly vulnerable to these stresses as it is generally of a lighter construction than the hull. Like the pendulum of a clock, the effects of hull stresses become more pronounced as they are transmitted further from their source to the superstructure.

Expansion joints are a rather undesirable feature of passenger ship design for a number of reasons. They add to the structural complexity and weight of the superstructure. There is also the tendency for some stresses to become focused around the bottom of the joint, eventually causing metal fatigue in this area. Expansion joints are usually concealed from view behind gusset plates, which are welded along one side of the join and free along the other. Their location can be spotted by the inevitable breaks in the regular pattern of the large promenade deck windows. In *Rotterdam*, however, her two expansion joints are fully exposed to view, where they serve as part of the ship's aesthetic appearance, imposing vertical relief to the strong horizontal expression of the double row of promenade deck windows.

On *Oriana* the overall strengthening potential of an integral superstructure built without expansion joints was carried a step further to function as the opposite structural element of her hull. It is framed horizontally, complementing the vertical web of the hull frames. This provides for the structural stresses normally absorbed by the strength deck alone to be taken up by the superstructure as well. A ship's strength deck is normally the uppermost full deck, forming the top of the hull. It is horizontally framed, and is often double plated to stiffen the hull and to support the mass of the deckhouses and equipment above it. In *Oriana* this function is effectively shared among the hull strength deck, C, and the three full decks in her aluminium superstructure, namely veranda, A, and B.

This boat deck view shows the very shallow incline of the lifeboat davit tracks, as can be seen at upper centre of the photo. Note also the location of the bimetallic joint in the superstructure wall at right. This appears as a white line at the level of the door sill far right. (Author's photo)

The same davits are used in *Canberra*, although their installation differs slightly. Here the number 8 boat is turned out and partially lowered, showing the extended davits at the top of the photo. (Author's photo)

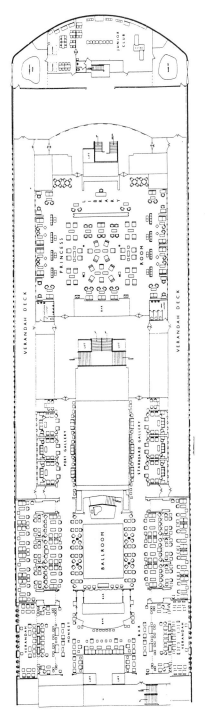

Plan of *Oriana*'s First Class public rooms on veranda deck. The Ballroom and Monkey Bar occupy the full beam of the ship in the same fashion as some of *Rotterdam*'s public rooms. Note the more traditional layout further forward with the port and starboard galleries flanking the funnel casing. The reason for the open deck space between the Junior Club and Princess Room was to provide access to the Number 3 cargo hatch. (Drawing – Orient Line)

The stresses are thus absorbed not just by the hull, but by the whole ship, which takes the strain in unison. This also allows for a certain degree of weight saving in the hull's construction, since the superstructure would provide much of the stiffening effect otherwise required of the strength deck alone.

There are a number of special technical considerations in using aluminium for ship construction. They have to do largely with special techniques for cutting and welding of the alloys under shipyard conditions. However, one of the most important of these is the very critical matter of possible chemical breakdown of these lightweight alloys where they come in contact with other parts of the ship. If attached directly to steel, electrolytic destruction of the aluminium will occur at sea when the joint comes in contact with salt water or spray. This can happen without the joint ever actually becoming inundated with or immersed in seawater. The airborne moisture alone at sea is saline enough to inflict severe damage to the bimetallic joint.

Any exposed join between the steel and aluminium parts of the ship must be made so that the two metals are insulated from each other. Direct contact can only be made in the interior of the ship where the bimetallic contact is protected from the elements. On earlier ships such as *United States* and *Bergensfjord*, neoprene sheets were sandwiched between the two metals where they were to be lap-joined. The stainless steel bolts which secured the joint were passed through plastic ferrules, completely isolating the alloy from direct contact with the fasteners.

The auxiliary stress-bearing function of *Oriana*'s superstructure makes a 'strength connection' necessary, demanding a rather different approach. Here isolation of the two metals is provided by a thin epoxy-resin-coated aluminium wafer placed between the overlap of the two metals. The top butt-edge of the steel plating, outside, and the bottom butt of the aluminium plating, inside, are each covered with a neutral cold-setting Araldite fillet. The join is secured by a double row of steel rivets passing from the outside steel plating, through the epoxy-resin shim, and the aluminium plating behind it. The only points where the two metals thus make direct contact are on the inside of the superstructure, away from the ravages of the elements. The join is also in a somewhat protected location externally, being located in the superstructure wall within the lifeboat recess just above the B deck promenade.

A further measure of protection is also afforded by the way in which the superstructure cantilever along the ship's sides was handled. Normally this added metre or so in the beam of a ship's deckhouse leaves the flat underside of the strength deck plating and outer supporting brackets at each hull frame exposed. In heavy seas, waves running up the side of the hull can be trapped by this recess, exerting substantial pressures on the ship to the point of breaking portholes and inundating the decks. On the recommendation of Vickers Armstrong, *Oriana*'s hull shell plating is curved outward below the superstructure, completely enclosing the overhang and effectively eliminating this 'wave trap'. Thus these waves are turned away from the ship's side. The instances of damage are reduced and the open deck immediately above, where the bimetallic joint is located, is less prone to being awash.

This particular feature, typical of many of the finer points in *Oriana*'s design, also contributes to the ship's aesthetic appearance. To the best of my knowledge, she is the only passenger ship to display such elegance in dealing with the otherwise rather unsightly overhang. Although it may lend some expression to a ship's lines when viewed underway at sea, in its usual undressed form it is least attractive when seen above from the vantage point of a pier or launch.

Internally, the structural integration of *Oriana*'s hull and load bearing superstructure is achieved by a series of crosswise or transverse

A general view of the Princess Room. The library is at the room's forward end, behind the mural. This arrangement continues the trend in open planning started with Brian O'Rorke's design of *Orion*'s interiors in 1936. (Author's photo)

Another view of the Princess Room as seen at night from the promenade deck. (Author's photo)

The starboard gallery, showing its attractive modern decor and functional layout as an anteroom to the larger lounges forward and aft. (Author's photo)

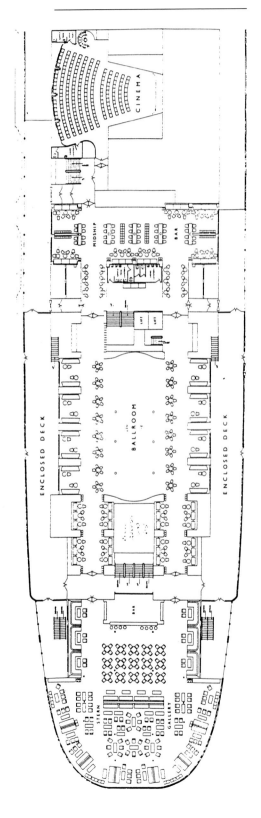

Plan of the Tourist Class public rooms
on B deck aft, showing the well articu-
lated integration of various spaces into
an essentially open plan. (Drawing –
Orient Line)

webs, extending from the head of her double bottom structure at E
deck, through the strength deck, and upwards through the entire aluminium superstructure. These web frames extend inboard as far as 3.6m,
on C deck, below the lifeboat recess. They effectively serve as a series
of enormous fence posts which anchor the superstructure securely to
the hull.

Oriana's structural arrangements were carefully studied by the British Shipbuilding Research Association (BSRA) at the time of her
launching. This is when a ship is subjected to some of the greatest and
most abnormal structural stresses of her career. The traditional launch
is a short transitional movement from dry land to the sea in which
some 15,000 tons of steel is rotated from an inclined launch to a dead-
level position floating in seawater. Instruments were rigged aboard the
ship to measure the stresses on her superstructure and hull during the
launch. The results of the tests were entirely satisfactory. In service,
Oriana proved to be reliable and highly manoeuvrable.

In view of the added height of the superstructure made possible by
using aluminium, it was realised that there were a number of worthwhile advantages to locating the lifeboats lower down than usual. This
is one of the most distinguishing features of both *Oriana* and *Canberra*.

The idea is not an entirely new one. It appeared as early as 1914 on
the Hamburg-Amerika Line's *Imperator* and *Vaterland*. Here the large
number of boats needed to cope with the ships' huge passenger
capacities resulted in a number of them being nested lower down along
C deck. The Rotterdam Lloyd liner, *Willem Ruys*, completed in 1947,
also carried her lifeboats lower down. The pronounced tumblehome of
the Dutch ship's hull allowed room for her boats to be half-nested
between A deck and her lower promenade deck. This arrangement
enabled the boats themselves to provide shelter from the hot tropical
sun in the cabins along these decks.

Normally, as a matter of convenience and economy, lifeboats are
situated on the uppermost deck, where there is ample space for the
davits and other equipment. However, on *Oriana* this would pose difficulties owing to the great height of the superstructure. The boats would
have to be carried some 26m above the water line. This would render
the entire ship rather top-heavy and was thought to present difficulties
in lowering the boats in an emergency, particularly if the ship were list-
ing to one side or the other.

A lower location of the lifeboats would contribute significantly to the
ship's stability, as the lightweight superstructure has the effect of
lowering the entire ship's centre of gravity. The substantial weight of
the boats themselves, along with that of their davits and other handling
gear, would be concentrated nearer the ship's low centre of gravity.
This is analogous to adjusting the counterweight on the pendulum of a
grandfather clock – the nearer the weight is to the fulcrum (centre of
gravity), the less the swing of the pendulum. By locating the lifeboats
on a lower deck, the ship, therefore, is less prone to rolling in heavy
seas.

The lifeboats on both *Oriana* and *Canberra* are nested at the base of the
superstructure, within a two-deck-high recess extending almost its full
length. As built, each ship had twenty-four boats, carried under specially
designed overhead-mounted gravity davits. Since becoming engaged in
full-time cruising with a reduced passenger capacity, two boats have been
removed from each ship in favour of stowable floating landing stages,
while a number of others have been replaced with launches.

Gravity davits have been in use almost exclusively aboard passenger
ships since the early 1920s. This type of device normally consists of a
movable boat cradle mounted on a fixed track, which is inclined at an
angle of 25 to 30 degrees. When the lifeboat is in its stowed position,

A partial view of the stern gallery, looking towards the sweep of windows completely surrounding the stern. Unfortunately the centre part of this has been obscured by a makeshift bandstand seen to the rear left of the photo. (Author's photo)

An exterior view of *Oriana* in the St Lawrence River during 1980, clearly showing the stern gallery from without. (Author's collection)

Port side enclosed promenade flanking
the Tourist Class Ballroom. This has
been attractively furnished to serve as a
café, rather than being lined with rows
of deck chairs. (Author's photo)

the cradles at either end are held at the upper end of the track by means
of a locking mechanism. When this is released, the weight of the boat
itself will cause the cradle to roll to the bottom of the track, where the
boat will stop beyond the ship's side in the 'turned out' position, ready
for loading and lowering.

The restricted height of the lifeboat recesses on both *Oriana* and
Canberra made it impractical to use standard davits. Forty-eight sets of
special davits were produced by the Welin-Maclachlan firm to meet the
special needs of both ships.

These work on the same basic principle, except that the boats are
counterweighted so that the angle of the track can be reduced to only
18 degrees. In the event of having to launch boats on the high side of
the ship, against a list exceeding this angle, the counterweights offset
the uphill travel of the cradles. To further save space, the boats are held
below, rather than above, the track.

The compactness of the davits allows the space below the boats to be
used as the principal outdoor promenade. This is particularly remarkable in view of the size of the lifeboats required on a ship as large as
Oriana and *Canberra*. The deck itself is almost entirely clear of the
obstructions normally found on ships' boat decks, thanks to the use of
overhead lifeboat handling gear. The lowering winches, usually fastened to the deck underneath the boats, were specially designed to be
mounted on the deckhouse wall at the level of the deck above the
promenade.

These davits have proved very reliable over the years. It is probably
only because of their additional cost and complexity that they have not
been used on a number of later ships of similar layout with fully nested
lifeboats. The advantages of this arrangement become even more significant in view of the still greater height of many new cruise ships and
ferries. Here, conventional gravity davits are normally used, often at the
expense of a three-deck-high recess.

Despite this rationalisation of the lifeboat location and other innovations in her structural design, *Oriana*'s internal arrangement is fairly
conventional. The layout of her passenger accommodations is solidly
committed to the traditional British tropical liner plan. The public
rooms are concentrated on the upper decks, flanked by deep promenades which in earlier days were essential to provide shelter from the
sun. The dining rooms on the lowest full deck, and the space between
these two strata is taken up with sleeping accommodations. On *Oriana*

this basic plan varies in scale and somewhat in detail from its earlier manifestation aboard her immediate predecessors *Oronsay* and *Orsova*. Its origins can be traced much further back to *Orion*, completed in 1935.

The majority of *Oriana*'s First Class public rooms occupy veranda deck, which is above the lifeboats and occupies the full width of the ship. The promenades extending along the greater part of the deck's length are, for the first time on an Orient Line ship, glass enclosed, owing to their vulnerability to high winds on account of the ship's great height and speed. The Tourist Class promenade aft on B deck is likewise enclosed. Open passenger spaces on the decks above and aft are also protected by strategically placed glass windscreens.

With the exception of a few deluxe and single First Class cabins on stadium deck, most other sleeping accommodations are below the public rooms. Passengers are berthed forward on A and B decks, inboard of the lifeboat recesses, and throughout the greater part of C and D decks. The division between First and Tourist accommodations here occurs at about the same point as it does in the public rooms above. Tourist Class cabins are also arranged aft of the dining rooms on E deck and still further down to G deck aft. The crew is housed forward on the lower decks, while the officers' quarters are immediately below the bridge. The overall interior layout of *Oriana* is, in fact, quite similar to that of *Willem Ruys*.

Popular features such as the Stadium, a deck sports area which was open above at its centre and covered around its periphery, were retained from Orient's earlier ships. A number of noteworthy new ideas were introduced too. Among these is the 300-seat two-deck-high cinema, which is the first of its kind in the Line's history. Originally, *Oriana* also had a premium service restaurant in First Class, served by a

This night photo of *Oriana* alongside in Montréal clearly shows her enclosed forward mooring deck. Its illuminated interior can be seen through the openings immediately below the ship's name. (Author's photo)

separate kitchen and its own bar. It was intended to be this ship's
equivalent of the famous Grill Rooms on several of the great Atlantic
liners such as *Queen Mary*, providing a alternative to the main dining
room or a venue for private parties and other special functions. However, this was short lived, and its space on A deck was later
appropriated for additional cabins.

One of *Oriana*'s most distinctive public rooms is the Tourist Class
Stern Gallery, fully aft on B deck. This large multiple function space is
housed in an extension of the lower superstructure reaching right to the
stern of the ship. The full height windows enclosing *Oriana*'s Stern
Gallery on three sides give a modern impression of the stern gallery of
an old sailing ship, perhaps one of those which carried settlers to
Australia in the nineteenth century. At the time the ship was built, this
was quite unusual. It is only recently that the superstructures of large
cruise ships and ferries have been extended so far aft. Among the first of
these was the *Scandinavia* (now *Stardancer*), completed in 1982.

The Stern Gallery is the farthest aft of a suite of three major Tourist
Class public rooms. These directly adjoin each other on an open plan
reminiscent of that adopted twenty-five years earlier on *Orion*. By
opening the doors connecting the Stern Gallery, Ballroom and Midship
Bar, they could effectively be combined into a single space when the
occasion warranted it. Their location in *Oriana* had the distinct advantage that it is far enough aft not to be perforated by the funnel uptake
and engine room casing.

However, *Oriana*'s number 4 cargo hold on H deck is directly below
the Ballroom. Its hatch trunking is brought up only as far as B deck,
where it is fitted with a flush cover which actually forms the dance
floor. A removable section of the Ballroom ceiling allows passengers'

hold baggage and general cargo to be worked through this room by the two electric cranes above on A deck. Since the Ballroom is hardly likely to be used in port during the turnarounds between voyages, this arrangement poses no danger or inconvenience to passengers.

Similar ingenuity is shown in the treatment of *Oriana*'s engine room casing. This is only trunked through C and D decks. In the Tourist Class dining room below, and in the cinema, Monkey Bar and Red Carpet Room above, hinged floor sections are fitted in line with the trunkway. This access allows the major pieces of machinery to be lifted for overhaul or maintenance, and is therefore required infrequently, if at all, during the life of the ship. The additional public spaces thus gained from the engine casing and number 4 cargo hatch freed more room elsewhere for revenue-earning cabins than would otherwise be available. Ventilation of the engine room is accomplished through two much smaller ducts fore and aft of the hinged deck openings.

There are, however, various other unique design features which were incorporated into *Oriana*'s overall structural design and layout. Since no ship of her size had previously been built specifically for the route she served, there were a number of special concerns which needed careful attention. Under the direction of a perhaps less experienced and vigilant naval architect than Charles Morris, these were things that could have been easily forgotten or overlooked.

Of these refinements, no doubt the most visually striking one is the shape of the superstructure, which is roughly pyramid-like in profile. Its apex is formed precisely amidships by the funnel and bridge housings. From here the decks are gradually terraced downward to the bow and stern of the ship. In reference to this, *Shipbuilding and Shipping Record* said of her in their issue of 1 December, 1960: 'She is unlikely to be hailed in daylight with "What ship is that?" for, once seen, she will never be forgotten'.

This rather unusual profile was adopted in an effort to improve the ship's handling, especially while manoeuvring at low speeds in and out of port or in other confined waterways. It is at these times that a large slab sided liner such as *Oriana* can be most susceptible to the power of the winds. Even a moderate breeze bearing broadside against a liner can make handling extremely difficult. When moving at less than 6 knots under these conditions, the side of the ship acts as a great immovable sail against which the rudder, propellers, and to some extent, even the transverse thrusters may be unable to compensate adequately. The

Oriana, seen here late in her career, making a once-only call at Quebec City in August 1980. The only visible changes in her appearance apart from the white hull are that the two aft life-boats have been removed and six others replaced with launches. (Author's photo)

General arrangement plans of *Oriana*.
(Builders' drawings, courtesy of Marine
Publications International)

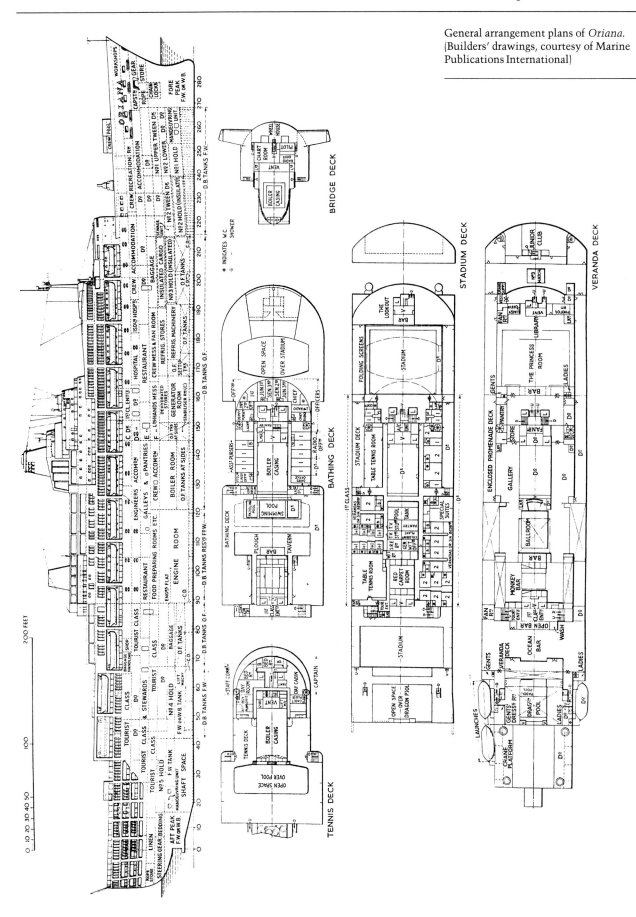

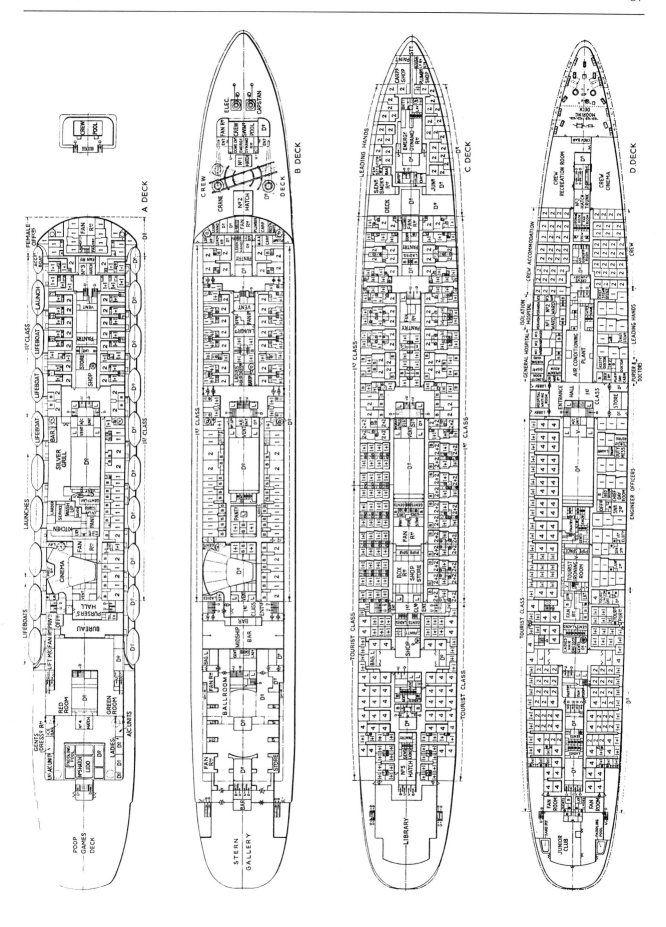

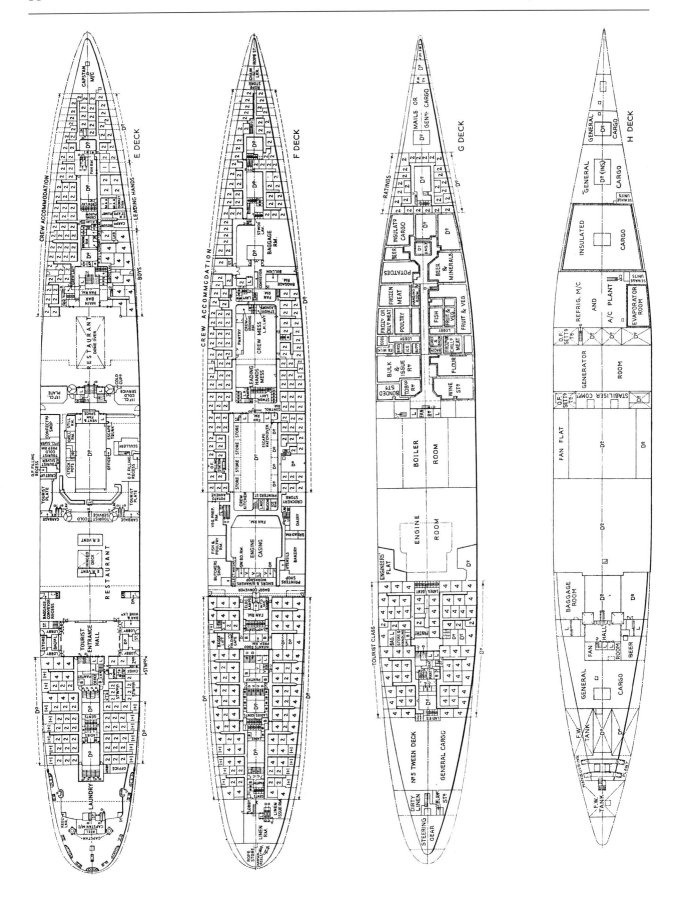

rudder's effectiveness is by its very nature reduced at low speed. While *Oriana*'s thrust units are capable of literally propelling her sideways, their power to do so is limited.

From his own intimate knowledge of the route, Charles Morris was aware that this phenomenon would pose potential problems for his new ship at a number of ports where she would encounter prevailing seasonal winds, such as the mistral off the south coast of France. By reducing the height of the superstructure towards the bow and stern, its sail effect is diminished at least where it is strongest. Since *Oriana*'s lifeboats are carried lower down than usual, a superstructure of this type was possible without the added complexity of having to locate them on different decks along the ship's length.

Another special consideration was that of mooring such a large ship at a number of the smaller ports along her route. At many of these the pier height is no more than 3m above water. The added height of *Oriana*'s hull would increase the angle at which her mooring cables are secured ashore, to the point of decreasing their effective purchase on the pierside bollards. This problem was solved by lowering the forward mooring deck from its usual location atop the hull by two decks, a distance of nearly 5m. The bow mooring gear is enclosed within the forward part D deck. Here the lines are worked through openings in the shell plating which are closable while at sea. Astern the ship is moored from the after part of E deck, which is also an open crew area.

One thing which Charles Morris had very definite views about was funnels, especially dummy ones. In his book, *Origins, Orient and Oriana*, he cites the examples of the old P & O Strath-class ships to illustrate the absurdity of bogus stacks. Of the three large funnels on each of the 1930s-built *Strathnaver* and *Strathaird*, two were dummies. The false sense of security that these were supposed to give was betrayed when the ships were viewed at sea against the sun. Light could be seen through the public rooms and other open spaces below the dummies, clearly indicating the absence of boiler or engine casings beneath them.

Oriana has a single funnel amidships, directly above her boiler room. It is a no-nonsense stack whose location, height and shape were determined by practical design rationale and extensive wind tunnel testing in the early planning stages. As a result of this research, the shape of the bridge housing was modified to include a wind trap at either side of the funnel's base. This was arranged so that the forward movement of the ship would force air to flow in between the stack itself and an outer fairing which doubles as the ship's name board on either side of the deckhouse. A solid wall closes the aft end of this space, breaking the airflow and forcing it upwards to join the funnel emissions, carrying them further up above the open decks.

The second funnel-like structure a little further aft and lower down is the engine room ventilation stack. Traditionally, engine room exhaust air is allowed to rise up the engine casing and escape through the skylights or other outlets atop the superstructure. However, on *Oriana*, the absence of such an escape route, and the excessive heat from her compact and powerful machinery made this stack necessary. The volume and temperature of this exhaust air were both sufficiently high that there was concern that if it were not discharged high above the decks it would be blown downward back into the engine room and accommodations.

Mr Morris was not tempted to turn the engine room exhaust into a second dummy funnel, balancing the real one. To have done so would have spoiled the ingenious pyramid profile of the ship. Also, weight economy was far too important to allow for any such structural excess. *Oriana* is able to stand as a timeless classic on the merit of sound and rational design without recourse to such decorative devices.

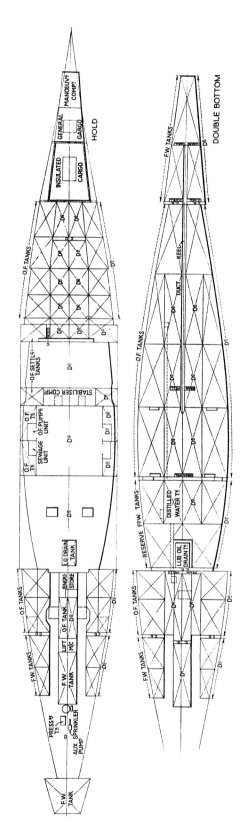

Chapter IV

WHY AND WHEREFORE MACHINERY AFT?

T HE conceptual design of *Canberra* emerged to a great extent as the brainchild of John West, the gifted young naval architect from P & O. He was only 29 years of age when he transferred from the company's Trident tanker design project in 1956 to assume the position of Assistant General Manager, in charge of the design and building of *Canberra*.

In physical terms, P & O's design brief which mandated Mr West's new job translated into a ship of about half *Queen Elizabeth*'s size, but with a slightly greater passenger capacity of a relatively high standard. This gave John West the opportunity he had been waiting for to design an altogether modern passenger ship with machinery fully aft and with top priority exclusively given to the needs of her passengers. Their accommodations would be consolidated into a single unbroken block of prime space amidships, as would be done in a tanker or other modern ship catering specifically for a specialised cargo requiring special care and handling. He demonstrated that his approach could meet the capacity criteria without compromise of standards of comfort.

In his personal notes on the project, John West explains how the concept was rationalised:

The designer must establish priorities out of the many and varying

Canadian Pacific Railways' Great Lakes steamer *Assiniboia*, with engines aft, arriving at Port Arthur (now Thunder Bay). (Gordon Turner collection)

demands connected with the project. It is logical to assume that passenger accommodation and the services connected with it should take priority. Passenger revenue is the 'life-blood' of the service, whereas the carrying of general cargo is of little or no importance. Carrying cargo at standard international freight rates is uneconomic in high speed ships. Carrying cargo also leads to delays at ports, and as time spent in port earns no revenue, it must be kept to a minimum. Cargo spaces in fast passenger liners are given over to baggage and cars of passengers, mail and 'exotic' cargoes.

The development of passenger liners has usually been dominated by considerations of accommodating machinery, but since the conception of *Canberra*, machinery spaces have become secondary and yet have remained adequate. It therefore seemed logical that the main accommodation should be in the form of a hotel block, with vertical ducting for services (including passenger lifts), public rooms interspaced at different levels; dining, kitchen and store rooms beneath. The resulting effort is to free the stern of the vessel for location of machinery.

The advantages of this design concept are as follows:

a. The main sources of noise, heat and screw activity are removed from the centre of the hotel accommodation.
b. The distance between power source and propellers is reduced.
c. Less volume is occupied by machinery since it is mainly located in a narrower part of the hull.

Disadvantages are:

a. Main propelling machinery is of greater density than other parts of a passenger ship. By installing boiler and turbines in the after part of the hull, unless corrected, the stern of the ship will be deeper in the water than the bow.
b. With electric power and steam produced in the after part of the hull, supplying energy to the forward part of the ship requires extra long runs of electric cables and insulated pipes as compared with the 'power source' located amidships.

Having decided upon the location of the main part of the passenger accommodation and the power plant, the remainder of the systems forming the overall design fell naturally into place.

A major difficulty for the creative designer is that, having devised a

An ocean-going adaptation of Great Lakes design, as embodied in the 1917 *Maui* of Matson Lines, shown here underway on her regular San Francisco–Honolulu run. (Matson Navigation Company)

new concept for the ship, a series of awkward situations result which have no ready made solution. One major example is the loading and discharging of stores, baggage, cars and special cargoes. Having removed large central ducts and casings above the engine and boiler spaces (to the rear of the ship in this new concept), it is necessary to load stores etc through the side of the ship, so eliminating the noise and interference of hatch trunks.

A precedent for modern passenger ships with their machinery fully aft had already been established nearly a decade earlier with the 7,608-ton French cargo/passenger ferry *El Djezair*. This attractive little ship, with her oil tanker-style engine layout was delivered in 1953 to the Compagnie de Navigation Mixte for service between the south of France and North Africa.

The actual origins of the idea go even further back, almost to the turn of the century. In the United States, the very progressive Matson Navigation Company adopted it on a series of their early liners, starting with the second *Lurline* of 1908. Matson's naval architect, Albert Diericx, derived his designs from the Great Lakes ships which were generally built with engines aft. He demonstrated to Matson that such an arrangement would increase the ship's potential capacity by one-eighth and provide improved passenger comfort. Altogether, there were five Matson liners built from this plan. The last of them was the *Maui*, completed in 1917.

The Great Lakes ships which were the prototype of Mr Diericx's ideas were in effect powered barges, hence the aft location of their engines. However, in some notable cases the rationale of their machinery location was dictated by special circumstances. With the Canadian Pacific's passenger vessels *Assiniboia* and *Keewatin*, it was rather a case of necessity being the mother of invention. These particular ships, which were built in Britain, had to be delivered in halves. In those days, prior to the present St Lawrence Seaway, they were too big to navigate the Lachine and Welland Canals in one piece. Each was built so that she could be separated amidships to undertake this stage of the delivery voyage. To make this possible, it was necessary for all the machinery to be completely selfcontained in the aft part of the hull.

After crossing to Quebec City under her own steam, each ship was dissected just ahead of the boiler room and floated upstream through the canals in two pieces. Final assembly took place in Buffalo. Once

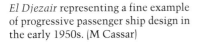

El Djezair representing a fine example of progressive passenger ship design in the early 1950s. (M Cassar)

rejoined, and their fitting out completed, they were obliged to remain in the Upper Great Lakes, as much as 500ft above sea level, throughout their long careers.

Although successful in its own right, the layout of those early Matson liners and of the Great Lakes steamers did not universally revolutionise passenger ship design. Even the later Matson liners, *Malolo* and her successors, reverted to a conventional midships machinery arrangement.

The basic problem lay with the heavy and cumbersome nature of early ships' machinery which dictated a traditional layout on board. For an increased capacity of little more than ten per cent, its concentration aft simply was not worthwhile. Much later developments in engineering and in the specialised design of oil tankers would be the key to establishing a lasting trend towards ships with machinery aft.

It is an essential matter of fire prevention on tankers to locate the machinery aft, as far as possible from the highly volatile oil cargo. Advances in the form of lightweight high-pressure superheat watertube boilers, compact and efficient geared turbines and improved diesel

The modern liner with engines aft began to assume her ultimate form as adopted in *Canberra*'s design with *Southern Cross*, shown in this aerial view. (Skyfotos Ltd)

Although the product of a rather different design approach, Holland-America's *Rotterdam* of 1959 also makes a bold modernistic impression. (Skyfotos Ltd)

engines made it possible for the machinery to be situated much farther aft. In turn, this gave way to a more progressive approach to machinery layout as a means of gaining maximum fore and aft space for cargo. For instance, it became standard practice on tankers for the boilers to be situated aft of the engine room and above the propellers.

El Djezair was the first ship to adopt the tanker-type engine layout and demonstrate its structural feasibility aboard a passenger ship. Her two watertube boilers were arranged in tandem, fore and aft of each other on a platform deck above the propeller shafts. The main and auxiliary machinery was located forward of this, in two adjacent compartments. The main turbines, whose location was largely dictated by their size and alignment with the propeller shafts, were in reality little further aft than normal. The real advantage lay in the use made of the narrower aft compartments for the boilers and auxiliary machinery, whose layout is less critical. The beam required to house the boilers was achieved by locating them almost completely above the waterline, where there would be sufficient widening of the hull.

The machinery arrangement gave *El Djezair* substantial cargo and passenger capacity for a ship of her size. The advantages that this could have also given to the layout of her passenger accommodations were, however, not fully developed. The problem lay in providing access to the extended cargo space below the passenger accommodations. Thus the intrusion of a traditional funnel casing through the accommodations was merely substituted for that of a cargo trunkway. The number

Canberra, shown here in 1966, creates a lasting impression of the modern liner with engine located aft. (Skyfotos Ltd)

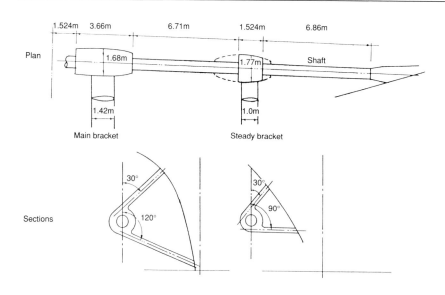

The carefully planned arrangement of *Canberra*'s exposed shaft and its supporting brackets. (Drawing by John West)

3 hatchway extended up through the middle of the passenger decks to a point on the boat deck well behind the bridge. The layout of the accommodations was thus rather ordinary and uninspiring.

El Djezair herself did not engender any great public enthusiasm for more ships with engines aft. Apart from the position of the funnel, the advantages of her design were not readily apparent to the average passenger. Once on board, she looked much like any other new ship of the day, but her example was duly noted in the industry and did foster considerable technical interest in further development of the idea. However, a more creative approach in accommodation layout would be necessary to stimulate any real public enthusiasm for such ships.

A further manifestation of the *El Djezair* design was embodied in the two-thirds aft machinery arrangement of the slightly larger *Lyautey*, also built in France, for the Marseilles to Casablanca service of Compagnie de Navigation Paquet. The Norwegian Hurtigruten coastal motorships, *Finnmarken*, *Harald Jarl*, *Lofoten*, and *Ragnvald Jarl*, followed as later diesel versions of the same basic idea. All of these were similar in that they were dual purpose cargo and passenger ships designed for coastal or short international voyages only.

The larger and better known Shaw Savill liner, *Southern Cross*, emerged from Harland & Wolff's Musgrave Yard in 1955 as a far more progressive example. This ship was built for a one-class around-the-world passenger service.

Southern Cross took a further leaf from the design philosophies of tankers and other highly specialised cargo carriers in that the whole ship was designed around the requirements of her single specialised human cargo. She was revolutionary because, unlike most passenger ships built up to that time, there was no commercial cargo or mail space at all. The passengers were given first consideration, rather than being just 'fitted in' to the left over spaces around the funnel casings and above the engines, bunkers, cargo and mail sacks. There were no engine casings and funnel uptakes protruding through their spaces, and no sources of heat, noise and vibration below; all that sort of thing was well aft and out of the way.

She introduced a number of fresh ideas in interior layout and passenger facilities. The plan was opened up and simplified. It emphasised large and bright public rooms. The accommodations were fundamentally Tourist Class, with the vast majority of cabins being without private toilet facilities. Nonetheless, they were laid out for the most part around a single central fore and aft passageway running practically the full length of each deck. Her open decks were also well planned, spacious and uncluttered.

While the technical merits of her design won her much acclaim, *Southern Cross*'s greatest success lay in her public appeal. Everyone could plainly see that she was an altogether modern ship which represented perhaps the greatest break with tradition in British shipbuilding since *Lusitania* and *Mauretania*. The fact that she is still trading successfully in today's American cruise market as *Azure Seas* further attests to her sound design and construction.

The example of *Southern Cross* spawned a number of concept designs based on her progressive layout. Among these was a 30,000-ton Atlantic liner, where the weight of the main machinery, located aft, was to be balanced by the auxiliary and hotel machinery located fully forward. Externally she would have had a very conventional three-funnel profile, with the forward and aft stacks serving the two machinery installations. The centre funnel would have been a dummy, housing an observation lounge for passengers. Another was Edgar Detwiler's vast 120,000-ton United Nations-class Atlantic liners, proposed in the late 1950s, which bore a strikingly strong resemblance to the progressive *Southern Cross* profile. Interesting as they were, unfortunately none of these plans ever materialised.

Of the four yards who tendered for building the then unnamed *Canberra*, it was Harland & Wolff who submitted the winning bid. Certainly their experience with *Southern Cross* would be a key element in the success of the new P & O ship. When the building contract was signed in January 1957, hull number 1621 would be the largest passenger liner to be built in Northern Ireland since the White Star *Britannic*, completed in 1914 within sight of *Canberra*'s birthplace.

Two years later, when construction of hull number 1621 was well under way, Holland America Line's new flagship *Rotterdam* made her debut. She was then the largest and most luxurious ship to be built with engines aft. What was most noteworthy about *Rotterdam* was the absence of conventional funnels. Although those on *El Djezair* and *Southern Cross* were fully aft, they were both rather squat and unattractive little conventional stacks. *Rotterdam* sported a pair of tall, slender, side-by-side 'goal post'-style exhaust uptakes. This gave the ship a futuristic profile, with the illusion of the machinery being much further aft than it really is.

The starboard main turbo-alternator showing the 6,000-volt generator, left, and the turbine at the right. (Author's photo)

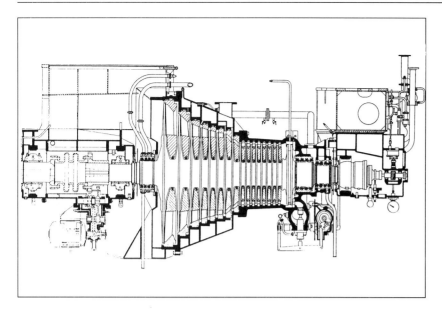

Longitudinal section through one of the seventeen-stage main turbines. (Drawing – BTH Ltd courtesy of Schiffahrts-Verlag 'Hansa')

The port-side propeller shaft where it emerges from its forty-two-pole synchronous motor, seen at the right. (Author's photo)

Although concentrated farther aft than usual, *Rotterdam*'s machinery was of a traditional layout, with the boiler room forward of the main turbines. This still provided for an excellent layout of passenger accommodations, featuring a number of outstanding public rooms and a magnificent double main staircase.

To design *Canberra* as a ship with engines aft involved a good deal more than simply copying the examples of *El Djezair*, *Southern Cross* and *Rotterdam*, or of combining the best features from all three ships. While much could be learned from these examples, nobody then had any experience with machinery located aft in high-speed passenger ships. *Canberra*'s projected schedule demanded a relatively high service speed of 27 knots, which called for a sophisticated hull form and extremely powerful machinery.

Of the literally thousands of passenger ships which have been built worldwide, the majority were designed for speeds of about 20 knots. Only a dozen or so of the greatest North Atlantic greyhounds and a very few other long-range and special express liners have ever been built for higher speeds. For each additional knot above the 18 to 22-

knot average, the price is heavy, both in terms of building and operation costs. For instance, *Canberra* requires 2.3 times the power of the
slightly smaller *Rotterdam* to drive her the additional 6 knots faster.

In the design of a high-speed ship, the shape of the hull becomes
about as sophisticated in its own right as does the aerodynamic form of
a supersonic aircraft. While the hydrodynamics of the underwater body
of the hull are important, its shape at the water line is perhaps the most
critical. Here, at the surface, where the divergent media of air and water
meet, is where the effects of drag caused by the ship's forward motion
are most serious. It is a well known fact that submarines yield their
best speeds only when fully submerged in the single element of the sea.

On surface craft, the flank turbulence, created between the outer 'V'-
shaped bow wave and the sides of the hull, has the greatest tendency to
slow the ship's progress. The higher the speed, the more pronounced
the effect becomes. To overcome this, the hull has to be specially
shaped at the water line so as to minimise the extent of the bow wave.
Its form below the water line is determined by the altogether different
considerations of hydrodynamic performance and of providing sufficient buoyancy to support the ship. Above, the rationale of payload
capacity and aerodynamics hold greatest influence.

The ingenious Yourkevitch hull of *Normandie* succeeded in combining these divergent and seemingly incompatible shapes into an inspired
unity of form. This type of hull is particularly effective at high speed, as
its waterline shape is derived from the principle of an airfoil. Like the
top surface of an aircraft wing, the side of the hull is shaped so that the
natural flow lines of the bow wave will closely follow its contour.

At the waterline, the sides of the hull begin to curve inward towards
the bow and stern from the middle of the ship in a single sweep, rather
than extending straight and parallel along the ship's middle body. The
forward lines of the hull are slightly concave, creating a hollowness
which makes the bow much narrower. The reduced angle of the bow
cuts through the water with a proportionally narrower bow wave,
which in turn more closely follows the contour of the hull.

Below the water line, the bow is shaped into a small bulbous forefoot. There is also a spreading outward, or flare as it is called, of the
bow above the waterline. This increased fullness of form both above
and beneath the surface improves the hull's stability at sea by reducing
the tendency of fore and aft pitching movements.

In the midships region, there is a tumblehome of the sides from

Although really intended for handling
automobiles, the lateral transporter is
seen here being used to load deck chairs
aboard. (Author's photo)

above the bilge keels. In cross section this gives the hull something of a pear shape. It is a means of providing additional buoyancy amidships to offset the lack of it in the refined shape of the bow and, to a lesser degree, the stern.

This refined and highly sophisticated hull design was the brainchild of the Russian-born naval architect Vladimir Yourkevitch, from whom its name is taken. In support of his design, Mr Yourkevitch was fond of pointing out that *Normandie*'s British rival, *Queen Mary*, needed an additional 40,000hp to drive her only a fraction of a knot faster. Hanging in his office, aerial photographs of both ships at sea served to dramatise his point. There was considerably less wake foaming around *Normandie*'s flanks.

With the exception of the Compagnie Sudatlantique's *Pasteur*, few of Vladimir Yourkevitch's later design proposals materialised. It is a credit to the man that his ideas have effectively remained as a fundamental theorem of modern express ship design. Elements of its basic design have since served to shape the hulls not only of *Canberra*, but of a great many other express ships of all types, right through to the present day.

Here again, precedent could provide only a partial solution to the specifics of *Canberra*'s design. Compared with *Normandie*, she is a slower and considerably smaller ship. Unlike the French liner, whose machinery was ensconced amidships in the most buoyant part of her hull, *Canberra*'s powerful engines were relegated to her confined and less buoyant aft compartments. This produced the double-barrelled problem of finding a workable machinery layout and redesigning the afterbody of the hull without seriously compromising her performance at speed.

Sufficient reserve buoyancy had to be maintained aft to keep the ship in proper trim, maintaining the Longitudinal Centre of Buoyancy (LCB) approximately amidships. The buoyancy of the stern also had to compensate for the opposing fineness in form of the bow, essential to the hull's overall hydrodynamic performance.

In other words, John West and his team were faced with a conundrum akin to balancing Jumbo and Twiggy at opposite ends of a playground seesaw. The seesaw can be balanced by moving the fulcrum on which it turns closer to Jumbo's end, thus giving Twiggy greater power of leverage. In general, and perhaps oversimplified terms, the position of the LCB can be altered in the same way, by making one or other end of the hull more buoyant in the water. Of course, this must be done without compromising the hull's performance as a transport.

Details of *Canberra*'s unique VertiVe-yors showing the pater noster lift above the receiving tray which is extended to mesh with its struts to receive the baggage for a given deck. At the lower left is a general arrangement showing the units location aboard the ship and its proximity to the conveyors on E deck. (Drawing – *Shipping World and Ship-builder*, courtesy of P & O Group)

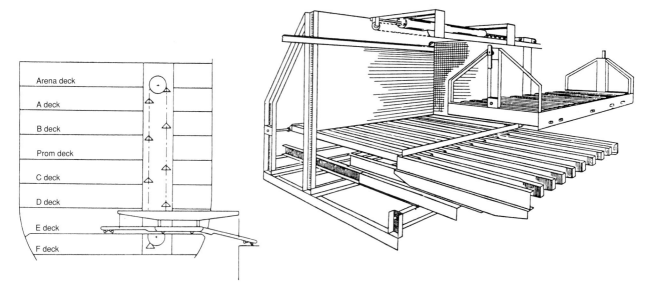

Two alternatives were explored as the most likely solutions to the question of *Canberra*'s hull form: a twin-skeg arrangement, somewhat resembling a catamaran, and a more conventional stern, but with the innovation of exposed propeller shafts, were both considered. Neither had previously been tried on a large and fast passenger ship. Both were thoroughly tested in the Model Tank of the National Physical Laboratory in the very early stages of *Canberra*'s design.

Experiments with various twin-skeg arrangements indicated, at best, only a marginal improvement in performance over conventional hull forms. More distressing though, was the revelation that the asymmetri-

Original wing-shaped funnels.

Alternative delta-wing funnels.

The ship's model, showing the alternative wing and delta wing funnel types along with the *Rotterdam*-style stacks finally chosen. (National Physical Laboratory, courtesy of Harland & Wolff plc)

Vertical twin funnels finally chosen.

cal water flow pattern inherent in the shape of any such arrangement could cause serious vibration on board while at speed. Even if the performance was outstanding, the discomfort of vibration aboard a passenger ship was reason enough to reject the idea.

The exposed propeller shaft alternative was found to yield the better performance without the vibration risk. Traditionally, on merchant ships these were enclosed within steel bossings from the point where they protrude through the hull's shell plating, aft to the stern bracket which supports the propeller bearings. At the modest speeds of most merchant ships, this provides added structural security with little compromise of performance. Conversely, exposed shafts were the preferred convention on naval ships, where performance and manoeuvrability are of prime importance.

In the case of *Canberra*, the advantages of eliminating the enclosing bossings are twofold. The line of water flow around the propellers would be less obstructed, producing smoother wake and consequently better propeller performance. Also, without the bulk of the bossings, a fuller stern form to accommodate the machinery was possible.

Of course, there is a trade off or compromise, as the improved performance is gained at some expense to structural security. Without their enclosing steel 'trouser legs', the exposed propeller shafts are vulnerable to risk of damage. This is most likely to occur while manoeuvring in port, while the ship is being assisted by tugs. The damage risk was minimised by fitting a support strut half way along the 18.5m length of exposed shaft. The profile and angle of this appendage was thoroughly tank tested to ensure that it would introduce minimum drag.

Tests at the National Physical Laboratory showed that in its final form, with the strut, *Canberra*'s exposed shaft arrangement would yield a 28 per cent performance margin. This meant that only 50,131kw (67,200hp) of shaft power was needed to move the ship at her rated speed of 27.5 knots.

Canberra's final hull form features a moderately bulbous forefoot below the water line. This is proportionally larger than that of *Normandie*, but still not the full bulbous type of today's cruise ships. Above, there is a pronounced flare, or spreading outward of the hull's forward body. The flare is brought out to a chine, or crease, two decks below the strength deck on top of the hull. The chine, which extends from just behind the bow, for about a third of the ship's length adds a distinctive touch to the ship's appearance.

Amidships, the sides of the hull are absolutely vertical, there being no tumblehome. Aft, the exposed shafts and their meticulously arranged centre brackets are concealed underwater, beneath a rather conventional-looking cruiser stern.

The power needed to move this elegant hull at its intended service speed of 27.5 knots, with a reserve margin to cope with the inevitable delays caused by bad weather and fog, amounted to 62,534kW (85,000hp). This amounted to slightly more than the individual shaft power per screw that was delivered by each of *Normandie*'s four motors.

Research was carried out at the Yarrow-Admiralty Research Department during the early stages of *Canberra*'s design to determine the best way of providing this power. This resulted in the recommendation of twin-propeller turbo-electric propulsion. Despite its additional weight and cost, this arrangement was chosen because of the flexibility it offered both in operation and in the layout of the machinery itself aboard the ship.

The choice of turbo-electric machinery was quite acceptable to P & O, since they were already familiar with it. As far back as 1929, their *Viceroy of India* and later the liners *Strathnaver* and *Strathaird* were similarly powered.

A detail view of the fully nested lifeboats suspended from their custom-
built davits. (Author's photo)

Turbo-electric propulsion consists of a steam turbine driving a alter-
nator to generate electricity which in turn runs an electric motor to
rotate the propeller. The apparent complexity of this system, which involves two transfers of energy – steam to electrical, and then electrical
to mechanical – is offset by its elimination of reduction gearing.

On ships with conventional steam turbine propulsion, the normal
turbine speed of several thousand revolutions per minute must be
stepped down to the propeller speed of around 120 to 140rpm. This is
done through reduction gearing, which can become a source of noise
and vibration, particularly on high-speed ships. Apart from these draw-
backs, one of the principal objections to reduction gearing is its inherent mechanical loss. The energy needed to turn the gear cogs
themselves detracts from the resulting shaft power at the other end of
the operation. Here again, the effect becomes more critical at higher
speeds.

Turbo-electric propulsion has the advantage that the alternators can
be built to run at the speed of the turbines, and the drive motors at the
chosen propeller speed. There is no need for gearing at all. The arrangement also offers the potential of greater operating flexibility as, for
instance, full reverse power can be obtained by simply reverse switching the motors. Canberra's motors can also be switched so that both
are powered at reduced speed from either one of her main alternators.
Apart from making slower running during cruises more economical,
this also provides opportunities for the alternators to be serviced while
at sea.

Since the link between the turbines and the propeller shafts is electrical rather than mechanical, the needed degree of flexibility in
machinery layout was possible. The comparatively small drive motors
could be positioned further aft than would steam turbines of similar
power. The choice of turbo-electric drive also eliminated the need for
the main turbines to be oriented along the axis of the propeller shafts,
allowing more flexibility in their layout.

Canberra's machinery is itself noteworthy as being the most powerful turbo-electric installation of any British ship. The power of her
motors has since been exceeded only by those installed aboard Queen
Elizabeth 2 during her conversion to diesel electric propulsion in the
winter of 1986/87. Canberra's main turbines are unique among
passenger ship installations in that they are of the single cylinder type
used in power generating stations ashore. They were custom built by
the British Thomson-Houston company, which specialises in stationary
power-generating machinery. These two seventeen-stage turbines are
far less complex than the double or triple expansion marine turbines
more commonly used on passenger ships. Since full reverse thrust can
be selected by electrical switching of the motor windings, there is also
no need for the added intricacies of reverse thrust turbines.

The overall layout of Canberra's machinery follows the oil tanker
design principle adopted on El Djezair and Southern Cross. While the
hull had been designed to accommodate a large engine installation,
great care still had to be taken in conserving weight in the machinery
spaces. Most critical were the boilers and the propeller shafts. As these
were the aftmost components, their weight would potentially have the
greatest effect on the ship's trim.

The weight of every item of machinery was carefully considered, and
in a number of cases ended up as the deciding factor in selection of
components. One measure adopted was to use hollow propeller shafts,
resulting in an economy in the order of 7.5 per cent as opposed to the
mass of solid shafts. While provision was made for the inevitable differences between estimated weights and the actual mass of the
installed equipment, deadweight ballasting of the forward compart-

ments was ultimately required. In this regard, every kilo of weight saved in the machinery installation itself paid off doubly, as it also diminished the amount of ballast required.

Forward of the engine spaces, there are three cargo holds with a combined capacity of 4230cu m. These were originally intended for passengers' baggage and automobiles rather than for commercial cargo. However, *Canberra*'s designers did not want to repeat *El Djezair*'s shortcomings in regard to the second and third holds which are beneath the superstructure. Apart from loss of valuable revenue earning passenger space, conventional trunkways would have placed the hatches some 25m above the water line. These holds would be difficult to work at such a height, and their access ways would have defeated the objective of an integrated and uninterrupted block of passenger accommodations.

The problem was solved by bringing the trunkways of number 2 and 3 holds up only as far as D deck, forward of the passenger accommodations. Here cargo would be handled through side ports in the hull by way of retractable lateral transporters. These are fitted with carriages which are raised and lowered to and from each hold through the centre line trunkway, as well as to and from the pier at a distance of up to 8m from either side of the ship. When not in use, the transporters are fully concealed within the hull, behind four sets of double shell doors.

When *Canberra* was completed in 1961, this was something of a novelty. Similar equipment has since become an integral part of containerised cargo handling both aboard ship and ashore. With the development of sophisticated cargo container ships later in the 1960s came much larger versions of these transporters in ports around the world. A further refinement came later in the 1970s with the containerised stores handling on the larger Scandinavian vehicle/passenger ferries. The first of these was the revolutionary Finnish express ferry, *Finnjet*, which carries all her stores in a set of six standard size containers. These are hoisted on and off the ship by a selfcontained larger version of *Canberra*'s transporters.

In view of *Canberra*'s large passenger capacity and the amount of port time allowed by her schedule, the whole question of baggage and stores handling had to be carefully considered. With the ship fully booked, this job could amount to as many as 5000 items of passenger baggage, in addition to large quantities of stores having to be handled in as little as eight hours.

The vast uncluttered promenade below *Canberra*'s lifeboats, shown looking aft from amidships, port side. (Author's photo)

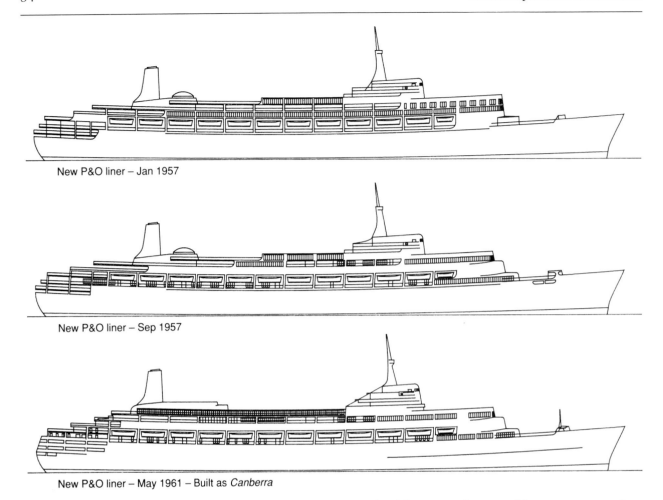

New P&O liner – Jan 1957

New P&O liner – Sep 1957

New P&O liner – May 1961 – Built as *Canberra*

Evolution of *Canberra*'s design. At its early stages in January 1957 (top) she bore a resemblance to *Oriana*, with vertical stanchions between the lifeboat recesses, and full-height windows on the deck above. By September of the same year (middle) she had taken on a more streamlined appearance with angled stanchions and a less severe treatment of the forward superstructure. Later modifications in the completed ship (bottom) included extension of the upper deck fully aft and raising the funnel housing, as well as the addition of an extra deck in the bridge structure. Other refinements were made in the grouping of windows and the shape of shell openings to the lower afterdecks. (Author's drawing)

This problem was solved by way of retractable conveyors and an automated system for internal distribution and collection of passenger luggage aboard the ship. Even so, human labour would still be the controlling factor. It was calculated that an experienced stevedore would need an average of six seconds to handle each item on or off the conveyors at either end. This information was used to determine the optimum speeds at which the mechanical equipment would be run. The speed of the conveyors was thus established at 18m per minute.

All conveyor access to Canberra is on E deck, where each unit is supported by a movable gantry which can be extended through shell doors on either side of the ship. The free end of every unit is suspended so as to allow for variations in pier height and changing tide conditions during the time spent in port. Stores conveyors on either side of the ship give access to the galley area amidships, where lifts are used to reach the store rooms and cold lockers below on G and H decks. Further aft there are separate conveyors for handling hold and cabin baggage.

The conveyor for hold items not wanted during the voyage feeds directly to a baggage room aft on F deck. Cabin luggage is handled from its own conveyor and distributed to *Canberra*'s various decks by a so-called 'VertiVeyor'. This patent device consists of a continuously rotating 'pater noster' series of luggage trays, arranged rather like the hoppers of a dredger. Items destined for any given deck are assembled and placed on one of these trays (or hoppers) as it passes, and the destination selected by pressing a button. The loaded tray will rise as the next empty one is presented at the loading station. On its descent, the tray will be automatically tilted, discharging its load at the selected deck.

A similar arrangement of conveyors and internal baggage handling was also used aboard *Oriana*. However, in *Canberra*'s case these facilities did not need to be augmented by as many deck cranes, resulting in a more clean-lined overall exterior appearance of the P & O ship.

The consolidation of virtually all *Canberra*'s cargo, stores and baggage accesses on her lower decks was a key factor in the design of her large dominant superstructure. Since the upper decks would thus be without the intrusion of hatch trunkways, and there would be no need for derricks, kingposts and other handling gear topsides, the designers were free to reflect the smooth lines of the hull form in the superstructure itself. In this regard the P & O ship represents a further development of *Southern Cross*'s design in that her profile has a more clean lined appearance. *Canberra*'s almost aerodynamic look is enhanced by her lifeboats being fully nested and the absence of exposed deck equipment, apart from her forward mooring gear and a single pair of electric cranes for working her forward most (and only) cargo hatch. The forward wall of the superstructure scribes a full semicircle from one side of the ship to the other, rather than merely being bowed or curved in shape. Unlike *Southern Cross* and *Oriana*, there is no terracing of the forward decks down toward the bow.

Two different alloys of aluminium, weighing some 1000 tons, were used for virtually all structures above the strength deck. This resulted in reducing the superstructure weight by about 1500 tons over steel deckhouses of the same size. The additional deck made possible by this magnitude of weight economy added accommodations for some 200 more passengers than could have otherwise been carried.

Although built without expansion joints, the superstructure does not form an integrated strengthening element of the hull as on *Oriana*. In this regard, *Canberra* is more conventional in that her hull and strength deck are of heavier construction, yielding sufficient stamina themselves without additional stiffening topsides. Although there are many factors involved, this point bears some consideration in view of the longer service life of the P & O ship over her Orient Line counterpart.

The profile of *Canberra*'s superstructure basically follows that of *Southern Cross*, with a forward bridge structure which aesthetically provides a visual balance with the funnels fully aft. While quite controversial at the time of *Southern Cross*'s debut, such departures from tradition were by *Canberra*'s time becoming more acceptable.

General view of *Canberra*'s vast top deck as seen from the port bridge wing, showing its subdividing screens and the windbreak faring. Note also the curved lines of the bridge bulwark. (In the right-side background is the Spanish sail training ship *Juan Sebastian de Elcano*). (Author's photo)

The first model and artist renderings of the ship shown in early 1957 bore a marked similarity to *Oriana* with a double row of large, full height openings on the two decks above the lifeboats. At this early stage, before *Canberra*'s internal arrangement had been finalised, this created the impression of a ship following *Oriana*'s more traditional layout. A second model and renderings shown by the time the keel was laid in September the same year, illustrated a more refined profile. The deck above the lifeboat recesses was fully enclosed, and the forward part of the superstructure was stepped back at games and B decks. The original *Oriana*-like vertical supports separating the lifeboat recesses and the openings above were angled slightly, giving a less severe streamlined appearance.

By the time the ship was launched, an extra deck was added in the forward bridge structure, and the sun deck and its glass side screening were extended fully aft, past the funnels. Other refinements in the shape and arrangement of these structures evolved as construction progressed.

The superstructure consists of a four-deck-high main body, extending the greater part of the ship's length. Above its forward part there is a smaller four-deck-high bridge structure housing the navigation bridge, and officers' living quarters. This provides a better arrangement of the officer accommodations than is afforded by their usual location along one of the uppermost decks. Apart from providing more privacy for the ship's officers, it has the advantage of leaving a greater amount of space available for passenger recreation.

Before settling for the *Rotterdam* style of tall goal post stacks various wing-shaped funnels were investigated. One of these was a pair of rather aerodynamic-looking wings, resembling a larger version of those atop *France*'s funnels, projecting outward at about a 30-degree angle from the top of the aft deckhouse structure. They were designed to discharge exhaust gases over either side of the ship, and supposedly away from the open after decks. A more slender delta-winged version of this with exhaust outlets facing aft was also tried. No doubt these were both ultimately considered too progressive for the late 1950s. Aesthetically, they would not have provided the same visual balance of the funnels actually built. One can't help but wonder, though, whether these futuristic stacks would have been retained if *Canberra* were built today.

As on *Oriana*, the lifeboats are nested below, at the base of the superstructure. The promenade beneath them is a handsome wide 'avenue', which on *Canberra* completely encircles the entire superstructure. At its forward end it is routed through an enclosed veranda, while aft it extends right to the stern of the ship. It is one of the largest ship's promenades – only four times around equals a mile.

The absence of lifeboats on top of the superstructure made it possible to develop more fully the uppermost decks for passenger enjoyment. *Canberra*'s approach stresses a single unbroken expanse of open recreation area amidships, rather than the conventional series of terraced after decks.

Providing enough protection from the wind on so vast an area of flat open deck space as that on *Canberra* poses considerable difficulty. When the ship is under way at her full speed of 27.5 knots, the effects of a 20-knot head wind can produce airflows of 47.5 knots above the ship. If this were allowed to reach the recreation decks it would doubtless leave them unusable. The obvious solution is to arrange windscreens and superstructure elements such as the bridge to deflect the winds away from the decks. This approach is already inherent in traditional ship designs with terraced after decks, where the superstructure itself provides adequate cover for the relatively small open spaces aft.

The outer promenade on *Canberra*'s sun deck which provides a traditional open deck space beyond the sheltered enclosures of the glass windscreens. (Author's photo)

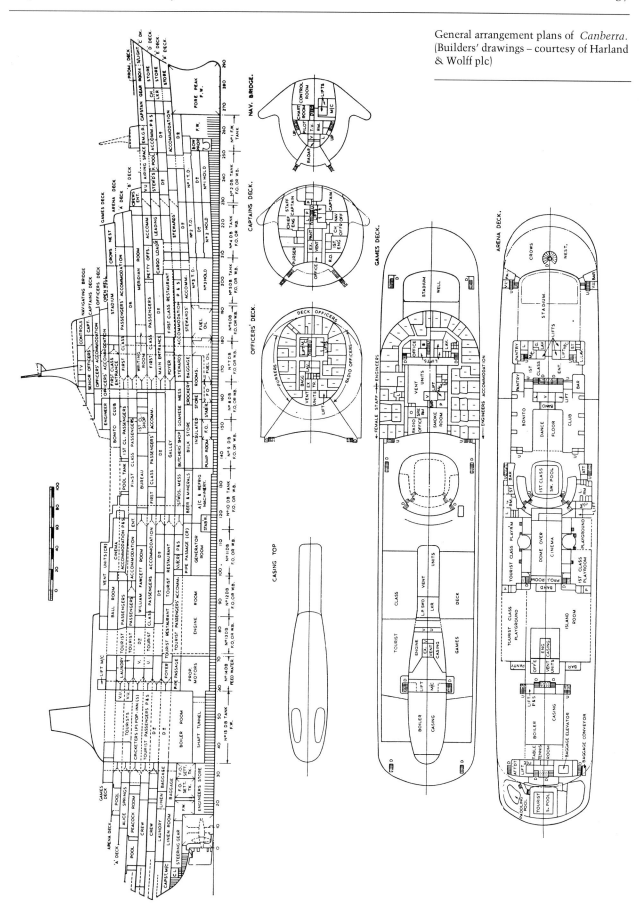

General arrangement plans of *Canberra*.
(Builders' drawings – courtesy of Harland & Wolff plc)

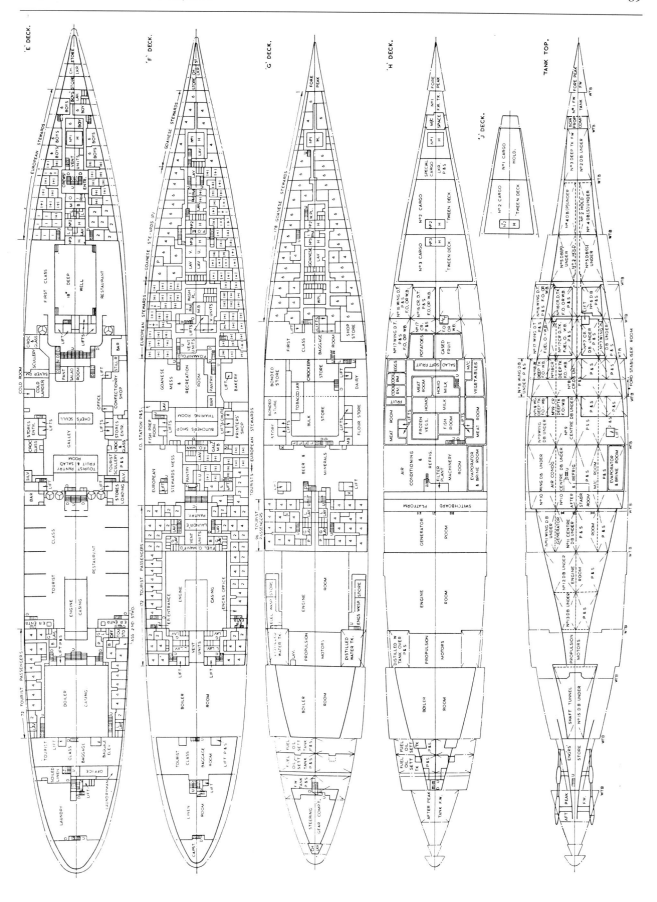

Canberra's four-deck-high bridge superstructure to some degree provides the same protection to the open deck areas amidships. However, it is comparatively small in relation to the more than 900 square metres of space requiring shelter. Wind tunnel tests made with a model of the ship showed that the most difficult conditions were produced with winds blowing from between 20 and 30 degrees of the bow. These had a particular tendency to create turbulence around the various deck structures and in the pool opening leading to the deck below. After experimenting with various arrangements of windscreens and other devices, it was found that a pair of diagonal fairings incorporated into the bridge superstructure produced the best results. Generally speaking, these reduced the wind velocities measured 2m above the deck spaces by about half.

The vast and uncluttered sun deck has proven to be one of the most admired, and consequently most influential, features of *Canberra*. Forward, there is a swimming pool which is recessed one deck lower down, with a series of terraces leading to it. This was planned to give added protection from the elements in the pool area.

Farther aft, flanking the funnel structure, there are enormous open spaces for deck sports and sunbathing. Protection from the ravages of high winds at sea here is also provided by glass windscreens which extend the full length of the open deck. These have been placed slightly inboard of the ship's edge to accommodate a narrow outer promenade. This feature, which is typical of the thoughtfulness of *Canberra*'s designers provides an alternative for those hardy souls who prefer a stiff sea breeze to sunbathing. These narrow outer galleries are also a great vantage point to watch the approach to ports and passage of the Panama and Suez Canals, when the attraction of clear and unobstructed visibility prevails over that of protection from the elements.

After twenty-three years in service *Canberra*'s timeless elegance still has not lost its appeal; she is seen here alongside at New York in April 1984. (Author's photo)

Chapter V

SIMPLE FORMS, CLEAN SURFACES, CLEAR COLOURS

EXCEPT for two lounges and swimming pools, all *Canberra*'s passenger spaces are consolidated without interruption throughout the centre part of the ship, fully ahead of the boiler uptake. The overall layout stresses easy and direct access to the ship's various public rooms and other common amenities. These are allocated to three complete decks, interspersed at the top, middle and bottom of the hotel block. The majority of passenger cabins are tucked into the intervening four decks, two above, and two below the middle strata of lounges. The cinema, along with the Tourist Class lido lounge, swimming pools and shops, are the only exceptions to this scheme, being located within the upper cabin block. There is also a small block of Tourist Class cabins much lower down, aft on the two decks beneath the lower public areas.

In principle, the three separate runs of public spaces serve the ship in the same manner as the major arteries of a town which bring together its various neighbourhoods. This scheme also diminishes the passenger's perception of the ship's huge capacity and gives a 'local' feeling to the cabin areas.

The main lounges contain a number of smaller quiet areas such as the libraries and writing rooms, as well as the ship's offices and shops which are all situated at the vertical mid-point of the hotel, on promenade deck. Topsides, on games deck, there is a second run of public spaces. Their proximity to the open sun deck immediately above and to the swimming pools dictates their more versatile and informal character. Below, on E deck, are the two dining rooms.

Apart from serving as the venue for entertainment, dancing and other organised gatherings, the main promenade deck lounges are the informal rendezvous point for passengers throughout the day. This is where people meet for morning coffee after swimming or sunbathing on deck, a cold beer before lunch, afternoon tea following the matinee film show, bingo or a hand of bridge, cocktails before dinner and so on. In this regard, the central location of these rooms is well placed for bringing people together within easy reach of all the ship's facilities. In turn, this reduces the likelihood of one having to ascend or descend the full height of the hotel block in a single move.

The arrangement of public rooms also coincides conveniently with *Canberra*'s lifeboat location on promenade deck. The three main rooms on this deck are thus ideally situated for use as emergency muster stations. There is the added advantage that the promenade itself is not immediately adjacent to cabins, whereby its use might disturb sleeping passengers or crew.

Canberra was designed both for First and Tourist Class operation in line service and for 'open' cruising with all passengers having the full run of the ship. When used, the class division forms a distinct vertical axis amidships, with First forward and Tourist aft. This allows for their easiest possible amalgamation during cruises by simply opening a few doors, as one would to connect First and Second Class coaches on a railway train.

In this regard, *Canberra* differs somewhat from other modern multi-class ships. *Rotterdam* and *France* had alternate decks allocated to each class. This was done to give the passengers of either class the impression of having the run of the entire ship. The value of this approach is only gained at the expense of added complexity in the overall layout. It usually entails providing tandem stairways and lifts so that those in each class can discreetly bypass the decks belonging to the other. This is especially evident in the close proximity of the two similarly planned stairways immediately ahead of and behind the aft engine casing on *France*.

This particular shortcoming was ingeniously resolved on *Rotterdam*, by way of her 'trick' main stairways. Two wide interleaving stairways are arranged like the up and down escalators in a department store, providing separate circulation of the divergent classes on a simple and compact plan. Holland America's designers were apparently inspired by the grand stairway of the Chateau de Chambord in France. The rationale of the sixteenth-century prototype was however rather different: The great overlapped spiral staircase was devised so that incoming lady visitors to the king's private chambers would not encounter those leaving.

The interior design and decoration of *Canberra* was undertaken by a team of professional architects assembled at an early stage of the ship's planning. The firm of Casson, Conder and Partners (later renamed The Casson Conder Partnership) were appointed as overall co-ordinators of interior design. They were teamed up with McInnes Gardner and Partners of Glasgow, who served as the executive architects responsible for specifications, technical and operational matters.

Casson Conder originally established a sub-office under the direction of one of their partners, Timothy Rendle, which was responsible for the *Canberra* project alone. Mr Rendle, who is himself a sensitive designer

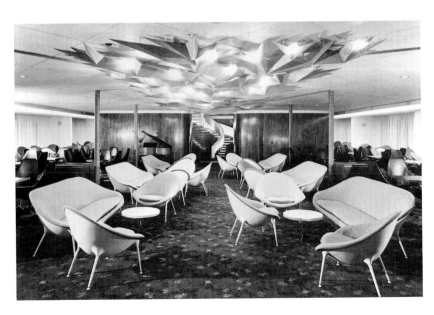

A view of the Meridian Room as originally decorated with its spindly-looking 'sixties' furniture and the central lighting fixture by John McCarthy. (Stewart Bale, courtesy of P & O Group)

of great perception, worked with Sir Hugh Casson as his executive associate. The design work was divided among three principal architects,
each in charge of a specific part of the ship. John Wright was responsible for the Tourist Class public rooms. Barbara Oakley's domain
included the passenger cabins, crew accommodations and the linking
element of all hallways and stairways. The First Class public rooms
were designed by Sir Hugh Casson himself, who was also responsible
for overall design co-ordination of the whole project.

A number of others were also brought in to handle the decoration of the
interiors and various other aspects of fitting out. Not least among these
was Sir Hugh's architect wife, Margaret Casson, who was responsible
fo designing *Canberra*'s distinctive crockery. Others included David
Hockney, Humphrey Spender, Audrey Tanner, and John McCarthy.

A concise appreciation of the architects' approach to this project is
given in a lecture paper, 'Problems and Solutions in Ship Interior
Design', written by Sir Hugh Casson at the time of *Canberra*'s completion:

> Ship's interiors demand simple forms, clean surfaces, clear colours and
> good serviceable materials left to speak for themselves. Gimmicks
> quickly become tedious. The latest fashion is within a few months a
> yawning bore. Too many patterns, too many colours, too much art, too
> much diversity of character – all devised in well-meant endeavors to
> achieve 'interest' – defeat in the end their own object. And if this sounds
> dull, remember first that a ship is full of people providing their own con-
> stantly changing pattern of colour and movement. Secondly that it
> moves constantly and often within only a few hours from one climate to
> another and thus from one quality and type of daylight to another, and
> thirdly that there is always the magical ever present background of the
> sea itself, with whose vanity of mood and colour no designer can ever
> compete and a spectacle of which the eye can never tire.

Sir Hugh went on to describe the specifics of how these principles were
interpreted in the design of *Canberra*'s interiors:

> Throughout the First Class in *Canberra*, for instance, ceilings are
> almost universally white and kept as flat and unbroken as it is techni-
> cally possible. The rubber floors of staircases, alleyways, entrances and
> the carpet of the principal public room (the Meridian Room) are the
> rich blue-green of the pacific. Walls are almost universally of dark
> smoky woods – Persian walnut, Indian laurel – or else white. Bright
> colours – flames, pinks and oranges are either (as in the Bonito Club)
> kept concealed by day and brought out only at night, or confined to
> areas (such as the cinema) untouched by daylight. Satin silver metal-
> work, opalescent glassfibre, polished glass and natural leather and cane
> almost complete the range of materials used in these areas.
>
> In the Tourist areas, by contrast, where spaces are larger and the
> required atmosphere is to be less discreetly quiet, colour and textures
> are used boldly and generously – gay mosaics and richly translucent
> gold-foil panels, murals – one more than 200ft long – and fountains,
> woods as pale as willow and as dark as rosewood, or stained to a
> strong stinging blue. Ceilings are sculpted to subtle forms.
> Throughout both areas the lighting has been flexibly devised to
> change to meet the mood of the moment or the time of day. Linked
> by the blue-green floors and predominantly white walls of the alley-
> ways are the cabins, large and small, mostly in natural woods set
> against white walls, where vivid colours are kept to occasional and
> very carefully considered points of interest.

The main focal point of the First Class public spaces is the elegant Meridian Room, located forward on the promenade deck. More than just a room, it is a suite of connected spaces arranged on an open plan giving an impression of infinite spaciousness. There is a large lounge area which one enters from either end at points on the centreline of the ship. The library and writing room are immediately aft of the lounge, flanking the central entrance hallway. The solid walls separating these rooms from the lounge stop well short of the side walls, creating a flow of space from one area to the other. Forward, the lounge is also carried on out of sight at either side, forming a loop which flows around an enclosed service island, also housing an intimate sit up bar and the ship's magnificent spiral staircase. The Meridian Room is in fact a space without inside corners, whose extremities carry on out of sight

The open planning is further stressed by the curved form of the service island wall. This sweeps away to the extremities of the room at either side and to the foot of the spiral staircase at the centre. Around the turns from the main room, the entrances to the service pantries are discreetly concealed within gentle 'folds' in the contour of the wall. At the opposite side, four centre pivoted panels open up other folds, revealing access to the dark and intimate Century Bar within.

Sir Hugh had achieved a similar sense of spaciousness, albeit on a much smaller scale, a few years earlier in his treatment of the state apartments of the royal yacht, *Britannia*. Here the layout of the drawing room, anteroom, main entrance and dining room emphasise a fairly open plan following the centreline axis of the ship. In these spaces, along with the much smaller private sitting rooms for the Queen and Duke, an added impression of spaciousness was gained by using rounded rather than square corners.

The spiral staircase as seen at B deck looking forward. (Author's photo)

In line with the decorative scheme throughout *Canberra*, the walls of the Meridian Room, Century Bar and the spiral staircase are panelled with dark Indian laurel hardwood. The panelling is stopped a few centimeters below the ceiling, where there is a flat recessed white cornice which gives an added impression of spaciousness. The monotony of what would otherwise be a dull and oppressive expanse of low white ceiling is broken by a wide border of diffused fluorescent lighting concealed by a cellular glass-reinforced plastic grillwork. The uniform medium-intensity lighting is carried along either side of the lounge, and beyond around the forward 'loop' encircling the spiral staircase and Century Bar, and alongside the outer walls of the smaller rooms aft. The flat centre part of the ceiling was originally fitted with an elaborate faceted metal-sculpted light fixture by designer John McCarthy. This proved to be visually rather overpowering, and was later removed. It was replaced by a combination of simple pot lights in the ceiling and free standing standard lamps.

The spiral staircase, which leads up from the Meridian Room to the Crow's Nest Observation Lounge on games deck, is doubtless one of the most dramatic architectural features of *Canberra*. The stairs rise through three decks within a large cylinder clad entirely in the same smoky wood as the Meridian Room. The stair treads, which are of white terrazzo marble, are suspended from deep aluminium-clad balustrades. Continuous indirect fluorescent lighting concealed in the soffit of the outer balustrade provides the only source of illumination. The effect is both dramatic and unusual, as much of the light is reflected upwards from the steps themselves, which appear to float in its glow.

Sir Hugh's treatment of the Bonito Club and its adjoining swimming pool on games deck also stresses open planning, although of a more informal nature than in the Meridian Room. This is a versatile multi-purpose area which serves as a lido cafe during the daytime and as a ballroom in the evenings. The pool lido is joined with the Bonito Club itself by means of a retractable glass wall which can be lowered vertically out of sight into the deck. Once this is out of the way, the lido and the dance floor within become a continuous indoor/outdoor area. The impression of openness and spaciousness is further enhanced by the series of terraces aft of the pool leading up to the sun deck above.

The pool lido is effectively extended into the room during the daytime when, for instance, the Bonito Club is used for the lunchtime poolside buffet. In the evenings the role is reversed with the dance floor flowing outside, encompassing the lido.

The Bonito Club's teak dance floor-cum-indoor lido is surrounded on the remaining three sides by a solid teak balustrade separating it from raised seating areas to either side and a bandstand forward. Here, as in the Meridian Room, there is a flat white ceiling with an expanse of diffused lighting to break the monotony. The centre area above the dance floor is evenly lit from behind a honey-coloured fibreglass grille. This is the reverse of the perimeter lighting scheme used in the Meridian Room. In the perimeter areas, lighting comes from small fixtures within the fibreglass table tops designed by Humphrey Spender. These have been decorated with coloured patterns based on Australian aboriginal drawings.

There were two additional features of this area that were considered, but which unfortunately never materialised. The first was a retractable glass dome covering the entire swimming pool recess at the sun deck level. The other was a movable floor section, concealed beneath the lido, which would have allowed the dance floor to be extended covering the pool. Both features would have added to the area's versatility and, at that time, been of great interest themselves. No doubt they were foregone out of concern both for their technical complexity and their

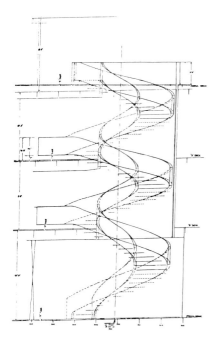

Architect's working drawing of the spiral staircase showing its complex geometric relationship to the steep sheer of *Canberra*'s forward decks. (Drawing – Casson Conder Partnership)

cost. The dome idea did eventually materialise elsewhere a few years later in the form of the retractable Magrodome roof over *Oceanic*'s top deck swimming pools.

Canberra's dining rooms are arranged following traditional liner convention, on E deck, otherwise known as the bulkhead deck. The size and location of these rooms presented special problems as to their interior lighting. Portholes or sidelights would, of structural necessity, be restricted in their numbers and size. At best, they could only provide natural light to a small part of these enormous spaces. Furthermore, on the lower decks they quickly become smeared and salt streaked at sea, offering little or no view. The designers decided to dispense with them altogether, and to rely entirely on artificial lighting. This taxed their resourcefulness to avoid creating the impression of huge factory canteens, an all-too-easy pitfall in view of the low flat ceilings of *Canberra*'s E deck.

Although attractive and functional lighting schemes were devised for both dining rooms, Sir Hugh Casson's treatment of the First Class Pacific Dining Room is the more ingenious. Generally, the room follows the same scheme as his other interiors on board *Canberra*.

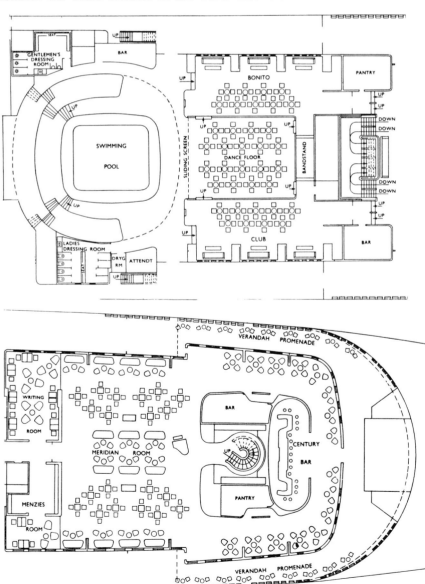

Plans of the Bonito Club and pool (above) and of the Meridian Room with its surrounding area (below). (Drawing – P & O)

There is the same dark Indian laurel wall panelling, Pacific blue carpeting and resourceful ceiling design.

The room has two distinctly different characters or moods, created by the lighting, which is bright and cheerful during the daytime, subdued and romantic during the evening dinner hours. The brighter daytime scheme comes from ceiling fixtures and from translucent wall panels lit from the back.

The overhead illumination comes from clustered fibreglass cylinders of varying diameters and lengths. These have the appearance of stylised stalactites covering the centre part of the ceiling, above a shallow floor recess of corresponding dimensions. The surrounding ceiling is slightly lower, and is the only deckhead on the ship to be clad in the same dark wood as the walls. Here the overhead light source consists of narrow recessed fluorescent strips extending athwartships. Continuous back-lighted wall panels along both sides of the room radiate a medium-intensity ambient glow like warm sunlight filtered through Japanese-style woven straw screens. This effect is produced by using textured fibreglass.

The 'dinner hour' mood is achieved by darkening the wall panels and

Architectural rendering of the Bonito Pool area. Here, the artist's conception of the site conveys a rather exaggerated impression of the ship's beam. (Ink and water colour by Heather Blake-Smith – Casson Conder Partnership)

An architect's impression of the adjacent Bonito Club in its evening role as a ballroom. (Ink and water colour by Heather Blake-Smith – Casson Conder Partnership)

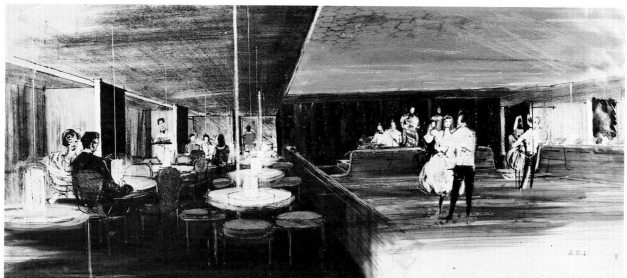

The Bonito Pool as seen from above on sun deck, looking down the terraced recess leading to games deck. The retractable glass wall is in its raised position separating the Bonito Club from the outdoor lido. (Author's photo)

The First Class dining room showing its daytime lighting scheme used for breakfast, lunch and afternoon tea service. (Author's photo)

Evening lighting scheme in the same room, with the wall screens darkened and table lamps used as at the right. (Author's photo)

switching to small electric lanterns on each table. Fluorescent 'wall washers' at the foot of the wall screens are used along with reduced ceiling lighting to give the room a warm low level ambient glow.

Both lighting moods are effective, and the visual impact of switching from one to the other is dramatic to say the least. *Canberra* was the first British ship to use so elaborate a lighting scheme. It took some convincing of the owners on Sir Hugh's part, as they feared that the crew would simply disregard a 'theatrical lighting plot' such as this. Stewards are in the business of catering rather than mood lighting, therefore they might be inclined to keep all lights switched on to make their work easier. Proof of the success of the Pacific Dining Room's lighting plot lies in the fact that it still continues to be used twenty-five years later!

The cinema, which is designed by John Wright, is *Canberra*'s only room in line service which is shared by both classes. It differs considerably from its counterparts on *Oriana*, *Rotterdam* and *France* in that there is no balcony, despite the room's height reaching through A and games decks. All seating is on a single, slightly inclined plane with the First Class entrances at the front of the room and those for Tourist at the rear. Like the dining rooms below, its interior is never reached by natural daylight.

Appropriately, the interior styling of the cinema is somewhat technically inspired. Its most notable feature is the ceiling which is fashioned as a suspended acoustic shell. The curved lines of its sculptured form sweep upwards from the sides of the room into the central clerestory dome. Along either side of the clerestory ventilation is provided through narrow elongated round-cornered openings. The ceiling itself is stopped short of the walls by a distance of a few centimetres, where concealed perimeter lighting is effectively used to pick up the grain texture of the longitudinally planked wooden wall covering. In its own right, this is one of the most innovative and attractive rooms on the ship.

Of the other public areas designed by John Wright for Tourist Class, the Peacock Room and Cricketers Tavern were the most noteworthy. While the decor of the Peacock Room has changed over the years, the 'Cricketers' has fortunately remained unaltered.

The Peacock Room was originally intended as a smoking room and a quiet alternative lounge to the larger William Fawcett room. Its curved walls and flat ceiling were clad with blue dyed veneer. The same colour was continued with added stripes of orange and gold in the curtains, which could be drawn along the entire length of the side walls. The floor was white, with black diagonal stripes marking one section of it for dancing. The room was decorated with a relief on its end wall and a latticed ceiling canopy, both done in blonde woods.

The canopy was one of a number of fixtures removed shortly after *Canberra* ran her sea trials. This, along with the two elaborate glass and aluminium fountain fixtures from the William Fawcett Room fell unfortunate victim to the ship's initial imbalance of trim afloat. Loss of the fountains was particularly unfortunate as they were a key element of the larger lounge's stylised palm court decorative scheme.

The Cricketers Tavern was designed as the Tourist Class pub, and has in fact become one of the entire ship's favourite 'watering holes'. This is a bright room panelled in willow, which flanks the port side of the boiler casing. It also serves as the main thoroughfare between the William Fawcett and Peacock Rooms. Colin Cowdrey, the England cricketer, served as a consultant on its decoration. The long inside wall displays a montage of genuine cricket bats, balls, gloves, stumps and club caps. A wide hand grip recessed into the outer edge of the white marble bar is twine-wound in the fashion of a bat handle. The outer side of the room is divided into semicircular bays. The screens separating these each bear specially commissioned lifesize portraits of cricket immortals, W G Grace, Sir Donald Bradman, Learie N Constantine and K S Ranjitsinhji.

The decoration of this room is successful in creating a genuinely club-like atmosphere without recourse to the overworked stereotype of ersatz 'Ye Olde English' pub rusticity. The cricketers theme creates a unique and congenial setting without gimmicks.

The prize for the most short-lived decorative scheme on *Canberra* must surely go to the Pop Inn, across the boiler uptake from the Cricketers. The walls of this teenagers' room were adorned with hot poker-work graffiti that 'may encourage or inhibit teenagers from extending the design on a do-it-yourself basis'. The artist was a then young and relatively unknown David Hockney of the Royal College of Art.

The story is that P & O's marine superintendent was not in favour of encouraging passenger graffiti – not even in the Pop Inn. He ordered the walls to be repanelled before the ship entered service. One wonders whether this work would have been saved if the artist's future fame could have been foreseen.

The cinema, which is the only room on *Canberra* of double-deck height. This fact is not obvious owing to the single level seating arrangement and the ceiling treatment. (Stewart Bale, courtesy of Merseyside Maritime Museum)

The Peacock Room as originally completed with its canopy ceiling and indirect lighting scheme. (Stewart Bale, courtesy of Merseyside Maritime Museum)

Canberra's unusually high passenger capacity, originally some 2200 persons, gave rise to a number of cabin design innovations. Among the problems to be overcome were those of providing as many cabins as possible with a view of the outside world. This was particularly important in First Class, where the price paid was higher. Tourist Class accommodations had to cater to the high volume of government-assisted Australian emigrant trade as well as to meet the somewhat higher expectations of cruise clientele. Cabins in all classes and price ranges had to serve the passengers' home needs over longer than usual periods of time – nearly four weeks for the whole passage from Southampton to Sydney or vice versa.

The majority of First Class and Interchangeable cabins on *Canberra* are arranged in 'court' groupings of from four to eight units each, which provide the inner rooms with natural daylight and a view through the large windows at ship's side. The idea is in reality a modern derivative of a turn-of-the-century innovation known as the Bibby cabin. The name comes from the Bibby Line, whose ships are credited with having first introduced this particular quirk of shipboard layout. It was a compromise arrangement of providing a far greater proportion of 'outside'

The Peacock Room after the floating ceiling had been removed following *Canberra*'s sea trials. (P & O Group)

The William Fawcett Room with its original furniture, and the 'fountains' (centre right) which were removed after the ship ran her sea trials. (Stewart Bale, courtesy of Merseyside Maritime Museum)

Canberra's unique Cricketers Tavern, which has turned out to be one of her most enduring interiors. Even its original furniture has been retained. (Author's photo)

accommodations. Fresh air and daylight were admitted to the inside rows of cabins by way of a short narrow alleyway in each extending to the ship's side, past the legitimate outside room. These Bibby alleyways, as they were called, were usually given a sense of purpose by placing the wash basin or a chest of drawers at the far end, beneath the porthole.

Although arguably a waste of valuable space, the Bibby cabin was nonetheless very popular. Literally thousands of them were built into ships the world over, until as recently as the 1950s. *Canberra*'s cabin arrangement is but one of several innovations spawned from the original idea.

The court arrangement is based on an idea promted by the noted American naval architect, George G Sharp. It effectively turns the original arrangement inside out so that the private Bibby alleyways are opened up to form the communal court. The side-to-side or athwartships corridors giving access to the cabins are thus progressively widened towards the side of the ship. Where the dimension of the passage increases at each row of cabins, there are outward-facing vertical ribbon windows in the private accommodations to either side. The court itself fulfils the function of the original Bibby alleyways for all six to eight rooms. Sharp's philosophy was that of 'bringing the side of the ship, in effect, to the rooms'.

Limited use of this arrangement was made on a number of American ships built during the 1930s. First to do so was American Export Line, on their original Four Aces which were built in 1931. *Excalibur*, *Exochorda*, *Exeter* and *Excambion* each had four 'veranda' groupings of cabins. These were laid out in groups of five to six cabins either side of the single centreline passage on A deck. The line's brochures proclaimed this as 'the ultimate in stateroom comfort and a privacy and spaciousness hitherto obtainable only at great expense'. At about the same time, veranda cabins were also featured on Moore McCormack's *Scanpenn*-class cargo/passenger vessels. Later, similar cabins were also built on the three American-built Panama Railroad liners, *Panama*, *Ancon* and *Cristobal*.

The basic cabin layout for *Canberra* represents a refinement and greatly extended use of the idea. During the early stages of her construction, full scale mock-ups of groups of cabins were fabricated ashore. Different units were furnished and decorated by Sir Hugh Casson, John Wright and Barbara Oakley, with each designer incorporating his or her own ideas. These were complete in every conceivable detail, right down to the placement of light fixtures and switches, loudspeakers and telephones, clothes hooks and towel rails, bedspreads and curtains.

The mock-ups were carefully studied by P & O management. Their recommendations were passed back to the designers, with Barbara

Development of the court cabin arrangement from its Bibby-style predecessor. (Drawing – John West)

Cutaway illustration of a veranda cabins grouping from the American Export Lines' second *Excalibur* and *Exeter* of 1948. (American Export Isbrandtsen Lines, courtesy of Gordon Turner)

Artist's impression showing an isometric view of a typical six-cabin court grouping on *Canberra*. (P & O)

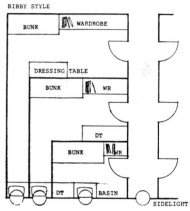

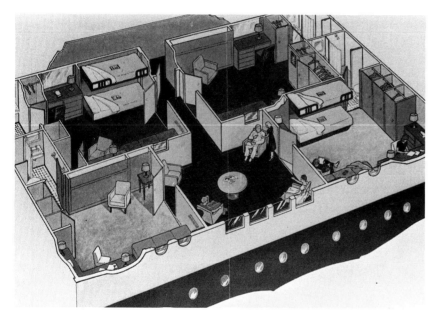

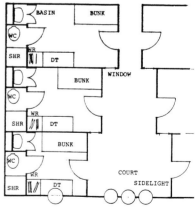

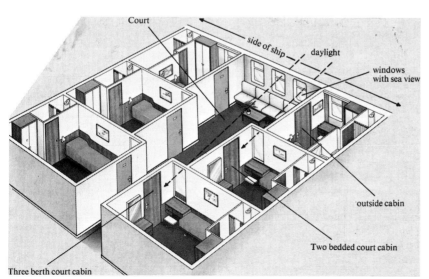

Oakley ultimately being given responsibility for all passenger and crew cabins aboard *Canberra*.

By nature of the court layout, the inner cabins tend to be larger, providing space for two to four passengers. The outside cabins are generally singles, some of which are fitted with upper pullman berths. The arrangement works best in the semicircular forward part of the superstructure on A and B decks. Here the greater radius of the outermost cabins compensates for the added space taken up by the court alleyways and facilitates a more uniform size of the outer and inner accommodations. Throughout *Canberra*, the courts are large enough to accommodate a settee and coffee table beneath the windows at the ship's side. The court thus serves as an informal reception area for the cabins surrounding it – a touch of luxury which compensates, psychologically at least, for the reduced size of many outside cabins.

Although not part of her preliminary plan, this type of accommodation was incorporated into *Oriana*'s layout at a later stage of building, following the example being set round the corner at P & O. Daylight is admitted to the Orient Line ship's courts through her distinctive elliptical double sidelights which are paired one above the other. However, for a number of the smaller cabins the effect was achieved not by a court as such, but rather by setting the walls of the alleyways at a slight angle rather than dead athwartships. The additional passage width so gained at the inner side of each pair of rooms was sufficient to accommodate the required windows in the rooms further inboard. Similar bulges in a number of the corridors aboard the *Imperator*-class ships and in

A 1947 plan showing possible arrangements of Sharp's 'air-light' concept (top) in contrast with the court cabin plan realised on B deck aboard *Canberra* (bottom). Note also the radial layouts forward in both plans. (*Marine Engineering and Shipping Review*, P & O)

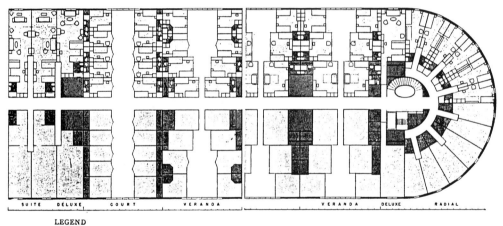

FIG. 1.—APPLICATION OF AIR-LIGHT ARRANGEMENTS TO VESSEL OF 90 FEET BEAM

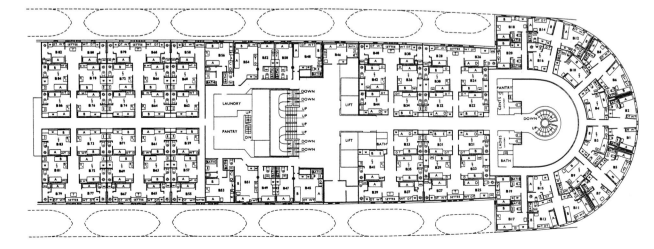

Looking across the entire beam of *Canberra* through one of the courts on C deck forward (cabins C-15 to C-27). (Author's photo)

One of the inner court cabins (A-69), showing its window in the corner above the bureau to the right of the door. (Author's photo)

Admiral von Tirpitz (delivered to Canadian Pacific as *Empress of Australia*) would suggest that perhaps the whole idea may have originated with those early German ships.

The court arrangement also has the advantage of admitting intervals of daylight to the long fore and aft passageways. This feature is somewhat reminiscent of Edwardian ships' interiors, where it was still customary for the athwartships alleyways to be carried to a porthole in the side of the ship. It is a welcome throwback, a departure from the claustrophobic fluorescent monotony of most ship's cabin passageways. Such contact with the outside world from within the belly of a large ship is a source of reassurance and orientation. If the position of the sun, tone of the sky and colour of the sea can at least be periodically glimpsed, then one is perchance reminded of which side of the ship one is on, whether walking fore or aft and if it is lunch or dinner time.

The court cabin arrangement is not featured aboard other ships built since *Canberra*. This is through no fault of the design itself, but rather a function of other changes which have ocurred in ship design. A variation of the idea might have materialised in Knud Kloster's futuristic *Elysian* cruise ship if she had actually been built in the 1970s.

A fore and aft passage on A deck, looking forward towards the spiral staircase. Although extending along the ship's centre, this is reached by intervals of daylight from the courts at either side, as seen in the foreground and again near the stairs. (Author's photo)

Diagram of a convertible cabin, showing how it can be made up as either a two-berth unit with shower and lavatory or with its plumbing fittings concealed by two extra bunks. (Drawing – John West)

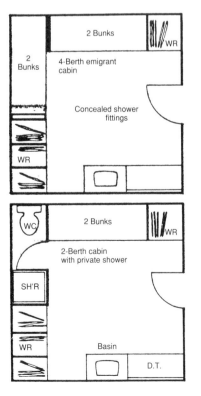

The idea has since come ashore, where it has appeared in various forms. James Stirling's design for the student residence at St Andrews University in Scotland is based on a plan resembling an open hand with its fingers outstretched. The walls of its 'fingers' are zig-zagged in the manner of some of *Oriana*'s courts so that the windows of the student rooms face a view of the North Sea and the mountains beyond, rather than the walls of the adjacent wings of the building. This resembles the window arrangement of *Canberra*'s inner court cabins, except here the court is a real open space.

A closer resemblance of *Canberra*'s plan is to be found in Maison Alcan, the new Montréal headquarters of The Aluminum Company of Canada. Here the architects, Ray Affleck and Peter Rose, have used the court arrangement for offices so as to gain the maximum benefit of daylight within a comparatively low twelve-storey structure in the city centre. The building is by no means Alcan's only link with *Canberra*, since the company supplied much of the aluminium alloy used in her superstructure.

Although the layout of Tourist Class cabins on *Canberra* was generally more traditional, there was one notable innovation in the form of a convertible two-to-four berth cabin. This was devised to satisfy the divergent needs of emigrant and cruise passengers. During line voyages to Australia these served as four-berth accommodations, without private toilet facilities. For cruising or upgraded line service, these rooms could be quickly turned into two-berth units with their own lavatory and shower.

The switch can be easily affected by a cabin steward in less than one minute. It involves simply folding one set of upper and lower berths away into a wall recess, thereby revealing the concealed lavatory and shower fixtures. A retractable partition with its own door is then unfolded from one end of the space to divide it from the rest of the room. It is a sea-going version of the type of ingenuity which is indigenous to the design of North American railway sleeping cars. Since *Canberra* entered full time cruising service in the early 1970s, most of these convertible cabins have remained permanently in their two-berth arrangement with private facilities.

Apart from the court and convertible cabins there are vast numbers of standard Tourist Class cabins of various sizes, with and without private toilets, inside and outside. Additional First Class accommodations included four deluxe and eight intermediate suites, along with a number of small inside singles along the ship's centreline. There were also special 'nursery cabins' for families travelling in First Class with infants.

Acoustics and noise suppression were given thorough consideration in *Canberra*'s planning. The normal mechanical sources of shipboard noise had to a great extent already been dealt with by virtue of the ship's aft machinery location. The turbo-electric plant was by its design inherently less prone to vibration than were geared steam turbines or diesel installations at the time. Care was also taken in the placement of other auxiliary items such as airconditioning units, stores lifts, galley and laundry equipment, etc, so as to keep them as far as possible from passenger and crew sleeping accommodations.

The use of airconditioning itself also served to make the accommodations much quieter. Less frequent changes of air are needed than with the old mechanical ventilation systems. The volume and velocity of air moving through the ship's ductwork are thus reduced, along with its own sound and tendency to carry machine noise. Gone was the characteristic eternal shipboard hiss emanating from innumerable bulbus inlet jets and punkah louvres in the days before airconditioning.

There remained the passengers themselves as the only major source of noise to be dealt with. This involved the normal issues such as proper acoustic treatment of public areas like the cinema and lounges used for live entertainment or dancing. The dining rooms were critical, owing to the inherent noise level of several hundred passengers handling cutlery and crockery. Added to this is the level of dinner table conversation which must also be dealt with in those spaces with their low ceilings.

It was, however, the generally quieter sleeping accommodations which presented the greatest difficulties. With the reduced levels of mechanical and airborne noise from the ship herself, it was domestic sounds from adjacent cabins which became the major issue. Passengers, even in the most expensive suites, are unlikely to complain about engine noise. However, if snoring, giggling or argumentative shipmates can be overheard from the room next door, that's a different matter!

With the type of plywood or marinite partitions traditionally used in ships' accommodations, even normal conversation would be likely to carry in *Canberra*'s quiet surroundings. This was overcome by designing a double-skin partition with its two sides fully isolated from each other. This would prevent the transmission of sound through the intervening free air space. To further suppress resonant sounds, each side of the partition was detuned by building it up from a series of randomly spaced marinite strips bonded to an open weave canvas facing.

These partitions were assembled using specially designed tracks, which were first fastened to the decks and the deckhead beams. The two sides of each wall were then assembled and screwed into place, making sure that they did not make internal contact. Decorative wall coverings were likewise fastened to either side, with plastic dividing strips fitted to conceal the panel joins. The finished ceilings were then attached directly to the overhead structure, but were isolated from the walls by a 6.35mm gap filled with compliant plastic sealing.

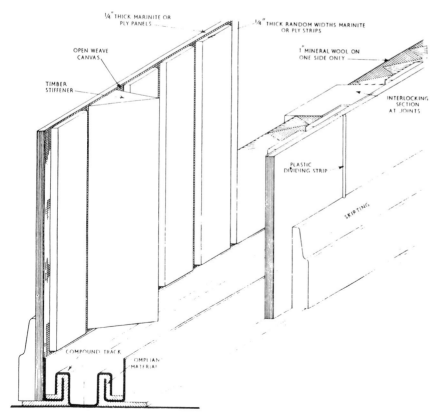

Diagram of the double-skin partitions used in *Canberra*'s accommodations, showing how the two completely isolated sides are attached to a special compound track. This provided the needed sound proofing without significantly increasing the thickness or weight of the partitions. (Drawing courtesy of the Royal Institution of Naval Architects)

There are one or two other features of *Canberra*'s accommodations which are particularly worthy of mention. They are typical of the care that went into the practical aspects of her planning. Throughout her many corridors and alleyways recesses were provided at regular intervals containing several shelves placed conveniently at about chest height. These were intended to give the stewards somewhere to put linen, tea trays and other items used in their work, rather than having to pile such things on the floor, as was the usual practice in older ships. It was a novel idea at the time. However, the cabin stewards' lot has been improved on later ships by simply providing the same type of service trolleys used in hotels.

Another practical matter that was addressed was that of lavatory odours. This was of particular concern in Tourist Class where there was a high dependency on communal toilet facilities by those occupying cabins either without their own plumbing or those convertible units which were being used in their four-berth mode. The solution was found by fitting small diameter ventilation pipes to openings in the rear of each lavatory bowl just below the seat. These toilets had to be ordered especially for *Canberra*, and were fitted throughout the entire ship regardless of the type and class of accommodation, or whether it was for passengers or crew.

Although perhaps very small matters in themselves compared with *Canberra*'s major design innovations, these last mentioned points represent the sort of finishing touches to the creativity and progressive thinking that went into the ship.

C M Squarey, a well-known marine writer and ship critic of the day, used a theatrical analogy to sum up his impression of *Canberra* in the 1 June, 1961 issue of *Shipbuilding and Shipping Record*:

> In the theatre world quite often the judgement of the dramatic critics does not tally with what the public thinks of a play. And what does matter about this ship is what the public is going to think of her. And there one can only, in the light of one's experience, indulge in predictions. But I do venture to predict she is in for a very long and a very successful run because, as I judge it, she has in her so very much of what the people want and look for and are prepared to pay for. In theatre language the script is very good, the production brilliant, the cast (ship's personnel) well chosen and determined to send the customers away happy.

Shelves placed in the cabin alleyways as a working convenience for the stewards. (Author's photo)

Chapter VI

FROM GRAND HOTEL TO MODERN RESORT

C ANBERRA's recognition in the architectural press was perhaps one of the most significant and incisive pieces of publicity to come from her debut in 1961. Extensive coverage was also given in newspapers and popular magazines, including a specially commissioned four-page pictorial feature in the *Illustrated London News*, showing interior renderings by artist H J Neave, and a superb cutaway view by G H Davis. *Punch* published a most amusing article by J B Boothroyd, in praise of the ship's many outstanding design features. Similar enthusiasm on the part of the shipbuilding and marine engineering press, including special souvenir numbers of several technical journals, was also her just due. However, *Canberra* is one of the very few ships to have achieved recognition in architectural circles. She was described in *The Architectural Review*, the *Architects' Journal* and one or two other publications.

The Architectural Review is one of Britain's finest architectural journals. It has been in circulation now for more than one hundred years, dealing with all aspects of architecture, interior and industrial design. Coverage ranges from details of the latest buildings in Britain and abroad to historical features on architecture and architects of the past; from the use of steel and glass in America to descriptions of traditional mud dwellings in little-known parts of Africa and Asia. Events of great architectural significance, such as the completion of Edwin Lutyens's public buildings and city plan for New Delhi, the Festival of Britain, and the design of Cunard's *Queen Elizabeth 2*, have warranted entire special issues.

Prior to the interest in ship design which surrounded the building of *Oriana*, *Canberra* and *Queen Elizabeth 2*, this prestigious journal seldom dealt with the subject. There had been a general article on ocean liner interiors in 1914, quoted earlier in this volume, and coverage of the Orient Line's *Orion* and *Orcades* in the 1930s.

The truth of the matter was that the majority of ship's interiors were considered to be of little architectural merit. As part of a movement to foster a greater general awareness of the situation, a number of articles on the subject appeared in *The Architectural Review* starting in 1956 and concluding in 1969, when *Queen Elizabeth 2* was delivered.

Although Cunard's two great 'ships of state' were still very much in their prime, the company's design department had been developing ideas for new Queen-class liners since 1951. As detailed plans slowly began to take shape towards the middle of the decade, the architectural profession became increasingly worried that they were going to, so to speak, 'miss the boat'. Without the influence of first-rate architectural and industrial design, modern materials and colours, they feared that these future ships would demonstrate to the rest of the world an unjustly poor impression of British architectural and industrial design. Above all, they wanted to eradicate the tired and hackneyed floating Grand Hotel style which had become so ingrained in the nation's shipboard architecture.

Those first floating hotels such as *Umbria* and *City of Berlin* belonged to an age when passengers still felt that they faced considerable discomfort and peril in going to sea. Mindful of this, shipowners sought to reassure their clientele with surroundings on board that at least looked something like home. As the size and sophistication of liners increased, so their interior decor progressed from reassuring homeliness to unabashed grandeur.

The philosophy was that, given surroundings resembling perhaps the London Ritz or some great country house, the passenger would enjoy the same feeling of security and well-being that such places could offer ashore. Here the steward could draw heavy damask curtains against the churning North Atlantic outside the windows, whilst the passengers sipped their brandy amongst the potted palms in the glow of a bogus fireplace. Such interiors were skilfully contrived to minimise as far as possible any impression of being on a ship at all. It was only upon venturing out of those plush sanctuaries to the honest nautical milieu of a teakwood deck that the passenger was re-united with reality.

This particular phase of design reached its zenith with the work of Charles Mèwes, architect to the renowned hotelier, César Ritz. This noted French designer was first engaged by Albert Ballin to replicate the style of his outstanding hotel work aboard Hamburg America Line's *Deutschland* in 1900. The enormous success of this eventually led to the formation of the Mèwes, Davis and Bischoff collaborative, which ultimately designed interiors for the majority of top Atlantic liners built during the following two decades.

These interiors reflected the understated good taste, refined elegance and sheer luxury of the hotels ashore. This rather scholarly style was based largely on period revival. Among its most famous manifestations aboard ship were the Palladian Lounge in *Aquitania* and the Pompeiian Bath aboard *Imperator*.

A traditional Grand Hotel-type interior in the Mèwes and Davis style. This example shows the First Class smoke room in *Mauretania*, designed by Harold A Peto. (Cunard, courtesy of Gordon Turner)

The next phase came during the highly competitive decades of the 1920s and 1930s. As individual nations and rival steamship lines competed fiercely for supremacy, particularly on the North Atlantic, there ensued a veritable battle of technical and architectural one-upmanship in shipbuilding. Each tried to create something grander and more awe-inspiring than the other.

The human scale of those Mèwes and Davis interiors became lost in the cavernous lounges, dining rooms and galleries of the larger liners. The decoration of these colossal spaces, some of which were as much as three decks high, continued however to build on the same basic hotel theme of their original work. Its artistic purity quickly eroded into what one architectural critic later described as 'a mixture of naive reminiscences, inappropriate artiness and bourgeois pretentiousness'. The public rooms on the larger ships were simply too big to carry off the style effectively without looking overdressed.

The Grand Hotel style of La Belle Époque had by then passed out of vogue ashore. It was no longer in keeping with the more informal lifestyles of the day, making its continued shipboard rendition a tired anachronism. With few exceptions, the later influence of modern and art deco styles aboard ship brought about little improvement. This only added to the artistic chaos, without asserting any identifiable sense of unity or direction.

When *Queen Mary* was being planned in the early 1930s, the architectural profession voiced its concern that such visual chaos might become much more pronounced aboard ship. An editorial feature published in the *Architects' Journal* of 15 January 1934 made stark comparison of the lamentable state of affairs in British ship design with the outstanding foreign examples of *Bremen*, *Europa* and *Kungsholm*. *Ile de France* was also cited as a bold expression of modern design, albeit rather garish. The author concluded his critique with the plaintive plea:

> Even if the new Cunarder must have an outlandish name ending in 'ia' (and how wearisome those obscure Roman provinces are becoming), let it be something nearer *Contemporania* than those hardy annuals on the slips, the *Jacobethia* and the *Georgiporgia*.

Of the more contemporary approach to interior design afloat, *Normandie*'s vast interiors were a great success. Her public rooms were generally modern in style and of a more informal character, despite the use of some rather old-fashioned furniture. Their layout was in geometrical unity with the structure of the ship herself, which contributed a further impression of good rationalist design.

The modern interiors of the first *Nieuw Amsterdam* and *Kungsholm* were more successful in making a nationalist statement through functional contemporary design. Among British owners, only the Orient Line had made any significant progress in this regard. The much admired decor of their *Orion* brought international recognition to her young designer, Brian O'Rorke, and established the line's reputation for progressive ship design.

In his coverage of *Orion*, *The Architectural Review*'s editor expressed an optimistic outlook on her design:

> Her interest, from the point of view of the travelling public, lies in the fact that for the first time a single architect, Mr Brian O'Rorke has been responsible for the passengers' accommodations. The ship therefore represents, not a hackneyed collection of decorators' effusions, but a unity. Mr Brian O'Rorke was consulted at the early stages of the ship's design and had considerable opportunities for controlling the disposition and shape of the different rooms he was called upon to dec-

orate. The *Orion* is consequently of interest to the profession in that she opens up a new territory in which architects are likely to operate in the future and enlarge their sphere of activity. She is of interest historically in that she continues a process which has been going on since 1911, when Walter Gropius designed his first factory, and is a further step towards the inter-penetration of Art and Industry.

Bremen, Nieuw Amsterdam, Kungsholm and *Orion* were but the very few exceptions to the general rule. Recollection of an over embellished pseudo art deco style became the legacy of the Cunard Queens and many of their contemporaries. This has since come to be referred to loosely as, ocean liner, or, New York skyscraper lobby, style. In spite of its shortcomings, fond reminiscences of it continue to be cherished by steamship enthusiasts and nostalgic romantics as the last fading vestige of a bygone era of ocean liner opulence.

The architectural profession's recollections were not so fond! More distressing was the fact that the approach to British ship design had since made little progress. Ian McCallum, *The Architectural Review*'s executive editor, published a scathing appreciation of the state of the art in his February 1956 issue. The question was asked:

Orion's First Class lounge, which itself was a fairly simple interior, but nonetheless one which is considered to be the turning point in British shipboard design. (P & O)

Why ... given a forceful, characteristic and entirely successful style outside does a ship have to have the worst kind of Grand Hotel style inside. Is it beyond all ingenuity to adopt and develop the nautical style, to provide interiors that are not such resounding anachronisms?

He went on to describe the 'antinautical' floating Grand Hotel style and its faults in no uncertain terms:

> A constant and particularly obnoxious influence ... is national and imperial propaganda. Since these liners constitute a permanent floating exhibition in which the passenger is imprisoned for varying lengths of time, it is neither possible nor necessary to resist the temptation to wave the flag. On such occasions, however, the conspicuous position of the flag waver should stand up to inspection – an overdressed vulgarian would clearly be miscast for the role. But, this is what these liners are, judged as examples of the best their countries can do in the decorative arts. Granted the craftsmanship is near faultless, the ship is a masterpiece of engineering, the navigation and service impeccable. The decoration is, as a rule, untouched by any acknowledged master of the art ...

The already strong rhetoric of this epistle was amplified by the accompanying pictures, which showed views of 'antinautical' interiors contrasted with 'nautical' examples. The best of these was a pair of photographs showing lounges on the *United States* and an unnamed British liner, also of the early 1950s. The American illustration was captioned, 'An interior that allows people to play the active part', while its British counterpart was caustically labelled, 'An interior which looks as if the mice had been at it'. However, on the 'nautical' side of the scale, Orient's then new *Orsova* was featured quite prominently, showing how this line at least had upheld *Orion*'s high standard of modern design in Britain.

Strangely, for many years the example of *Orion* was not followed by other British lines, including the owner's sister company, P & O. Nonetheless, Orient Line continued to back this same approach on all their later liners, right through to *Oriana*. Brian O'Rorke himself worked as consulting architect with Misha Black's Design Research Unit as principal interior designers, on what would be both his and Orient's last ship. Excellent though *Oriana*'s interior design was, it was rather a case of déja vu. This was what everyone already expected of a new Orient ship, even as late as 1960. The basic elements of *Orion*'s styling had over the years been quietly refined and kept up to date. It came as no surprise!

Encouragement was also to be found in the domain of the less expensive passenger classes. From the standpoint of Ian McCallum's critique, those below the salt, so to speak, at least had more appropriate shipboard surroundings, albeit largely without the convenience of en suite baths and lavatories. Although itself hardly appropriate in First Class, the white paint and linoleum habitat of Tourist Class demonstrated the honest value of simplicity and functionality.

Simple and unadorned interiors can be rendered with a sense of luxury and elegance through the use of serviceable top quality materials and fittings, comfortable furniture and an effective colour scheme. The fine example of the 1940s-built Danish North Sea ships *Kronprins Frederik* and *Kronprinsesse Ingrid* makes this point abundantly clear. The delightful interiors of these little liners were a study in simple elegance. What's more, the warm club like atmosphere of their public rooms was achieved without the adornment of window curtains!

Ian McCallum went on to examine the recent progress that had been made on a number of Italian and American ships:

> Both countries are, in a loose term, extrovert, delighting in bold colours and experiments in form. In the liner *United States*, for example, the Americans have shown what can be done in an idiomatic style of decoration, which though it may not exhibit the higher flights of imagination, is both luxurious and simple... The *United States* is a decorator's ship, and it shows the advantages of humility.

This and Italia's *Cristoforo Colombo* were cited and illustrated as good examples of what could be done on modern ships.

Mr McCallum concluded that, while these examples were indeed a step in the right direction, more could be done if the architects were to become involved at a much earlier stage of planning. This would allow them to have some influence over the structural planning, particularly in cases such as *Southern Cross* where the machinery would be aft, and there would be greater freedom to develop more exciting interior layouts. This was, however, a view that was not necessarily so enthusiastically shared by naval architects and shipbuilders.

As far as layout was concerned, it appeared that the tradition of the four-stacker still held sway. The plan was usually absolutely symmetrical with the peculiar shipboard oddity of those H- and U-shaped rooms worked in around the numerous casings and other interruptions. If there were not enough of these obstructions, it seemed as though substitutes were found in the form of ship's offices, shops, lavatories and so on, which were doggedly lined up along the centre line in their places.

These shortcomings in internal layout continued to prevail even on ships of advanced structural design, including many of the best known liners built during the 1950s and 1960s. For instance, the divided funnel uptakes on Canadian Pacific's latest *Empress of England* and *Empress of Canada* yielded little improvement in layout other than their centreline cabin alleyways. Here the opportunity to develop a *Normandie* or *Nieuw Amsterdam* style axial layout of the public spaces was somehow missed by a wide margin. Even where the decor was admirably modern, the layout remained rather old fashioned. *Oriana* still had glass enclosed promenades and galleries flanking her boiler casing on the veranda deck. A fairly traditional layout of catering facilities and dead centre location of the purser's office were still retained on the otherwise thoroughly modern *Canberra*.

Cunard, on the other hand, had good reason to defend their existing interior design standards, criticised as they were. The *Queen Mary* and *Queen Elizabeth* had virtually become institutions as two of the world's most famous and best loved liners. Arguably, the interior decor was itself an endearing influence which, for their American passengers at least, evoked a sort of romantic impression of the whole nation's strong sense of tradition. This was a quality which matured as the ships aged.

The *Ivernia*'s First Class lounge, which 'looked as if the mice had been at it'. (Cunard, courtesy of Gordon Turner)

Cunard rightfully perceived the distinct trading value of maintaining traditional styling and service as operators of the world's most famed Atlantic fleet. As late as 1961, a Georgian-style interior was reportedly favoured by the Line's then chairman, Sir John Brocklebank, for their new Queens. This would probably have been executed in the manner of other recent Cunarders, described in company releases as 'recreating the past in terms of the present by using modern methods of construction to interpret some of the gems of historical interior design and construction'. Even as late as 1967, when the architectural profession had all but won the battle, there was a short lived plan to decorate the discothque on *Queen Elizabeth 2* in a style resembling ye olde 'typically English' hunting stables.

Why change? Does it make sense to abandon an apparently successful aesthetic of tradition for some notion to prove the country's architectural and design virility overseas?

Lifestyles and the public's view of travel were changing by the 1950s. Thanks to higher personal incomes and more leisure time, people were becoming far more accustomed to travel in general. The development of long-range commercial air travel and the proliferation of the private motor car had also done much to assert public confidence in the means of travel, the vehicle itself. Travellers no longer needed the sense of security afforded by those lavish shipboard interiors, which were devised to distract them from any impression of being on the move. The technically motivated interior decor of the Comet and 707 aircraft made no pretence to conceal the impression of flight. Whatever reassurance the air passenger might still need was more likely to be provided by the carefully chosen rhetoric of prepared (and even tape-recorded) loudspeaker announcements.

Top rank industrial designers had for some time been employed to give a functional modern identity to various transport media. This was particularly prevalent in the United States, where Henry Dreyfuss, Raymond Loewy and Walter Teague were leaders in the field. The ergonomic design of seating for the Lockheed Constellation and Electra airliners was executed by Dreyfuss. Later, Teague used full-scale mockups to perfect his interior design of the Boeing 707. Here he succeeded in reducing the inherent impression of crowding in an aircraft interior by minimising the intrusion of visual detail. Light fixtures, air vents, emergency equipment and hand luggage stowage were recessed or flush mounted overhead to be as inconspicuous as possible.

The First Class main lounge aboard *United States*, which 'allows people to play the active part'. (United States Lines)

The simple elegance of Danish interior design as shown here in the main lounge of the DFDS ferry *Kronprinsesse Ingrid*. (DFDS)

Raymond Loewy, perhaps best known for his Studebaker designs and bottle styling for Coca Cola, was also active in the railway and motor-coach fields. He redesigned steam locomotives for the Pennsylvania Railroad in 1936 to portray a modern image aimed at keeping the railway competitive with its newfound airborne competition from the DC3 airliner. He also produced the unified aluminium coach body styling for Greyhound, along with the company's distinctive leaping dog logo.

A 'vehicle derived' metal and enamel aesthetic made its way into domestic industrial design. Many ordinary household appliances were clearly influenced by motor car design, with, for example, chrome refrigerator handles made to resemble the door handles of a Studebaker; many of these objects were in fact designed by the same people. In Germany, Dieter Rams produced the elegantly simple and functional design of Braun appliances, ranging from their famed Kitchen Machine to home entertainment equipment, cameras and electric shavers. Meanwhile the design philosophy of Italy's Olivetti was epitomised by the company's Lexicon and Lettera typewriter models. These machines demonstrated a perfection of unity between their complex inner workings and their functionally styled enclosures. With such a high standard of product design in the ordinary home and office, why should anyone be expected to settle for less aboard ship?

The time had come for a similar machine- or vehicle-conscious approach to ship design too. Liners now had to compete not only with air travel, but with sophisticated modern resorts ashore. In either case, the ship was no longer 'the only way', but rather an alternative, either to jet travel, or to holidays at resorts ashore. As such, the passenger ship had to compete on the basis of the singular travel and recreation experience that she alone could offer. To do this successfully, the surroundings on board had to enhance the passenger's perception of the unique experience of being at sea aboard a great ship.

Here too, American industrial designers had achieved some outstanding results. Raymond Loewy was among the first with his interior styling of the Panama Railroad's *Panama*-class liners completed in the early 1940s. Ten years later, Henry Dreyfuss's work on the American Export Line's *Independence* and *Constitution* also involved exterior styling of the superstructure and open decks. Moore-McCormack's new *Brasil* and *Argentina*, of 1959, also featured styling by Loewy. These were all ships of sound modern design which demonstrated a unity of their technical and aesthetic design elements.

By the close of the decade, there were signs of improvement on at least the two largest ships built in Britain since *Queen Elizabeth*. Predictably, *Oriana* continued the progressive modern style adopted by Orient Line twenty-five years earlier on *Orion*. P & O's decision to follow with a similar approach for *Canberra* came to the architectural profession as blessed relief indeed! The interiors of a spate of other new British ships completed around the same time, including the new Union Castle flagship, *Windsor Castle*, were not so encouraging.

While *Oriana* and *Canberra* were fitting out, *The Architectural Review* again raised the subject of interior design aboard ship. In November 1960, it compared the Orient and P & O interiors with those of other recently completed British liners:

> ... it is distressing to find interiors like those of the *Caronia*, the *Ivernia*, the *Carinthia*, the *Sylvania* and the rest – comprising a bewildering sequence of banalities – representing contemporary British design.
>
> Today [Orient] line has continued in the lead. Their *Oriana*, on point of completion, designed internally by a group of architects co-ordinated by Misha Black of Design Research Unit, promises to be the best designed British ship to date. And the P & O have followed with the *Canberra*, now being fitted out with interior designs by Sir Hugh Casson and Neville Conder.
>
> Britain now has a number of able architects with experience to take over from the contract furnishers and others (not excluding the directors' wives when it comes to cabin furniture and bedspreads) who have hitherto set the depressing standard of ship interiors. Given the opportunity, such architects can help shipping companies, whose building programme means so much to British prosperity, to restore to the term 'shipshape' something of the connotation it had in the past.

The completed *Oriana* and *Canberra* emerged as proof that British firms such as Design Research Unit and the Casson Conder Partnership could indeed take over and produce the type of shipshape interiors the architectural profession wanted. A critique of the two ships was published the following September. Apart from further preaching to the as yet unconverted, it concluded its praise of their interior design and decoration by saying:

> A shiplike interior starts from the unique conditions of shipboard life and shipboard spaces, and becomes expressive in so far as it enhances the life that is lived in those spaces. It needs to be businesslike and direct, particularly in the cabins, and mindful of the sea. In the public areas it needs to make excessively wide and low rooms humanely comprehensible before it begins to play games with port and starboard lanterns to remind passengers of something they already know – that they are on a ship. Indeed if ship interior architects would stop imitating hotels or falling over backwards to prove they have stopped imitating hotels and approach their design problems with the same honesty and purpose as the best hotel architects, a convincing shiplike character would emerge without strain and equivocation.
>
> Where *Oriana* and *Canberra* are most conspicuously successful is where this kind of result has emerged from this kind of thinking. The decoration of the rooms is based on their use, and stems from the way they work ... the fact that the designers have had some hand in the choice of all equipment seen or used by passengers means that there is equally a sense of visual unity of the whole ship.

Only three months after this was published, Cunard cancelled their plans to build Q3. A building contract was finally signed three years later for an altogether different ship, known at first as Q4, the fourth 'Queen-class' Cunarder. The ship's initial interior and decorative design team was appointed in late 1965, a few months after the first section of her keel had been laid down. By the time this ship was launched as *Queen Elizabeth 2*, in September 1967, she already showed great promise of becoming a worthy flagship for the nation. At long last, the architects were winning their battle – the overdressed flagwaving vulgarian had finally been slain!

The final chapter of *The Architectural Review*'s campaign was written in the June 1969 issue, devoted almost entirely to coverage of *Queen Elizabeth 2*. Some parting thoughts on the subject were expressed by Sir Hugh Casson, co-ordinating architect of *Canberra*. His article, 'A Ship is an Island', which revealed a masterful understanding of ships and their design, concluded on a note of admirable humility:

> In the end all the technical skills and inspired guesswork, helped here by a fine company tradition and public affection bequeathed her by her two great predecessors, can do no more than give QE2 a good start. The final test is when at last she is on her own, A ship – to use Kipling's words – has to be 'sweetened' at sea; 'Lay your ears to the side of a new ship at sea', he wrote, 'and you will hear hundreds of little voices in every direction thrilling and buzzing, whispering and popping... like a telephone in a thunderstorm... and all the bits and pieces of every size and weight and responsibility learn how to take individually or together the strains of movement'.
>
> Only when she talks with one voice can she be said to have found herself to be able to bear the crown which we all believe is her due.

Cover illustration of *The Architectural Review*'s September 1961 issue, showing a montage of *Canberra* seen through her own windows and appearing again in a bottle on the table; obviously the profession was pleased. (*The Architectural Press*)

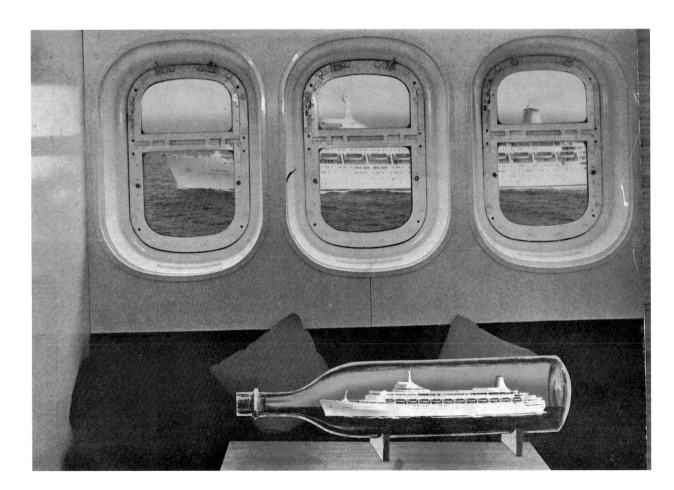

Chapter VII

A DUAL-ROLE FLAGSHIP

JAMES GARDNER was one of the first shoreside professional designers to be involved in Cunard's plans to build a ship which would replace *Queen Mary*. His earliest appearance on the scene came as soon as could possibly have been hoped for – the building contract had not even been signed. He recalls in his autobiography the initial visit he made to the Cunard building in Liverpool:

> ...(It) gives a friendly burp as I push through its swing doors and go up in a slow but sure mahogany lift, to be decanted into a world of brass doorknobs and polished lino. I fill the interval between Sir John Brocklebank's being made aware of my presence and the important moment when he is ready to receive me inspecting a beautiful model of the *Mauretania* hermetically sealed in a case like Snow White in her glass coffin.
>
> Brocklebank's purpose in meeting me was to make it clear that, whatever I did with the rest of her, the ship must have the traditional Cunard funnel. 'It is the insignia of the line you know, Cunard red.' Of course I know. Brocklebank must be wondering why a designer has been called in at all. Why can't they leave it to the yard? He has a point there. After generations of constructing ships, the yard men have built up a massive backlog of know-how. Once the underwater form has been determined by trials in a tank, the rest follows on the lines of the original clinker-built whale boat, with upswept bow and stern to take the seas – called sheer. This, even when refined and attenuated still gave the great iron ships some grace and a sense of riding the sea. Then the walls of the superstructure slope inwards very slightly – like the battered walls of old Paris apartments – to give strength. Shipbuilders call it tumblehome. Even the decks are cambered so they clear quickly when she takes the seas. All is fine curves, so to define her lines one is given sheets of numbers; so far along, so far in, so far up. The result can be a cobby bluffbowed coaster or a long slender ocean liner, and this is the way the *Mauretania* 'happened' – just as the elegant railway locomotives 'happened' in the early days of steam.

After meeting with the Cunard chairman he ventured into the drawing department to become acquainted with the 'happening' he was being asked to shape:

> I climb up the narrow stairs to the Cunard drawing office with some

Q3, the 'block of flats dumped in the sea' which confronted James Gardner on his first visit to Cunard. The top drawing shows the ship as he probably first saw her, before a funnel design had been chosen. Below, Q3 is shown with the large Strombos stack which the owners favoured. This funnel is an intrusion between the two tall masts. It was the first view which may well have inspired Gardner's adaptation of Q3 and the later Q4's designs. (Author's drawing)

James Gardner's original visualisation of Q3 with its tall slender stacks. Note the rendering of a Cunard house flag on the superstructure forward of the large windows. This attractive feature was later compromised to be replaced by the word 'Cunard' painted in its place. (James Gardner)

trepidation, as an outsider. Inside I find oak plan chests, high wooden stools and palefaced draughtsmen with a problem. The ship will have no sweeping curves; she is a block of utility flats dumped in the sea, and must ride uncomfortably high to pack in the essential accommodations – more like a piece of floating real estate.

The drawing office had put together a model in an attempt to make her look like a ship. One vent has been shaped like an obese 'streamlined' funnel, and the other which comes up at an unfortunate place, is disguised as a mast. For the rest it is an assembly of bits borrowed from the old *Queen Mary*. No longer on the defensive, I am itching to have a go, and am sure that she can still be shaped so she looks designed for the job or maybe even is in part. I parcel a stack of blueprints in brown paper and make for Lime Street Station feeling jubilant – or as near as I ever get to feeling jubilant. Something exciting is about to happen.

Certainly the following eight or so years would be exciting, not only for James Gardner and a handpicked group of his fellow architects and designers, but for everyone involved with the creation of the new ship.

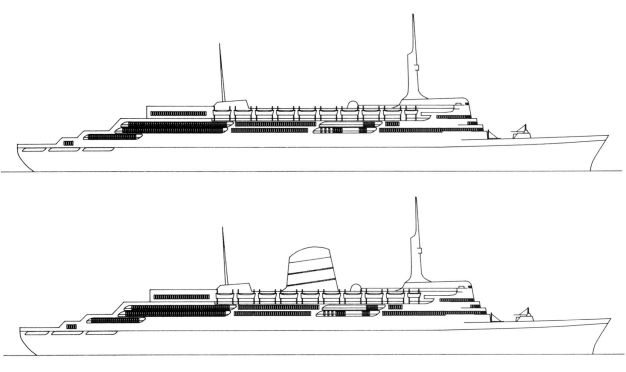

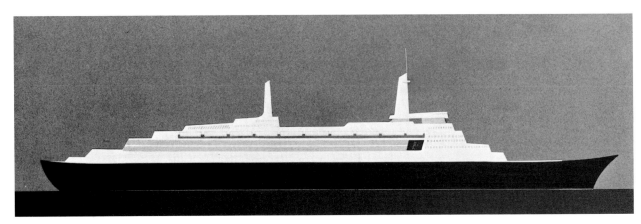

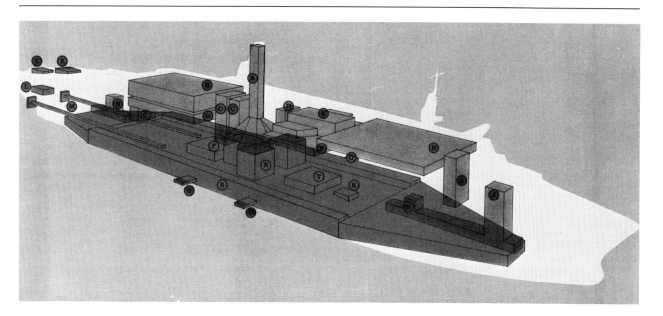

Ironically, the huge bundle of plans which he took on the train to London that night were for Q3, the ship which would never be built. His visualisation of her as a long slender liner with elegantly curved lines and a modern funnel was approved by Cunard only months before they declined to build her. Thus, at the end of 1961, the line had narrowly averted creating perhaps the greatest floating white elephant since Brunel's *Great Eastern*!

What was wrong with Q3 was that her design was based on a long-standing premise that a Cunard express Atlantic liner could not be made suitable for use in other trades. This supported the belief that a much higher standard of First Class accommodation was essential in North Atlantic service than in markets elsewhere. Together with the conventional approach to powering this ship with quadruple screws, the resulting 75,000-ton size emerged at only slightly less than that of her predecessors. As a virtual replacement of *Queen Mary*, she would have been too big and too conventional in concept. If built, she would probably have turned out rather like a larger version of *France*, which was under construction at the time. The example of the new Compagnie Générale Transatlantique ship has since demonstrated Cunard's wisdom in not building such a liner themselves.

It is doubtful that *France* ever turned a profit for her owners during her short twelve years in their service. After being laid up for the next five years, she luckily averted the inevitability of a premature scrapping when sold for conversion to the cruise ship *Norway*. Economically, it was largely due to the incredibly low price paid by Knut Kloster for her that such an extensive and costly refit was feasible at all. It is unlikely that a second latter-day Atlantic leviathan, belonging to Cunard or otherwise, would have also been so fortunate.

Although Q3 was rejected on the whole as the wrong ship for the jet age, her design embodied a number of progressive elements which survived. Indeed the later Q4 design, which eventually materialised as *Queen Elizabeth 2*, owes an important part of its origin to Q3. Much of the work done by Cunard's design department in reducing structural complexity and weight on Q3 would ultimately prove vital on the new ship. Since structurally Q4 would be no less a 'block of flats dumped in the sea' or a 'piece of floating real estate' than her unbuilt predecessor, then so too would James Gardner's ideas be kept. He was soon recalled to carry on from where he had left off with Q3.

When Cunard submitted their Q3 design for builders' tenders, they

Illustration of *Queen Elizabeth 2* showing the distribution of some of her main structural elements.

Legend

A- flue vents/uptakes; B- double room; C,D- passenger staircases/lifts; E- theatre; F- Columbia Restaurant; G- stabilisers; H- Britannia Restaurant; I- forward passenger staircase/lifts; J- cargo hatch; K- swimming pools; L- steering gear; M- propeller shafts; N- car lift/garage; O- engine casing/vents; P- turbines/condensers/gears; Q- Queens Room; R- three boilers; S- fuel/water/waste/ballast tanks; T- turbo alternators/refrigeration.

(Drawing by David Rock, *The Architectural Press*, courtesy of The University Archives, University of Liverpool)

encouraged the yards to put forward their own ideas on her overall design concept too. The winning bid came jointly from Vickers Armstrong and Swan Hunter & Wigham Richardson which, coincidentally, also offered the most progressive ideas on the ship's construction. After the dust had settled on the Q3 project, and Cunard had re-assessed their needs, Vickers Armstrong were again approached in May 1963, this time as consultants on the design of Q4.

Cunard's own naval architect, Dan Wallace, and chief marine engineer, Tom Kameen, headed the company's design team which was primarily responsible for the detailed planning and layout of the ship. Their work also involved collaboration with other specialists, including Parsons Marine Experimental Turbine Research and Development Association (PAMETRADA) which would design the machinery, James Gardner on the styling of the ship and the team of architects and designers responsible for her interiors. Vickers Armstrong's role was to implement their ideas on structural design, providing the optimum ratios of size, power and speed which would ultimately determine the ship's physical characteristics.

By this stage Cunard were thinking in terms of a smaller dual purpose twin-screw ship of around 50,000 tons – approximately the size of *United States*. The impetus for the twin-screw design came largely from the ideas put forward in the Vickers and Swan Hunter tender for Q3. Their proposal showed that the smaller ship was both technically and commercially feasible without seriously compromising Cunard's basic requirements. She would be large enough to maintain the company's prestigious 'big ship' image on the North Atlantic run. She would be equally suited for cruising, where the reduced overall dimensions and draught would enable her to navigate the Panama Canal and facilitate access to many more ports around the world.

Elevation and top views of the display model of Q4 which was first shown to the public in April 1967. (Cunard, courtesy of George Devol, World Ocean and Cruise Liner Society)

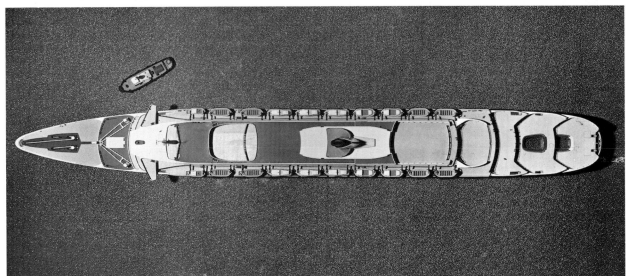

A twin-screw design would also offer a number of worthwhile economies for Cunard, provided that the stringent criteria of performance, passenger capacity and service could be met. The fuel consumption of such a ship could probably be reduced to about half that of the old Queens. It was reckoned that only four boilers would be needed, half the number required to raise full steam on the quadruple-screw *France*. Likewise, the number of main engines would be halved, making it possible for them to be housed in a single engine room. Conversely, the main engines of the old Queens and the newer quadruple-screw liners, *United States* and *France* were arranged two by two in tandem engine rooms – one each for the fore and aft pairs of screws. These economies along with recent developments in modern, powerful and compact machinery would significantly increase the amount of revenue earning space available on board for carrying passengers.

The advancement of modern lightweight engine and structural design was clearly demonstrated by a number of recently completed Atlantic liners. For instance, *France* represented an economy of 3000 tons in the weight of her machinery and a 40 per cent reduction in fuel consumption compared with *Normandie* built twenty-five years earlier. Although the newer ship was not as large, both were of quadruple-screw propulsion with nearly identical power and performance. Likewise a comparison of the smaller twin screw Holland America liners *Nieuw Amsterdam* and *Rotterdam* shows a reduction of 150 tons in the weight of the latter vessel's machinery.

These developments were of particular interest to Cunard in view of the performance that would be expected of Q4. The high service speed and large passenger capacity of the ship would require the most powerful and compact machinery of any passenger ship ever built. The design of this was contracted to PAMETRADA, who had been leaders in the field for some time, and who had recently done similar work for *Oriana*.

PAMETRADA was founded in 1944 to consolidate and rationalise marine turbine research and development in Britain. In the years which followed, it produced highly efficient marine turbine designs for both navy and merchant ships against stiff competition from diesel engine builders. Much of their success was achieved through the adoption of modern developments in industrial and aviation turbine designs for shipboard use. This largely involved metallurgical research in the use of lighter alloys for marine turbine construction. Chrome-nickel-vanadium was introduced for rotors and molybdenum steel for bearings. Special oil-hardened and tempered steels were also developed for use in other components such as reduction gears.

So far as providing a living prototype as the starting point for the new Queen's design, *Oriana* was almost ideal. She represented the type of dual purpose ship that Cunard wanted. Although a little smaller than what they had in mind, her speed and passenger capacity were also generally adequate for North Atlantic service. *Oriana* seemed to be proof enough that a twin-screw liner was a feasible option for Cunard.

Although *Canberra* has many of the same design features and a number of distinctive innovations of her own which were adopted, she was of heavier construction. On the question of machinery location, it was mainly for reasons of weight distribution and hull strength that an aft arrangement of *Canberra*'s type was avoided. Considering the greater length of Q4, balancing some 500 tons of propulsion hardware aft against a varying volume of fuel and water ballast forward would be difficult. The distribution of two major structural loads so far apart would be likely to cause excessive bending of the hull, particularly in North Atlantic service. A ship with engines aft designed for prolonged operation under such conditions would need additional strengthening, adding weight and in turn increasing her draught.

Another view of the model, conveying a sense of scale by way of comparison with the tug. (Cunard, courtesy of George Devol, World Ocean and Cruise Liner Society)

The location of *Queen Elizabeth 2*'s bimetallic joint beneath the lower row of large windows is clearly visible as caught by the sun in this view. The photo, which was taken in April 1987 upon her return to Southampton after re-engining in Germany, also shows the many other structural alterations made over the years. (Fotoflite)

Cunard's own quest for reduced weight had started in the early stages of the Q3 project. One of the most significant technical advances in the original Q3 design was the reduction of the ship's draught to about two metres less than that of the old Queens. This was particularly note-worthy considering the similarity of the proposed new ship's other principal statistics with those of her predecessors.

Dan Wallace began to address himself to this concern early enough on Q3 so that some of his ideas could be incorporated into *Sylvania*, an intermediate Atlantic liner completed in 1957. An improved structural girder form developed by the British Ship Research Association was widely used. Further economies were gained by using lightweight fittings made of modern materials, such as plastic bathtubs and domestic piping. As *Sylvania* was the last of a nearly identical four-ship class of liners, the success of these measures in service could easily be assessed and monitored against the performance of her three sisters. This experience proved beneficial as the whole matter of weight economy took on a much stronger significance on Q4.

Finally, there was the strong last impression of Q3 imparted by James Gardner's masterful approach to her exterior styling. This represented an important visual link inherited by her successor, which embodies his further development of the original ideas.

Artists renderings of the ship released in March 1961 depicted a rather conventional profile with an enormous single ovoid funnel amidships, Cunard red of course. Fully forward there was a second exhaust uptake incorporated into the mast. The double-deck promenades were glass enclosed amidships, but open fore and aft. This detail, combined with the streamlining of the superstructure, created the impression of a 1950s style *Aquitania*, a curious throwback in an otherwise modern, though rather bland, design.

The builder's model which was unveiled later that year showed a radically different profile which incorporated Gardner's ideas. The ship had clean crisp lines which bore little resemblance to her predecessors and which conveyed a modern impression of timeless elegance. The overall contour of the superstructure was refined and the double-deck promenades were fully enclosed. The navigating bridge had been given a modern cantilevered form which appeared to float above the forward superstructure. Below, the foredeck featured a whaleback similar to that favoured by the French on *Normandie* and *France*.

The most striking feature though was that the great red funnel was gone! It had been replaced by a second slender white mast-like exhaust. The forward mast-stack, was now visually balanced by the aft uptake, slightly abaft the midships line. This was probably the single most striking element in conveying the ship's new image. After all, within the preceding two years *Rotterdam* and *Canberra* had emerged without conventional funnels as the world's two most admired modern ships.

This was the last that was seen of Q3 before her demise in October the same year. It was not until late 1963 that detailed specifications and plans of the smaller and more versatile twin screw Q4 were first publicised. At this stage the new ship's size had increased to 58,000 tons. Her length and beam were established at 292.5 and 32m

Queen Elizabeth 2's hull in March 1966, at an early stage of construction. The boiler and engine compartments (foreground and background respectively) are assembled, showing the inner hull formed by the tanks at either side and the double bottom below. (UCS records held by Glasgow University, courtesy of the Archivist and with permission of the Keeper of the Records of Scotland)

The ship's hull at a more advanced stage of construction, showing the transverse webs to the left and right in mid-foreground. Those which can be seen are on two and three decks forward. (*The Architectural Press*, courtesy of The University Archives, University of Liverpool)

respectively. PAMETRADA calculated that the power needed to move the ship at a top speed of 30 knots would be 88,000kw. At a service speed of 28.5 knots the fuel consumption would be 492 tons per day. The weight of the machinery required was estimated to be around 5600 tons, about one-third the weight of *Queen Mary*'s machinery.

It was on the basis of these specifications that a building contract was signed between Cunard and John Brown and Company on 30 December, 1964. The contract design showed a slender ship which was 10 per cent narrower and more than 2m shallower in the water than the old Queens, though, as James Gardner had noted from his first glimpse of Q3, she too was to be of prodigious height above the waterline. Structurally, Vickers Armstrong's work had helped render her remarkably similar to *Oriana*. Bigger by half than the Orient Line prototype, she would be the largest and most powerful twin-screw liner yet built.

The ship's tonnage did rise still further, as it almost inevitably does in the process of building, until she was finally measured upon certification. When completed in 1969 as *Queen Elizabeth 2*, she was measured at 65,862 tons, closer to the size of *France*. Since then her tonnage has risen still further with various additions to the superstructure, to 67,139, as measured after she was re-engined in 1987.

Throughout the designing and building stages, weight saving was next to Godliness. No matter what other compromises might have to be made, the draught was not allowed to increase one iota. To do so would have jeopardised the ship's versatility as a cruise ship, denying her access to various ports throughout the world. In Atlantic service, the shallower draught of the new ship would make her independent of the tides for docking and undocking at Southampton and New York. This was a particular problem for the old Queens, since they were unable to enter Southampton at low tide, sometimes seriously disrupting their schedules. On one humiliating occasion in late 1946, *Queen Elizabeth* docked in Southampton nearly two days late after grounding at low tide nearby on Bramble Bank.

The approach to structural weight saving was based largely on the original Vickers Armstrong proposals, which by this time were well proven on *Oriana*. *Queen Elizabeth 2*'s structural design likewise

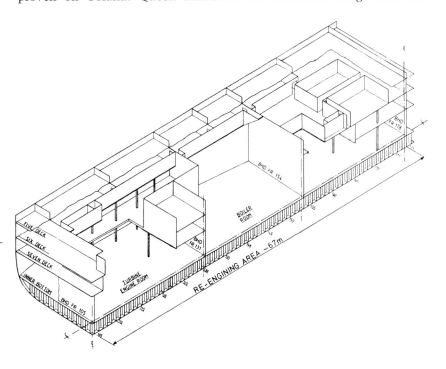

Isometric cut-away diagram showing the port-side half of *Queen Elizabeth 2*'s original engine and boiler spaces. As is indicated at the bottom of the drawing, this is the 67m long area that was rearranged to house the ship's new diesel-electric machinery in 1986/7. (Drawing – Lloyd Werft)

France, showing the tapering of the ship's after decks above the slender form of her hull. (French Line)

In contrast with the much wider decks afforded by *Queen Elizabeth 2*'s fuller hull form above the waterline. (Skyfotos Ltd)

stressed a dominant aluminium superstructure forming an integral stress-bearing element of the hull.

The topmost five decks of *Queen Elizabeth 2*'s superstructure are constructed entirely of aluminium alloy, with the exception of the funnel uptakes which are steel. The exterior bimetallic join with the steel hull is immediately beneath the row of large windows on quarter deck. The steel structure of the hull has been continued upwards to encompass the full height of one deck, which is actually the lowest deck in the superstructure. The normal stress bearing function of the strength deck is jointly borne by one and two Decks and the superstructure above. All decks from two deck upwards are framed longitudinally. Those below are transverse-framed, following the lines of the hull frames.

The structural unity of the hull and superstructure was made, as on *Oriana*, by a series of transverse aluminium webs placed at intervals along the length of the ship. These extend through ten decks, from the top of the keel and double bottom assembly below five deck up to signal deck, atop the main body of the superstructure. Apart from the difference in materials used, the structural arrangement of the hull is relentlessly continued upwards through the superstructure. Its outer shell is absolutely flush with the sides of the hull, with no overhang of the superstructure decks as on the old Queens and *Oriana*.

The internal layout of the entire ship is relentlessly regimented by a grid of square supporting columns, as used in a high rise building. These are arranged in five parallel files extending along the centre line and at distances of 4.25 and 9.75m to either side. Their fore and aft spacing varies between 6.1 and 9.1m, following the positioning of watertight hull bulkheads and the precise location of the major pieces of machinery in their compartments.

Strict adherence to a grid plan in designing a ship presents difficulties because her various decks are used for radically different functions. Some compromise of the plan is inevitable to accommodate the machinery and other vital working parts. Working out the diverse arrangement for several strata of cabins and large, attractive and functional public spaces above usually does not warrant structural concessions being made.

This was overcome largely by discontinuing the central row of columns at quarter deck, beneath the larger lounges and the dining rooms. It at least allowed the boundaries of the Double Room's well

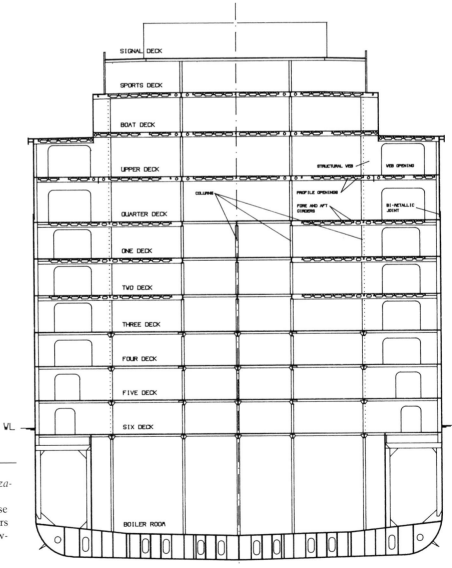

Structural cross section of *Queen Elizabeth 2*, showing the arrangement of supporting columns and the transverse webs. Note also the fore and aft girders used above three deck. (Author's drawing)

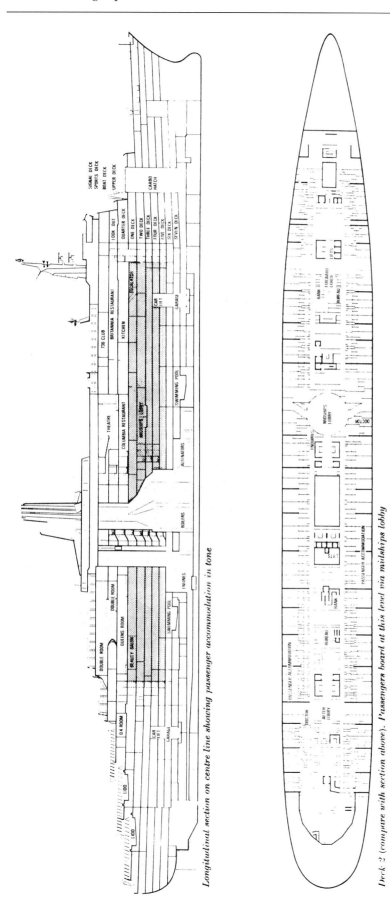

Longitudinal section on centre line showing passenger accommodation in tone

Deck 2 (compare with section above). Passengers board at this level via midships lobby

Longitudinal section of the ship and plan of two deck. The section clearly shows the straight upwards slope of the decks fore and aft, adopted in place of sheer. The shaded area designated the location of passenger cabins. As can be seen from this and the plan below, passengers are housed entirely on the flat portion of each deck. (Drawing – *The Architects' Journal*, courtesy of *The Architectural Press*) opening and the central floor areas of other spaces to be bounded by the outer rows of supports at either side. The only real exception was made for the theatre, which is completely unbroken by columns, and occupies most of the boat deck's enclosed width. Here extra girders were fitted above the ceiling to provide the needed strength. The dimensions of all other deck openings, including the boiler and engine uptakes, stairwells, lift shafts and hatchways, were limited to a distance of no more than 4.5m from the centreline.

The thickness of the upper hull plates was reduced slightly to allow the superstructure to bear some of the stress. The greater tendency for movement under stress so high up in the ship is compensated for by the greater degree of elasticity inherent in the aluminium alloys used. In spite of the weakening effect of the numerous large window openings perforating its shell, the superstructure also requires the intrinsic strength to withstand high winds at sea as well as the topsides load of twenty lifeboats and launches, along with their davits and launching gear.

To retain rigidity topsides as far as possible, the exterior shell plating of the superstructure is kept solid for a distance of at least 1m fore and aft of each web. This accounts for the irregular groupings of the large windows on quarter and upper decks since the spacing of the webs is varied. The windows themselves are rounded at the corners on a fairly wide radius, with the length of their top and bottom edges being slightly curved rather than flat. Apart from its purely functional purpose of relieving strain of the shell plating at the corners of these openings, the shape also serves to soften the aesthetic expression of the ship.

About 1100 tons of aluminium alloy went into building *Queen Elizabeth 2*'s superstructure, amounting to about half the weight of a comparable structure made of steel. The added advantage of its stress-bearing properties allowed for further weight reduction below, particularly in the structure of the strength deck. The conventional non-stress-bearing deckhouses of the old *Queen Elizabeth* were supported atop a heavy double-plated strength deck. This alone weighed some 2000 tons, nearly double the entire mass of aluminium used in *Queen Elizabeth 2*'s superstructure.

As with *Oriana* and *Canberra*, the weight saved by using aluminium allowed for an extra deck to be gained in the superstructure. The crusade to save weight and increase usable space in *Queen Elizabeth 2* also gained an additional accommodation deck within the hull. This

The arrangement of open deck spaces aft on *Queen Elizabeth 2* provides protection from the elements by way of the superstructure forward and the side windscreens as seen at the left. This view shows the quarter deck pool (now enclosed), with its one deck counterpart to the right below the glazed aft railing. (Author's photo)

was accomplished partly through careful structural planning and partly thanks to the reduced height of the PAMETRADA engine design.

Through detailed advanced planning of the machinery layout, electrical, plumbing and ventilation services, the overall height of each deck could be reduced by 0.15 to 0.22m without diminishing the finished ceiling height of the accommodations. The services trunk lines were generally routed above the corridor ceilings where a reduction in height could be tolerated. The type of structural girders first used by Cunard on *Sylvania* proved helpful here. These had deeper webs so that they could be perforated to reduce weight. Full advantage was taken of this feature for wiring and piping runs.

An additional metre of headroom was gained thanks to the compactness and meticulous planning of the machinery spaces. Here a detailed one-sixteenth scale plexiglass model of the engine room was constructed long before final drawings were submitted for tender. This enabled each component to be made to scale and test fitted on the model, making vital production data more quickly available, and reducing the instances of on-site alterations and wastage of materials.

Queen Elizabeth 2's powerful and sophisticated machinery was packed into three of her fifteen watertight compartments. The critical matter of positioning these spaces and their resultant bearing on the rest of the ship's layout were explained by Dan Wallace in an article he wrote for the January 1969 issue of *Shipping World and Shipbuilder*:

> Early strength calculations showed that for minimum weight the main machinery should be sited slightly aft amidships. Fortunately this also coincided with the optimum position of the machinery spaces so far as subdivision was concerned. Even a variation of a few feet in the position of the machinery spaces has a considerable effect on the strength and subdivision requirements. The position of the main machinery, of course, dictated the position of the funnel . . The lido decks can thus be arranged in a terraced fashion. This provides more sheltered decks than are available in liners whose machinery is aft. The terraced decks also allow for overlap, thus providing greater lido deck areas and also affording areas giving shelter from the sun.

The machinery itself was arranged, as in *Oriana*, with the boilers in the centre compartment, the turbo-alternators forward and the main turbines aft. This provided for the closest proximity of the boiler and

View of the boat deck, showing the effectiveness of the khaki paint scheme in reducing glare. This was a byproduct of its main purpose to camouflage the safety equipment from view when the ship is seen from a distance at sea. (Author's photo)

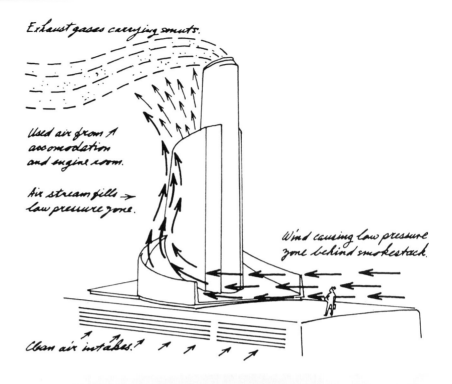

Exhaust gases carrying smuts.

Used air from
accomodation
and engine room.

Air stream fills
low pressure zone.

Wind causing low pressure
zone behind smokestack.

Clean air intakes.

Illustration showing the workings of
Queen Elizabeth 2's funnel with the
wind coming from the port quarter and
being taken up by the scoop at its base.
Note also the close proximity of clean
air inlets in the deckhouse below.
(Drawing – James Gardner)

The completed funnel after being
hoisted aboard in sections and secured in
place. This photo was taken in August
1968, while the ship was fitting out in
graving dock. (UCS records held by
Glasgow University, courtesy of the
Archivist and with permission of the
Keeper of the Records of Scotland)

engine uptakes to each other, thus minimising the extent of their intrusion through the accommodations above. These pass through the passenger decks at points immediately fore and aft of the E stairway and lifts.

The three compartments are flanked by side tanks for fuel which extend the full three-deck height of the engine and boiler rooms. These, together with the transverse bulkheads fore and aft and the ship's double bottom, encase the machinery within a complete inner hull which would enable it to remain operative even if the hull should become heavily damaged.

The original prime movers consisted of two sets of double expansion steam turbines with a shaft power rating of 44,000 kilowatts each. Full power was transmitted to the propellers at 174rpm through two-step reduction gearing. The machinery was designed for maximum operating efficiency at 85 per cent of full power, yielding a normal service speed of 28.5 knots. Steam was supplied by only three powerful Foster Wheeler boilers at 504 °C. (A fourth boiler was eliminated earlier as an economy measure.) Power for the ship's electrical needs was provided by three 5.5kw turbo generators, driven by steam at the same temperature and pressure supplied to the main turbines. All together this was the most potent power package yet installed in a twin-screw merchant ship the world over. It was also one of the most compact, occupying only half the volume of the old *Queen Elizabeth*'s machinery. Taking into account the reduced power needed by the smaller new ship, the end result was that her machinery accomplished the same result as the earlier *Queen* in terms of speed and performance.

Construction of the whole ship was simplified by completely eliminating the curved lines of sheer and camber in her decks. This served to reduce further the building costs because it made a great deal more standardisation and prefabrication of the accommodations possible.

The lines of sheer normally describe two parabolic curves upwards, one each from the middle of the ship to the bow and stern. The bow sheer is usually twice that of the stern. The purpose of sheer is to improve the seaworthiness of the ship. The extra depth of the hull towards its extreme ends serves to maintain a consistent freeboard height above the waterline against the vessel's natural tendency to pitch as it moves on the seas. Sheer also maintains a safety margin in the watertight subdivision of the hull, where flooding of the forward-most compartments would be more likely in the event of a collision. These compartments are thus deeper and better suited to keeping the ship afloat in a damaged condition.

Camber is the transverse curvature of a deck towards the sides of the ship, built primarily for the purpose of drainage.

Obviously fitting accommodations on decks which are curved upwards in one direction and downward in the other is both difficult and costly. There are no flat horizontal lines and few true perpendiculars. Worse still, since the line of sheer is parabolic, the geometry of fittings along its length is not constant.

For some time the problem was partly solved by eliminating camber altogether on enclosed decks and by flattening the sheer line of the upper 'tween decks and superstructure amidships. All decks from the bulkhead deck downward were fully sheered to meet the international regulations and conventions on seaworthiness. Above, the decks were carried straight and parallel to the keel between two points approximately in line with the ends of the superstructure. This had the added advantage of giving more headroom amidships on the bulkhead deck, where it was needed for the galley and dining rooms usually situated there.

This practice was first adopted by Vickers Armstrong on Orient

Line's passenger ships with the building of their second *Orcades* in 1947. It was subsequently adopted on all their new ships, including *Oriana*. Conversely, P & O's *Canberra* was built with all her decks fully sheered.

In *Queen Elizabeth 2* this was handled in yet another way by building all decks absolutely flat and horizontal along the entire middle body of the ship. Forward, the effect of the sheer line was achieved by a straight upwards slope of the decks from a point approximately below the main mast. Aft, it was done by a shorter slope and a step above the propellers. Camber was eliminated altogether, with the exception of a slight sloping of the outside area of the boat deck. *Queen Elizabeth 2* was the first large liner to dispense completely with the traditional curves of sheer and camber; a technique later to prevail in cruise ship design.

Despite their structural encumbrance, the lines of sheer can contribute greatly to a ship's aesthetic appearance. The *Queen Mary* and *Queen Elizabeth* each had a beautiful sheer, sweeping from the bow to the stern. *Canberra* and *Rotterdam* too are particularly outstanding in this regard among the more modern ships. *Queen Elizabeth 2* needed to be given at least a visual impression of sheer for her to look right. This was an important part of James Gardner's role in designing the ship's structure.

The effect is achieved in part by simply painting a sheer line along the sides of the ship. It is traced by the join of the charcoal grey hull colour with the white superstructure. This forms the prescribed parabolic curve, sweeping forward gradually up across the line of portholes on two deck to the peak of the bow at one deck. This is visually strengthened by a chine forming a similar curved line in the shell plating of the forward quarters at one deck level.

These lines are reflected by the gentle downward curve of the bulwarks above. The converging curved lines serve to conceal the straight slope of the forward decks. Aft, a similar effect is achieved by the gentle tapering of the glazed windscreens flanking the terraced open decks. This particular refinement has subsequently been lost due to the aft extension of the superstructure to incorporate a glass roof over one of the swimming pools.

A further impression of sheer is given by a slight upturn in the forward end of the open boat deck promenade. Although a straight slope, it originates from about the same point aft of the mainmast as the other two superimposed sheer lines. To the skilled eye, however, this particular piece of deception is betrayed by the dead straight line of upper deck windows immediately below.

The arrangement of *Queen Elizabeth 2*'s open deck spaces as originally built generally followed the *Oriana* approach, stressing a long series of terraced open spaces aft. This began with the games area on sports deck, immediately aft of the funnel, and continued downwards to one deck in a progression of five long steps. The most remarkable feature of this virtually uninterrupted series of terraces was their size, especially from side to side. Although basically following *Oriana*'s plan, they lacked the clutter of her two crane platforms and other deck gear. Compared with *France*, their breadth was not restricted by the taper of the French ship's hull lines. Despite her refined waterline profile, *Queen Elizabeth 2*'s upper hull shape maintains nearly maximum breadth for a surprisingly long distance aft.

The lower three levels, two of which contain swimming pools, are protected from the elements by the tapered windscreens mentioned earlier. Similar windbreaks are fitted alongside the games area and the small boat deck veranda inboard of the lifeboats. The only unprotected areas are the boat deck itself and the forward gallery on sports deck, just below the bridge.

Originally, *Queen Elizabeth 2* was also given a sheltered well deck topsides aft of the main mast, resembling the Bonito Pool area on *Canberra*. Unfortunately this was not provided with a swimming pool, direct access to any public spaces other than the children's room, or, for that matter, any other real sense of purpose. It was rather out of the way and awkward to get to. Consequently this area was seldom used, and its location eventually became appropriated for the penthouses which were added a few years later.

James Gardner was instrumental in introducing a number of other ideas which refined the *Queen Elizabeth 2*'s overall exterior appearance, giving her a less severe visual expression. A dark charcoal grey colour was used for the hull, compensating for the reduced visual balance topsides of the single slender funnel. It was thought that black would have produced too overwhelming an effect without the balancing force of a couple of big red funnels above.

The lifeboats also needed special consideration so that the irregular line of boats, excursion launches and work boats would not spoil the otherwise smooth and uncluttered appearance of the ship. These were arranged with the larger covered launches amidships, following the top contour of the superstructure with the funnel's base structure amidships. To obscure the clutter of davits and other boat-handling equipment from view, the walls of the superstructure along the boat deck and the handling equipment itself were painted khaki instead of the usual white. The effect of this was quite remarkable when the ship was viewed at a distance, since the boats appeared to be freestanding. On deck it also served to reduce glare from the sun, a welcome touch no doubt on tropical cruises. The deckhouse below the bridge was also painted the same colour, giving the bridge itself a distinctive cantilevered appearance.

The visual impression of the lifeboats was also diminished by coincidence of the large windows on the decks below being grouped independently of the arrangement of lifeboat davits. Since the days of the Pretty Sisters, *Caronia* and *Carmania*, it had been traditional practice for the arrangement of lifeboat davits to prescribe the positioning of supporting columns and openings on the decks below. On the old Queens, for instance, there was a constant number of windows directly beneath each boat, with a separate group of two or three more panes

Queen Elizabeth 2 as she appeared upon completion in 1969 and for the first four years of her service life. (Beken of Cowes, courtesy of Gordon Turner)

between it and the next boat. This tended to give the whole ship a more severe visual impression than was wanted for *Queen Elizabeth 2*.

Perhaps the most powerful aesthetic feature of the entire ship was James Gardner's treatment of her original funnel. It was an outstanding example of form following functionality, with but minor concession to appearance – beauty in functional perfection. The funnel was left to a fairly late stage in the ship's design. At the pre-tender stage the builder's model had no funnel at all.

It seemed at first that the task of adapting his original tall slender stack from Q3 would be simple enough. There was still some resistance to such a design from the more conservative factions within Cunard, but this was no real threat. The greatest difficulty was that none of the various model funnels tested in the National Physical Laboratory's wind tunnel seemed to overcome the old problem of keeping soot and smuts away from the after decks.

Various types were tried, including thin mast-stacks, fat ovoid forms, some with air vents, others without, and so on. The aerofoil-shaped Strombos type, adopted for Holland-America's *Maasdam* and *Ryndam*, as well as the French ships *El Djezair* and *Lyautey*, was also tried. It all really did not seem to make much difference. Under the worst wind conditions the smoke always ran down the back of the funnel and onto the open decks. What about 'those ungainly projections on the funnels of the *France* and the flat mortar-board tops on the *Michelangelo*', asks Gardner? Nobody seemed to know or care; they were foreign anyway! Apparently everyone had forgotten about *Oriana's* made-in-Britain funnel design.

The real cause of the problem was that smoke has a tendency to flow down the leeward side of the funnel to fill in an area of low pressure there. If the prevailing winds are blowing from either side of the ship, and are strong enough, then a greater low pressure area will occur around the opposite aft quarter of the funnel. Under these conditions, when the winds do not reinforce the ship's own enveloping airstream, the smoke may well lack the velocity to get fully clear of the decks. This was observed by one of the shipyard's research people, who then worked with James Gardner to find a funnel design that would work properly under such circumstances.

The eventual solution that evolved was based on three elements. The funnel itself was made as tall and thin as possible, somewhat resembling Gardner's original visualisation of it for Q3. The trick was to fill its relatively small low pressure void with used air from the accommodation ventilating and airconditioning systems. This was done by enclosing the aft half of the stack within a cowling through which the return air was pushed by powerful exhaust fans. Where this forced airflow was vented just below the top of the working funnel, it would give the engine exhaust smoke and gases the needed push to carry them up and away from the ship.

However, further wind tunnel tests of this arrangement showed that under some unfavourable wind conditions the outer cowling created its own low pressure area. At first the two men experimented with various arrangements of windscreens on deck to overcome this. What finally emerged was a wide wind scoop on top of the deckhouse. This solved the problem using the Venturi-effect, with the narrowing form of its curved lines increasing the airflow from deck level and forcing it up around the back of the whole funnel structure, cowl and all.

It was a combination of new and old ideas. The stack itself embodies the old idea of a tall thin funnel which would discharge steam, smoke and soot well above the ship, rather like those of, perhaps, *Campania* more than half a century earlier. The outer cowling and wind scoop were modern refinements which made it work more effectively.

In the Cunard boardroom there were still those who needed convincing. Sir Basil Smallpeice, then the Line's chairman, asked that a conventional Cunard funnel also be made to show on the model for comparison, and to pacify the traditionalists. As James Gardner recalls, the matter was soon irrevocably resolved once and for all:

A week later he [Sir Basil] rang. Apparently he was a buddy of the Queen and wanted to show her the model (to ask if she would acquiesce to her name being linked with it, I guessed). I was to meet him with it at the side door of the Palace, and, 'oh bring both funnels please, your first one and the one in Cunard house colours'. So, he would ask the Queen, and my guess was she would plump for the red one; after all to anyone not practised at the objective visual design it would look more like a Cunard funnel is expected to look. At the appointed hour my modelmaker and I were gingerly steering the fragile model into the hands of a flunky, when Smallpeice asked: 'Where's the

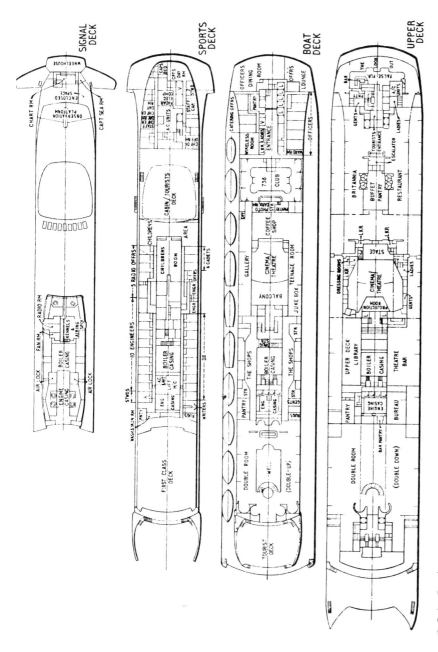

General arrangement plans of *Queen Elizabeth 2* as completed. (Builders' drawings, courtesy of Marine Publications International)

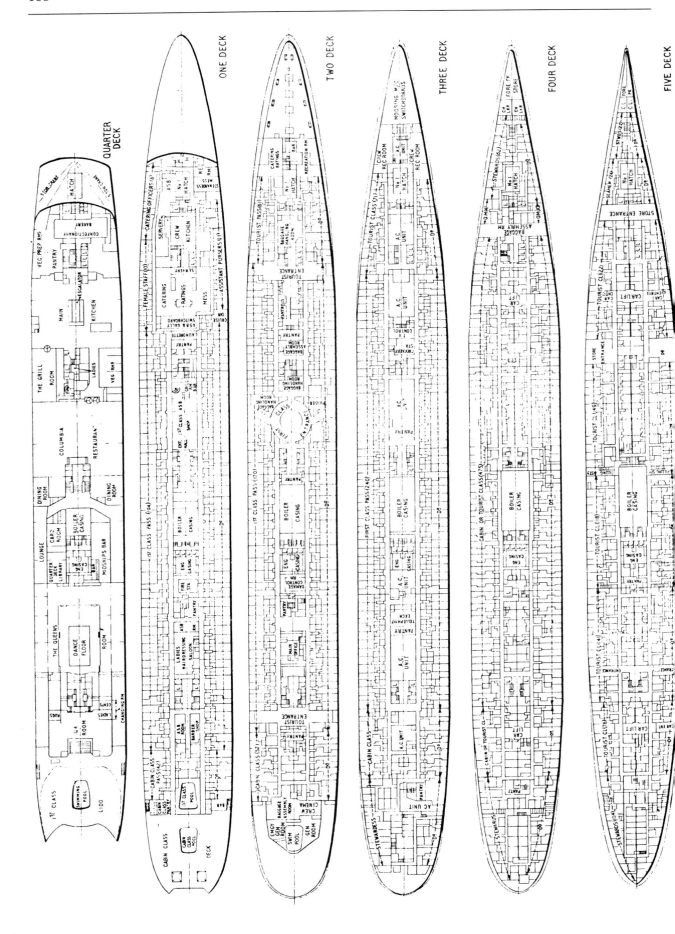

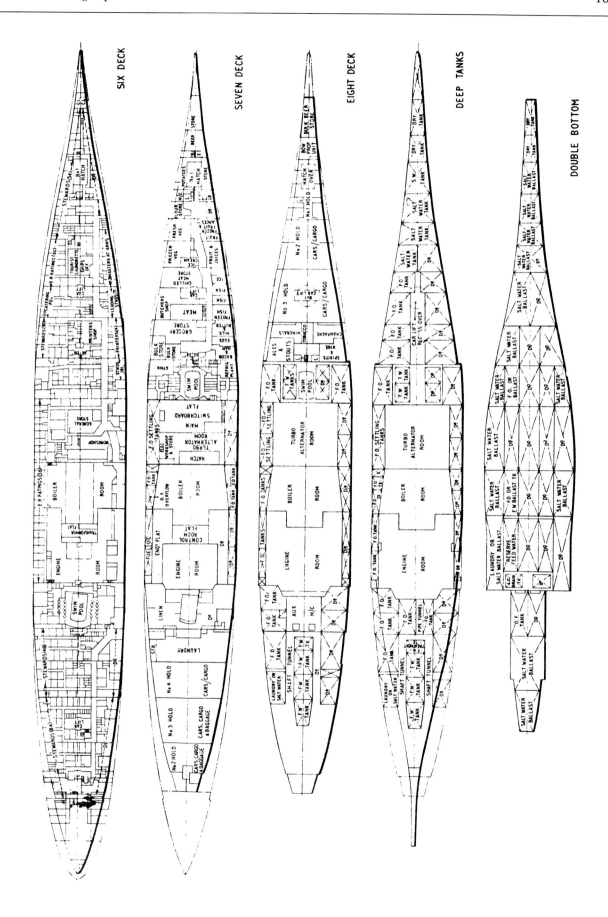

red funnel?' 'Awfully sorry,' I said, 'It fell off this morning – and some-
one trod on it. Absolutely useless, I'm afraid.' Smallpeice just gave me
one look.

On the finished ship, the funnel was hailed as a triumph both in the
technical and popular press. There was some lamentation at its distinctive black and white colour scheme which had replaced the traditional
Cunard red and black. Unfortunately the old colours did eventually
return as part of a post-Falklands tinkering with the ship's image. They
are still there, only now on a broader funnel which was an unavoidable
side effect of the conversion to diesel engines. The basic idea and shape
has since also appeared in various mutations on a variety of other ships,
ranging from the handsome funnels of the Royal Viking Line ships to
the side-by-side stacks of the Japanese ferry *White Sampo 2*.

Whatever advances are made in the structural and technical design of

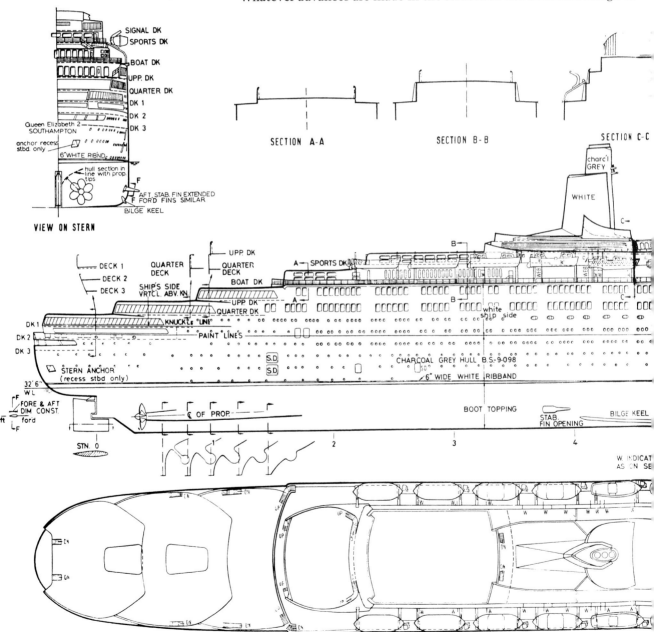

a ship, the end result must be pleasing to the eye if the ship is to be a success. In this regard, the well known marine author, Lawrence Dunn, made the following remarks in *Shipbuilding and Shipping Record* on 28 September 1967:

> Indeed, it is remarkable how quickly one becomes adjusted to, and able to appreciate, new shapes. This ability has probably been aided by the constantly evolving design of cars. So with ships and funnels, to the point where a vessel with two funnels conventionally placed fore and aft looks somewhat old fashioned.

Despite major differences in silhouette, detail and size, it is interesting to observe that the new *Queen* has most in common with the *Rotterdam* (a compliment to both) the French *Ancerville* and, to a lesser degree, the *Galileo Galilei* class. All have excellent overall balance and a refreshing touch of the severe.

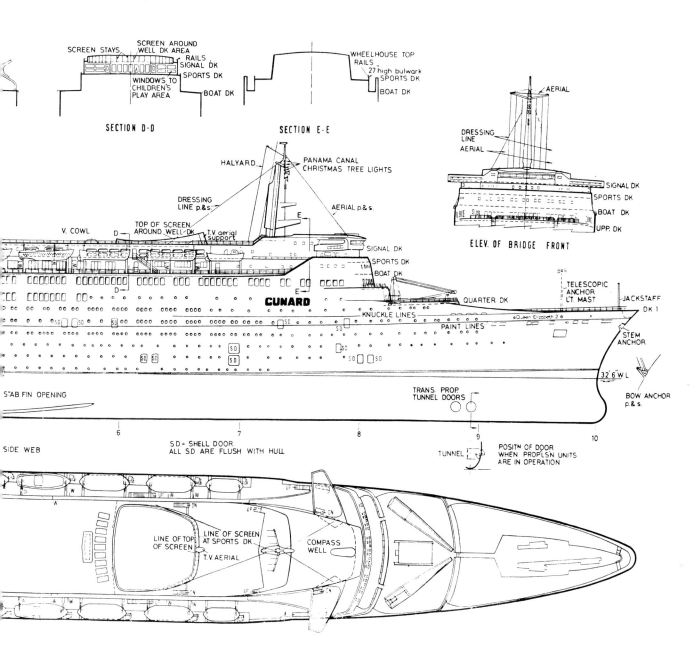

Chapter VIII

THE MOST EXCITING THING SINCE APOLLO 1

SHIPS have been boring long enough; so proclaimed a Cunard brochure introducing *Queen Elizabeth 2* and advertising her first sailing schedules for 1969. Inside, the text went on to say:

> From the 1860s to the 1960s ocean liners have been boring their way across the seas. Cunard has launched the ultimate weapon against boredom at sea. The new Cunard *Queen Elizabeth 2*. Whatever your pre-conceptions about *QE2*, she is bound to take you by surprise. It's like climbing into the most exciting thing to be launched since Apollo 1.

To encapsulate the entire history of steam shipping into a single word, 'boring', takes nerve. It dismisses the influence of such great ships as *Mauretania*, *Normandie*, *Nieuw Amsterdam* and *Canberra* out of hand, to say the very least. Nonetheless, with these sweeping statements Cunard's publicity people were making a bold claim that their new flagship really would be something different, and that a great deal was expected of her. The reference to America's Apollo spacecraft, designed for voyages to the moon, was perhaps appropriate.

The difference in *Queen Elizabeth 2*'s rational internal layout and modern design to that of her grand predecessors made them seem like the great rambling manor houses of Olde England, which could only survive any longer thanks to organisations such as the National Trust. The old Queens had indeed become as outmoded as those once-great homes for most of the same reasons – they were simply too large, had too much wasted space, and were far too labour intensive to be run economically.

For instance, passengers and crew on *Queen Mary* were served from five separate galleys spread about the ship, as opposed to the centralised catering of virtually all dining and messing facilities on the new ship. Likewise, on the *Queen Mary* there were countless pantries, bars, stores and other amenities scattered about the accommodations, without direct access to any centralised flow of services. This all added to the numbers of crew needed in the hotel department, not to mention the extra work load of fetching and carrying goods and materials about the entire ship.

The First Class public rooms, many of which were two and three decks high, usually accounted for the greatest waste of valuable space. Apart from the sheer interior volume of the main lounge, smoke room and dining saloon, there were lesser excesses elsewhere, including the

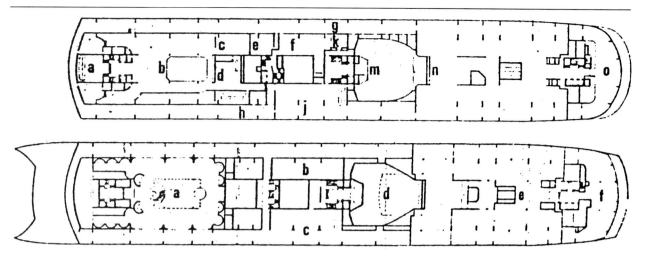

cabins for all classes, resulting from a persistently old-fashioned approach to layout. Enclosed promenade decks were another waste, and by 1969 these had become about as passé as the morning rooms and conservatories of those old houses.

A number of the new ideas which appeared aboard *Queen Elizabeth 2* had actually originated with the earlier Cunard Q3 project. Relocating the dining rooms to the upper decks was one example. This was done so that these spaces would be on the same decks as the other principal public rooms whose size demanded some additional deckhead or ceiling height. The lower headroom acceptable for cabins could therefore be maintained universally below, throughout the 'tween decks. The passenger public areas and sleeping accommodations were thus divided virtually horizontally, which simplified things considerably. Each deck would be for either one purpose or the other, and a constant height would be maintained throughout its entire length.

Dining saloons, or restaurants, as shipping lines often prefer to call them, have in the past occasionally been located high up the ship, notably in a number of European liners. Among these were the Hamburg Sudamerika's *Cap Arcona* and Lloyd Triestino's *Victoria*. Built in 1927 and 1931 respectively, these were tropical ships, in which high-ceilinged dining rooms were designed to be naturally cool and airy in the days before airconditioning. The restaurants were located aft on the promenade decks, with their ceilings pushed up through the deck

Plans of *Queen Elizabeth 2*'s upper deck showing the progression from the early stage of design (above) to the layout actually built (below). Note the elimination of the enclosed promenades, g and h:

Legend

First plan – a- Cabin Class bar; b- Cabin Class lounge; c- Cabin Class library; d- Cabin Class shop; e- Cabin Class teenagers room; f- Tourist Class teenagers room; g- Tourist Class promenade; h- Cabin Class promenade; j- Cabin Class cocktail lounge; k- First Class teenagers room; m- Theatre; n- Cabin/Tourist Class restaurant; o- Tourist observation lounge

Final plan – a- lounge; b- library; c- cocktails; d- theatre; e- restaurant; f- observation lounge

(Drawings – Cunard, courtesy of *The Architectural Press*)

The enclosed promenade on quarter deck, showing how it is routed through openings in the ship's structural web. The dark and intimate Midships Bar is to the right within the smoked-glass doors. (Author's photo)

above. First Class dining rooms were also located on the upper decks of the later Norwegian America Line ships *Oslofjord* and *Bergensfjord* completed in 1938 and 1956 respectively.

However, in these cases the location of the dining rooms had nothing to do with any overall rationalisation of the ship's catering arrangements. In most instances they were catered from their own separate galleys, while on *Bergensfjord* service was by way of a lift and dumbwaiters connecting an adjacent pantry with the main galley three decks below.

Apart from locating the passenger restaurants at the top of the ship, the Q3 plan called for crew messing facilities to be grouped nearby, with the crew cafeterias forward and below in the upper 'tween decks, and the officers' mess higher up, beneath the bridge. Together all these facilities were to form an integrated catering complex, organised around the central nucleus of a single galley and its related pantries, bars, serveries, bakery, larders and so on. This was planned to be as far forward as possible so that the mast above the bridge housing could also double as an exhaust stack, and to provide direct access to the stores and cold rooms below from the forward hatches.

The most progressive ideas in Q3's layout and planning were brought forward and rescaled to the reduced overall dimensions of Q4. The efficient and compact arrangement of catering facilities and the need to save space became even more important in view of the smaller size of the new ship. As her first keel sections were laid in July 1965 and as the hull took shape in the months which followed, the ship's internal design still had a long way to go. At that time she remained firmly committed to Q3's three-class Atlantic service. There would have been a large number of interchangeable cabins and some common public facilities. At best, this would have made it possible superficially to retract the class barriers for cruises. With work well in hand, and a stringent deadline for the ship's completion to be met, she may well have entered service that way.

However, in late 1966, with about two-thirds of the hull completed, the builders informed Cunard that they would be unable to deliver the ship by May 1968, as had been agreed. While this meant that the already financially beleaguered owners would loose the lucrative 1968 summer North Atlantic season, it allowed enough extra time for some very important changes to be made. Research undertaken by the Economist Intelligence Unit showed that, in view of changing lifestyles, the

On upper deck passengers enjoy the timeless shipboard pastime of watching a sunset at sea. Note the lifeboat embarkation hatches at left and centre. (Author's photo)

original three-class plan was potentially less profitable. This was consequently modified in favour of a far more flexible two-class arrangement. A virtually open range of passenger facilities for cruising would be stressed, with provision for the dining rooms and a few other spaces to be segregated by class on North Atlantic service only. A complete rationalisation in the layout of all public spaces, especially those originally allocated to the two lower classes, was also undertaken.

By the time Q4 was launched in September 1967 as *Queen Elizabeth 2*, she had been transformed into a very different ship. Her hull was by then completed with some cabins already finished, one of the indoor pools in place, and much of the superstructure erected, While the lengthy delays in building were extremely costly, especially as the old Queens had already been disposed of, the improved design of the new ship has no doubt compensated considerably in the long run.

The traditional practice of giving the highest deck to First Class was completely reversed. This was done to provide the premium-fare passengers with an added measure of comfort by locating their spaces nearest the centre of gravity. Despite the use of stabilisers, everyone was still worried about the ship's great height, particularly since the topsides public spaces for each class were to include the restaurants. The rooms on quarter deck, as it was named, would be used exclusively by First Class in North Atlantic service. Tourist Class would then be relegated to the two decks above.

The First Class rooms on quarter deck were retained in their original layout and concept. Above, on upper and boat decks the plan was completely revised. Here the separate facilities at first planned for Cabin and Tourist Class were amalgamated to either serve Tourist Class in Atlantic service or to complement the facilities below on quarter deck while cruising as an open-class ship.

On upper deck, the triplication of First, Cabin and Tourist Class teenagers' rooms was eliminated, along with the duplication of shops, bars and other smaller rooms belonging to the two lesser classes. The combined Cabin and Tourist Class dining room was redesigned as the Britannia Restaurant. The main Cabin Class lounge was broken through to its Tourist counterpart on the deck above, forming what would become the Double Room. Forward of this room's upper level on boat deck, space formerly allocated to other Tourist Class facilities became the shopping centre. Further forward were the coffee shop, an art gallery, teenagers' room and the night club. These, along with the two-

The convergence of port and starboard promenades on quarter deck occurs here at the D stairway amidships. The promenades turn diagonally inwards to the portals at either side of Helen Banynina's launching tapestries in the background of the photo. (Author's photo)

deck-high theatre, were available to all passengers without class barriers of any kind.

The most outstanding feature of these redesigned decks was their simplicity of plan, replacing the old-fashioned layouts with their numerous vestibules, galleries and other wasted circulation spaces which had no purpose. *Queen Elizabeth 2*'s rationalised plan presented a sequence of bright modern rooms, of appropriate size and proportions for their special purpose. These were integrated into a practical scheme which used a minimum of space for access and circulation, whilst at the same time conveying a strong impression of diversity and spaciousness.

This effect was achieved largely by restyling the glass-enclosed promenades left over from the heyday of the old Queens. Those teak and metal verandas of the North Atlantic, with their long files of empty wood and canvas deck chairs, by then abandoned as centres of shipboard social life, were revitalised as indoor circulation arteries. The need to duplicate those earlier unheated, essentially outdoor, spaces with parallel inner access alleyways and galleries was eliminated. On quarter and upper decks, the promenades were opened up to the ship's

Right: Cabin 3076 on three deck, looking inboard towards the entrance vestibule, walk-in wardrobe and bathroom which isolate the sleeping area from the corridor. Designed by Jon Bannenberg, this represents the most ubiquitous cabin type let to First Class in line service. (Author's photo)

Below right: Another view of the same cabin, showing the functional arrangement of dresser and writing table beneath the solidly nautical feature of two portholes. *Queen Elizabeth 2* was the first major British liner to dispense entirely with the old boarding house practice of placing wash basins in the cabins proper. (Author's photo)

Below: Cabin 2008 on two deck is a compact single-berth room; one of the few to offer an additional fold-away upper pullman bed. Although this is one of the smaller examples, the average cabin area per passenger in *Queen Elizabeth 2* was originally 6.7sq m as opposed to only 4.4sq m on the old *Queen Elizabeth*. (Author's photo)

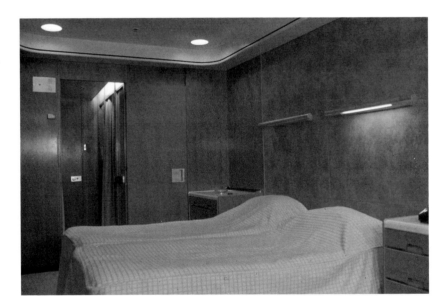

climate-controlled interiors and fully incorporated into their architectural design, decoration and colour schemes. Direct access was provided to the various public rooms from both sides of the ship rather than its centre.

Enclosed promenades had by that time also been done away with on a number of notable Scandinavian ships, including Norwegian America's *Sagafjord* and Swedish American Line's latest *Gripsholm* and *Kungsholm*. However, in most of these cases this was done by simply extending the public rooms out to the ship's sides, while retaining a classic inboard circulation pattern flanking the normal centreline stairways and uptakes.

Meanwhile, perimeter access had been successfully adopted ashore in a variety of buildings. Perhaps most outstanding among these were the Thomas J Watson Research Centre for IBM in Yorktown, New York, and the Bell Laboratories building, at Holmdel, New Jersey. Both were designed by the noted Finnish-American architect, Eero Saarinen. Their plans stressed wide 'avenues' surrounding each floor within the exterior glass curtain wall, giving perimeter access to the laboratories and offices within. In Britain, a similar effect was achieved by James Sterling at St Andrews University. Here, the passages giving access to the various common rooms and entrances to the residences above were arranged along one side of each arm of the building to convey the impression of a ship's enclosed deck.

The advantage that this same approach offered on *Queen Elizabeth 2* was that its perimeter circulation pattern retained the basic function of an indoor promenade. Here, in the comfort of the ship's interior, passengers can still take a stroll around the deck, or sit in complete comfort and indulge in the timeless shipboard pastime of watching the sea beyond the large full-height windows. The promenades also serve as overflow seating areas for entertainment and other gatherings in the larger lounges.

The smaller spaces such as the conference centre, card rooms, libraries and several bars, along with services such as pantries and lavatories, were arranged alongside the centreline uptake casings, stairwells and lift shafts. Access to these is generally from one or other of the promenades flanking their outboard side. Here, the quiet atmosphere of the libraries, card room and conference room, or the dark intimacy of the Midships Bar, are assured by solid walls enclosing their outward-facing sides. These partitions have soundproof windows corresponding to those in the ship's side, admitting a view of the traffic arteries and the outside world beyond. Conversely, the starboard-side Theatre Bar on upper deck has been left open to the promenade like the larger full-width rooms.

Only the dining rooms and galley were excluded from this scheme, where they occupy the whole width of the ship, fully forward on these decks. Further aft, the promenades enclose about two-thirds the length of upper deck and about half that of quarter deck.

The design and layout of *Queen Elizabeth 2*'s cabins did not undergo the same extensive rationalisation, except that they were no longer to be divided among three classes. The most expensive accommodations were arranged amidships, along the greater part of one, two and three decks, comprising the First Class bloc in Atlantic service. However, all cabins, regardless of their category, were designed to uniformly high standards. Each was equipped with its own private toilet facilities (itself a 'first' in British liner design), ample storage space and good lighting. The cabins themselves, along with all corridors, stairways and other common areas are fully carpeted throughout.

Extensive research was carried out during the earliest stages of the Q4 project to determine what the passengers themselves expected and

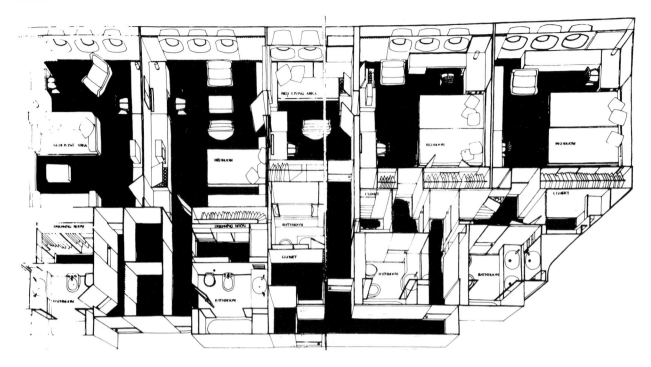

Diagram showing the layout of cabins designed by Gaby Schreiber. This grouping is located on two deck, port side and immediately aft of the Midship Lobby. The arrangement of the access alleyways allows these five rooms to be combined in various ways to form suites of two or three cabins. (*The Architectural Press*, courtesy of The University Archives, University of Liverpool)

wanted of their shipboard lodgings. In response to this the designers worked to provide the greatest possible number of cabins with twin lower berths and natural daylight. Four-berth cabins, which featured prominently not only in the old Queens, but more recently in *Oriana* and *Canberra*, were limited in number to serve the very small portion of the market which demanded such accommodations for families or students travelling together. It was also found that there were very few people travelling alone who would require single rooms.

Over three-quarters of the cabins have portholes or sidelights, then representing an unusually high proportion of outside accommodations on a ship of such size. The more expensive rooms follow a straightforward hotel-like layout, having two or three side ports. Most of these are rectangular in plan, with their bathrooms, walk-in cupboards and entrance vestibules further inboard, between the rooms themselves and the corridors. In the standard accommodations on four and five decks, the proportion of outside units was achieved by some clever, if not rather tricky, layouts. Many of them are arranged in pairs having sleeping alcoves which were 'dove-tailed' one inboard of the other. There is also a variety of interlocking L and T shaped rooms further fore and aft, in the narrower parts of the hull.

Despite the unprecedented standard of these accommodations, their complicated overall layout remains somewhat old-fashioned. This point is illustrated by *The Architectural Review*'s critic, Sherban Cantacuzino in the magazine's *Queen Elizabeth 2* issue of June 1969:

A comparison with the layout of the *Canberra* reveals a fundamental difference of approach. The *Canberra* has a central corridor and groups of six cabins (three deep) planned around public 'courts' which break up the endless corridor and provide regular glimpses of the sea. The shape of the rooms was considered more important than portholes. The QE2 has two corridors (the width of the two ships is roughly the same), and a continuous row of narrow cabins one or sometimes two-deep. Notwithstanding the pleasing character of some of these rooms (often an area no larger than 6ft × 6ft with a desk and chair as the only excuse for the porthole, while the main part of the cabin lies further back), it is a pity that they did not undergo the same sort of rationalisation that Dennis Lennon brought to the design of the circulation areas ... The large number of variations in cabin type (50–60) must have been costly to build and will be costly to maintain. The variety desirable in public rooms is unnecessary in private cabins, which need only to be simple and comfortable.

Although the interior decoration of the cabins was ultimately to be executed by designers appointed at later stages of building, they still reflect much of the work done by the original design team. This included many practical ideas on layouts and storage space made by Lady Tweedsmuir, who was appointed as Cunard's first lady director in 1965. Despite the criticism of some rather complicated layouts, the accommodations on *Queen Elizabeth 2* were, as a whole, in a class of their own for many years, and still rank with the best new cruise ships.

By the time *Queen Elizabeth 2*'s plan was being rationalised, changes had also taken place in the design team itself. At first, the ship's interior design was co-ordinated by Cunard's own people. These included the chairman's wife, Lady Brocklebank; vice-chairman, Anthony Hume, and the line's naval architect, Dan Wallace. Despite their progress, Cunard was perceived in some quarters to be mishandling the job, in the words of one critic, 'as casually as they would lay out for stalls at a village fete'. The Council of Industrial Design expressed concern about whether or not the nation's top designers were to be engaged, and wanted to ensure that the best British-made fittings and equipment would go into the ship. The matter was even discussed in Parliament, where the government felt that they had a vested interest in the project as they were financing it with the loan of public money.

Lady Brocklebank was probably victimised most, simply for being the chairman's wife, at a time when derisive remarks were being made in architectural circles about steamship line directors' spouses choosing the curtain and bedspread materials for their husbands' liners. In fact, quite the opposite was true of Lady Brocklebank. She was a well-travelled lady who had a practical understanding of the traveller's point of view, but she was also reasonably conversant with the more technical aspects of ship design work. She too was responsible for much of the progress that had already been made in designing the cabins.

Cross section through the 736 Club showing the sunken central area of the room. This feature was used in a number of spaces set aside for entertainment to provide improved visibility and increased headroom. (Drawing – *The Architectural Press*, courtesy of The University Archives, University of Liverpool)

A detailed plan of *Queen Elizabeth 2*'s very elaborate childrens' complex, consisting of a big playroom, creche and cinema with projection booth. (Drawing – *The Architectural Press*, courtesy of The University Archives, University of Liverpool)

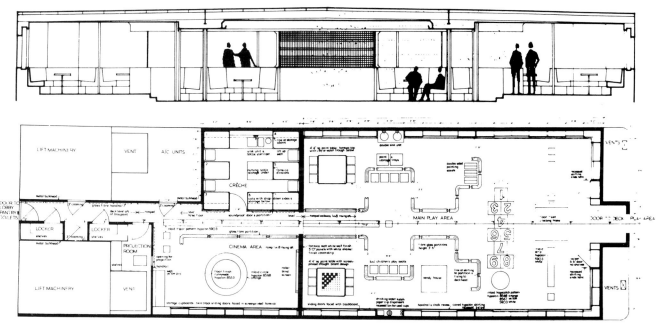

Looking from the Queens Room into
the promenade at right, where it
extends beyond the room creating an
impression of openness and infinite
spaciousness. (Author's photo)

The first change came in October 1965, following discussions which
had been held between Cunard and the Council of Industrial Design at
the height of the controversy. James Gardner was appointed to super-
vise the exterior styling of the ship as he had done with Q3, and to act
as an adviser on other aspects of her design. At the same time there had
been a management reorganisation in Cunard, when Sir John Brocklebank stepped down owing to poor health. Sir Basil Smallpeice, who
emerged as director, had moved quickly to change the concept and
design philosophy of the project. Before the end of the year the design
team was completely reshuffled, with some of its members, including
Lady Brocklebank, being dropped and others appointed. Among those
who remained were Dennis Lennon and Jon Bannenberg.

The new team was headed by James Gardner and Dennis Lennon as
joint design co-ordinators working in close collaboration with Dan
Wallace. James Gardner would continue to be primarily responsible for
the outside styling while Dennis Lennon was to co-ordinate the interior
design. Of his partner's approach, James Gardner noted:

> ...in a project as complex as this, whoever did the job was bound to slip
> a bit here and there. Most designers I could think of would either slip
> 'Scandinavian' or 'Bauhaus' – and this wouldn't appeal to Cunard's
> American customers. If Lennon slipped I guessed it would be in a safer
> direction towards international Hilton (the best international Hilton).
> In practice he didn't slip at all, so we will never know.

The remainder of the team was made up of professional architects and
designers who would work on individual parts of the ship within a unifying overall design theme defined by Dennis Lennon. The principal list

of designers and the areas they were responsible for was made up of:

Jon Bannenberg	– Double room, card room, indoor pool, some First Class cabins.
Sir Hugh Casson	– Children's and teenagers' rooms designed by his students.
Michael Inchbald	– Queens Room, quarter deck library
Dennis Lennon & Partners	– Restaurants and Grill Room, Theatre Bar, Midships Bar, First Class luxury suites, Captain's quarters and all linking elements such as stairways, corridors, etc.
Jo Patrick	– Officers' and crew accommodations, hospital.
Gaby Schreiber	– Theatre, conference rooms.

Others included Professor Misha Black, Stefan Buzas, David Hicks and Jean Munro. The partnership of Crosby, Fletcher, Forbes was given responsibility for all lettering, signposting and graphic design work.

Although none of these professionals was a specialist in ship design work, as are Njal Eide, Joseph Farcus and Robert Tillberg today, collectively they brought along considerable experience in this field. Misha Black had co-ordinated the interior design of *Oriana*. Sir Hugh Casson's experience included *Canberra* and the state apartments of the royal yacht, *Britannia*. Michael Inchbald had designed the interiors of the Tourist Class public rooms on the Union Castle flagship, *Windsor Castle*, as well as doing some earlier redesign of Cunard interiors. Jean Munro had also designed a number of interiors for Union Castle, including *Transvaal Castle* and *Windsor Castle*.

Dennis Lennon had to play the important, and no doubt sometimes diplomatic, role of integrating the creativity of a group of distinguished designers whose work was already well known both in Britain and internationally. He explains:

> I didn't want to put too heavy a hand on the whole project... I preferred the designers to suggest their own interpretations. At the same time I established the principle that what we were trying to do was to give

The Queens Room as it appeared in 1979, still with its original furniture. Although the room itself remains more or less intact, the furniture was replaced during the 1986/7 refit. (Author's photo)

A corner of the Queens Room showing it closed off from the promenades with the drapes drawn. In this way it becomes a smaller and more intimate space. (*The Architectural Press*, courtesy of The University Archives, University of Liverpool)

the ship character and that it was not just an opportunity for individuals to put across their own ideas... We realised we were not only working for Cunard, for we were conscious of the fact that the *QE2* will be taken as a national symbol, something which will show people everywhere what Britain can do in the way of design.

To help set the right overall tone for the project Mr Lennon sought to inspire his designers with examples of contemporary architecture and design which he felt were most appropriate. An exhibition of this work was set up in his studio, and visits were arranged to places such as the Royal College of Physicians in London, designed by Dennys Lasdens, one of Britain's top modern architects.

To impart an overall sense of unity to the ship, Dennis Lennon's office assumed responsibility for all connecting elements, such as corridors, stairways, promenades and entrances throughout the ship. The visual chaos that might otherwise result from a wide diversity of designs was avoided by uncompromised standardisation of these elements, including their deck and wall coverings, colour schemes, and lighting, right down to details such as door hardware, and signposting. Without this it would not have been possible to accord as free a hand to the individual designers.

The design of the public rooms was developed with the help of many large-scale models. These were constructed as great as one-sixteenth scale, and in many instances were fitted with ceilings which simulated their lighting schemes. The interiors of the models could be studied and photographed either through window and door openings or by way of removable wall sections. The photographers' lamps could be adjusted and moved to give accurate impressions of how the completed rooms would look at eye level, as seen under various conditions of daylight and with their intended electric lighting schemes.

These models served the same purpose as the cabin mock-ups usually used in the design of a large liner. The full-size sample cabins often built at the shipyard during the early stages of construction allow for defects in design or outfitting to be identified before they are repeated, maybe hundreds of times, aboard the ship. These plywood facsimiles, which are fully decorated, furnished and equipped, even with bed linen and hand towels are expensive, but far less so than correcting minor problems or oversights later. Obviously this is not practical for the public rooms because of their size and because each is unique. However, their accurate reduction to lilliputian scale does suffice as a reasonable substitute for full-scale mock-ups.

Apart from helping the designers and builders in their work, these models, along with the cabin mock-ups, were valuable in demonstrating the proposed designs both to Cunard management and to the contractors involved. Elaborate slide presentations showing these and numerous other general views and exterior details of the ship model were prepared for the owners by James Gardner and Dennis Lennon's studios. Later, much of this same material was also used in brochures and other general publicity, including an exhibition of *Queen Elizabeth 2*'s styling and interiors at the Design Centre in London.

That exhibition and the press coverage which it generated gave the public its first real impression of how much *Queen Elizabeth 2* would differ from her predecessors. Her smart, crisp and modern decor stressed top quality serviceable materials such as fibreglass, metal, plastic and leather. Gone were the myriad veneers of the old Queens, 'in homage to the fecund vegetation of the Empire', as Ian McCallum had put it in his 1956 *Architectural Review* article. Banished as well were the old-fashioned decorative trappings with their overdone artiness and excessive bric-à-brac in favour of clean unbroken lines and functional forms.

The whole scheme of *Queen Elizabeth 2*'s interiors stressed a strong sense of unity with her structural design. The same rounded corners and clear unbroken forms characteristic of her functional exterior lines were emphasised inside too. This can still be clearly seen in the quarter and upper deck promenades, which are routed through the ship's structural web. Here the wide-radius curved corners of openings in the aluminium web itself are features of the finished interior cladding enclosing them. The series of archways so retained along each promenade reflect the shape of the full-height windows, and make no pretence at concealing a definitely shipboard expression. Elsewhere, as in the trumpet-shaped columns of the Queens Room, the lines of the upper deck Look-Out and the unique circular entrance hall on two deck, the expression is equally shipshape. The same 'vehicle conscious' functionality of form ran throughout details such as the stairway designs and various other linking elements as well. There were few sharp corners and angular shapes to be found anywhere in the passenger spaces.

The large superstructure and boat deck windows are an important design feature of most public spaces. Glass is also widely used in elements such as the numerous frameless door panels and the original balustrade and stair banister of the Double Room. In consideration of this and the number of entrances and other interruptions, the decorations were generally not embellished with paintings, pictures, murals or other artwork. Instead, the design scheme tended to emphasise making the structures themselves as elegant and visually appealing as possible.

Another general design feature was that in a number of the public rooms part of the floor is sunken by a step or two. While this does give some impression of added height in low-ceilinged rooms, its main purpose was to increase visibility. In the 736 Club, which was the

One of *Queen Elizabeth 2*'s more attractive and enduring smaller interiors is that of the quarter deck Library, adjacent to the Queen's Room. This elegant modern room with its quiet club-like atmosphere has changed little from its original rendering by Michael Inchbald. (Author's photo)

The Double Room in its initial form as seen at boat deck level looking forward. Bannenberg's epic staircase (removed in 1987) is in the foreground, with the original bandstand and Double Up Bar at the far end. (*The Architectural Press*, courtesy of The University Archives, University of Liverpool)

A longitudinal cross section diagram of the Double Room. This gives a good impression of the balance of elements in its original arrangement. The spiral staircase is balanced by the bandstand at the opposite end of the central well through boat deck. Note the Double Up Bar which is to the right of the semicircular glass screen enclosing the bandstand. (*The Architectural Press*, courtesy of The University Archives, University of Liverpool)

ship's original night spot, and in the Queens Room it was done to give good visibility for live entertainment. In this regard, *Queen Elizabeth 2* was among the first modern ships to make specific provision for professional-quality passenger entertainment. A similar effect is also achieved in the Grill Room, where the innermost tables are on a raised floor, providing a better view of the sea.

As originally completed, *Queen Elizabeth 2* offered a staggering array of public areas and other facilities, amounting to some twenty-five different rooms, including the indoor pools. Since then a number of these have been changed considerably, and not necessarily for the better. New ones have been added, while others such as the Q4 room, Upper Deck Library and Look-Out have disappeared altogether; there would be almost enough material here for a full chapter on 'Lost *Queen Elizabeth 2'*. However, the ship's most noteworthy rooms and the majority of her linking elements have survived the periodic overhauls more or less intact.

Highest up, on sports deck, is the children's room, which, along with the original Coffee Shop on boat deck were designed by two of Sir Hugh Casson's students of interior design at the Royal College of Art. The idea was originally proposed by Dennis Lennon at an early stage when these spaces on the ship had not even been defined. The students were, at first, asked to submit only general concepts. On the basis of this work, Elizabeth Beloe and Tony Heaton were chosen to work at Dennis Lennon's studio during their summer holidays to develop their designs.

One of the most attractive and enduring interiors is that of the Queens Room, one of two spaces designed by Michael Inchbald. It is used as the First Class main lounge in Atlantic line service and as an al-

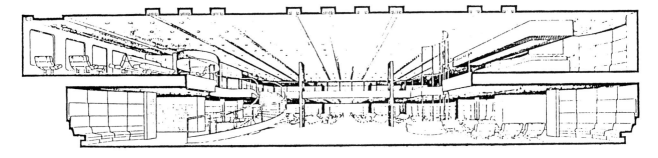

A close-up view of Jon Bannenberg's Double Room staircase. Note the port-starboard run of the floor planking, lighting fixtures and ceiling serrations. (*The Architectural Press*, courtesy of The University Archives, University of Liverpool)

ternative showplace to the Double Room (now restyled and renamed, Grand Lounge) on cruises. This was an especially difficult interior to deal with, being one of the largest spaces to have only a single-deck height and being of greater width than its fore and aft dimension. As Mr Inchbald describes his approach:

I have emphasised a fore and aft lengthened look by incorporating mirrors at the perimeters of each end to dissolve the excessive width. I overcame the disadvantages of the extreme lowness of the ceiling, which is now only 9ft 2in, in three ways: by perforating it in the form of a lattice, by the up-swooping effect of inverted white trumpet shaped structural columns, and flanking the sides of the room in specially designed fine wool curtaining with immense random vertical stripes of white, honey, lemon, and pale flame. The fluid lines of this white and silver aerodynamic room are anchored by the rectangular strength of the sculptured 'woodblock' end walls, veneered in walnut which partly mirrored, suggest massive, but open screen walls, rather than solid blank ones.

This scheme also has something of the illusionary properties of Sir Hugh Casson's Meridian Room on *Canberra*. In the Queens Room the promenades extend the room to the ship's full width, giving an impression of infinite spaciousness where they reach further fore and aft out of sight at each corner. The effect is heightened by the way in which the room dissolves into the promenade spaces and the sense of openness created by the large windows adding an airy and spacious indoor/outdoor impression. In the central part of the room the perforated fibreglass ceiling is silhouetted against concealed electric lighting, giving the impression of filtered sunlight.

This very flexible room can also be shut off from either one or both of the wide promenades flanking it. Sliding glass doors concealed within the stanchions can be used along with the room's curtains to isolate its centre area as a smaller and more intimate space when needed. The effect of this easily-made change is quite remarkable, as the reduced room so created loses its fluid sense of openness and assumes the feeling of a classic and very much smaller ship's interior enclosed within traditional glassed-in promenade decks.

The Architectural Review praised the Queens Room, describing it as being, 'in many ways the most exciting and probably most admired

room on the ship'. Going on to describe its huge upper deck counterpart, the Double Room, the same article said:

> But Bannenberg does everything the opposite way to Inchbald...
> Although the lower level is the same square shape as the Queens
> Room (also incorporating the promenades), Bannenberg goes against
> tradition and emphasises the width by running the ceiling ribs, the
> furniture layout and even the boarding of the dance floor in the port-
> starboard direction.

This was claimed at the time to be the largest room in any passenger
ship then afloat. It had grown that way in the rationalisation of the
ship's interior layout. The difficulty here was to organise this vast
amount of space to suit a variety of functions, any number of which
could be going on at the same time, from dancing or formal entertainment, to quiet conversation in small gatherings or drinks at the bar.
The mezzanine on boat deck helped out by providing a degree of distance from whatever activity might be going on below. The bar was
originally on this level, along with a number of the room's semicircular
seating alcoves. More of these intimate little recesses were also worked

The view which greets passengers as
they enter the First Class Columbia
Restaurant by way of its raised
platform. The alcoves formed by the
ship's structural web can be seen to the
left of the photo. (Author's photo)

A similar arrangement of alcoves was
used in the Tourist Class Britannia
Restaurant. In its original configuration
this room was essentially doughnut
shaped, with alcoves such as this
forming a series of smaller rooms
surrounding a central service core
which was connected to the main
galley below. (Author's photo)

Queen Elizabeth 2's original discotheque was the 736 Club, as depicted in
this architectural rendering, probably
from Stefan Buzas's office. (*The Architectural Press*, courtesy of The University Archives, University of Liverpool)

into the plan at upper deck level, where they offer a degree of intimacy
without being too cut off from the centre of things.

One of the main pitfalls which beset rooms of this type is that of
providing an adequate vertical link between the two levels. All to often
the upper level ends up being underused. Mr Bannenberg endeavoured
to overcome this with a wide sweeping circular stairway, which was
also a visual focal point of the whole plan. He created it to be 'something which women could sweep down, feeling elegant and regal. I
wanted it to be an epic staircase'. The Double Room has since changed
radically, with its upper level having been appropriated by the shopping
arcades and its epic stairway replaced by a pair of much smaller ones
half encircling the bandstand at the room's opposite end.

The Columbia Restaurant on the quarter deck is another of the ship's
more sophisticated interiors, as well as being among those whose
original design has survived more or less intact. It was designed by
Dennis Lennon for First Class on Atlantic service or those berthed in
premium-rate accommodations at other times. Originally the restaurant had a seatingcapacity of 500, enough to serve all First Class
passengers at a single sitting, while an additional 100 could be catered
for in the adjacent Grill Room. Both rooms have since been extended to
cope with the additional demand from cabins added on boat deck and
the penthouses.

Passengers enter the Columbia Restaurant aft, from the central point
where the two quarter deck promenades converge. The entrance itself
is from a slightly raised podium incorporated into the adjacent stair and
lift landing. It represents a scaled- down version of the *grande descente*
so favoured on French ships, where ladies arriving for dinner were able
first to survey the scene from on high, and could then make their regal
debut in view of those already seated. In the Columbia Restaurant the
four-step elevation was just enough to give a pleasant perspective view
without being overly dramatic.

The restaurant consists of an open and uninterrupted central area,
flanked on either side by smaller alcoves divided by the ship's structural web. Again, the web openings are retained, although here bronze-
tinted glass panels are fitted. Colour has been used effectively to change
the character of the room at different times of the day. Lemon-coloured
linen was chosen for the tables in the centre part of the room during
breakfast and lunch service. These are the times when the restaurant is
least busy, and its peripheral areas need not be used. At dinner time

pink would be substituted, while the colour in the alcoves was always beige. The remainder of the colour scheme was donkey brown for the carpeting, hide wall covering and chairs while the curtains were pale apricot.

Dennis Lennon also used colour to help passengers and crew navigate their way around *Queen Elizabeth 2*'s many stairways, lobbies and passages. Each of the four main stairway and lift groupings has its own unique colour scheme. Going from stem to stern, these are red, blue, white and yellow. In each, the colours are extended to the lift doors and cab interiors, as well as the adjoining entrance lobbies. The design of stairways is otherwise uniform, stressing a streamlined shape for the balustrades, rounded corners, and recessed stainless steel strips dividing the wall panels.

The circular Midships Lobby on two deck, which is part of the blue stairway, is especially noteworthy. Again, quoting *The Architectural Review*:

Here passengers will get their first impressions, and in the Midships Lobby the designers went all out in their way to create a stunning effect. The drama lies both in the form – a concentric floor and ceiling plan pivoted around a single white fibreglass mushroom column – and in vivid contrast between the apple green hide of the seating and the dark blue of the carpet and hide wall panels. Both the sinuous chrome handrail which protects the sunken seating area, and the concealed perimeter lighting emphasise the circular form.

The serrated ceiling was to have been of silvered fibreglass. Dennis Lennon wanted this to create the illusion that 'you have dropped a pebble into the sea, the rings getting bigger as they circulate'. Although this appeared to work well in the model, the difficulty of applying large enough foil covering at full scale could not be overcome. As substitute materials could not be found, the magical shimmering effect created in the model did not materialise in reality.

Throughout much of the ship's interior, colour schemes which by themselves might otherwise appear dull are enlivened by a variety of reflective surfaces and effective lighting. In the Columbia Restaurant, for instance, there is the solid perspex hand rail of the entrance balustrade, and the aluminium cladding of the columns and the ribbed cedar veneer ceiling. These metallic surfaces were universally anodised to give a silver lustre, which as *The Architectural Review* noted was

Originally the ship's unique floating art gallery, this space had become a reading room by 1979, as seen in this view. It has since served as a computer learning facility, and is now an Executive Services Centre. (Author's photo)

'known euphemistically as Q4 gold'. Metal surfaces used elsewhere in corridor ceiling coverings and the fibreglass stair balustrades are of a standard glossy white finish.

Lighting played an important role in many of *Queen Elizabeth 2*'s interiors. The success of her Queens Room and Midships Lobby, in particular, owe a large measure of their visual impact to the effective use of this medium. In both of these spaces the overhead sources are augmented by concealed fixtures which illuminate the ceiling itself from below.

The Queens Room has lamps which face upward hidden inside the white fibreglass plant troughs surrounding the large sunken dance floor below Mr Inchbald's latticed ceiling. Additionally, fluorescent tubes beneath the settees and tables cantilevered from these same troughs illuminate the floor, heightening the 'floating' impression achieved by suspending the furniture in this way. A similar technique was adopted in the Midships Lobby, where much of the light is directed upwards from low banquettes surrounding the backs of the circular seating arrangement.

In the original 736 Club, lighting was used to change the character of the room to suit its use either as an informal lounge, bar and discotheque or as a night club. The scheme stresses indirect low-level ambient lighting from fixtures behind the curtain pelmets and the ceiling coves. A change of mood for the nightclub role was made by switching to direct table illumination from lamps recessed into the ceiling and to three ship's lens lamps focused onto the room's columns.

Throughout much of *Queen Elizabeth 2*'s interior, spot lighting was used to emphasise the bright metal accent strips in her wall panelling, along with such features as columns, handrails and balustrades.Wherever artwork was used, it too was highlighted by the use of effective lighting. A number of the ship's interiors, among them the Grill Room, actually looked their best after the sun had gone down and the lights came on.

When *Queen Elizabeth 2* was finally handed over to Cunard in 1969, her styling, both inside and out, showed great promise of making her 'the most exciting thing to be launched since Apollo 1'. However, as Sherban Cantacuzino pointed out in the closing remarks of his critique, design alone is not enough:

What will count ultimately is whether the design is capable of fostering the quality of life on board.

The striking first impression made by the Midship Lobby upon entering the ship, despite the fact that the ceiling did not turn out as Dennis Lennon had wanted it to. (Author's photo)

Chapter IX

IN THEIR WAKE

THE 1960s were surely one of the most progressive periods in the history of modern passenger shipping. This was a time of transition in which the last round of great liner building took place. The most outstanding achievements of this era were *Oriana* and *Canberra* at its beginning and *Queen Elizabeth 2* at its conclusion. They stand like great book-ends bracketing the history of the transition to full-scale cruising. *Canberra*'s daring structural design and modern profile was a catalyst in shaping a number of the most noteworthy ships of the 1960s. Both she and *Oriana* were also of particular interest to Cunard in the planning of *Queen Elizabeth 2*. Elements of *Canberra*'s layout, styling and interior decor are still being exploited in today's sophisticated cruise ships.

In the years immediately following her completion, *Canberra* made a strong impression with the Italians who were among the most prolific builders during the period. They produced a number of large and noteworthy liners, including *Oceanic*, *Eugenio C* and Italia Line's final North Atlantic sister ships, *Michelangelo* and *Raffaello*. The unmistakable influence of *Canberra*'s distinguished profile and innovative internal layout is most readily discernible in *Oceanic* and *Eugenio C*.

These two ships were completed in 1965 and 1966 respectively by

Home Lines' *Oceanic*, seen here at New York in April 1982, alongside her younger sister, *Atlantic*. In this view the angle of the sun shows the semi-nested arrangement of her lifeboats. Here repairs are being affected to the number 1 and 3 boats following an Atlantic storm. (Author's photo)

Cantiere Riuniti Dell'Adriatico at Monfalcone on Italy's northeastern Adriatic coast. The same yard had also built the Lloyd Triestino sister ships *Guglielmo Marconi* and *Galileo Galilei*. A month after *Oceanic* was commissioned, Italia's elegant *Raffaello* also emerged from the same builder's San Marco yard near Trieste.

Oceanic was ordered by Home Lines, originally for North Atlantic service between various European ports and Montréal. Her accommodations were thus designed for two classes, based on the *Ryndam* and *Maasdam* example. This gave Tourist Class virtually the complete run of the ship while restricting one or two patches of prime space as an exclusive retreat for a small number of First Class passengers. Ultimately, *Oceanic* entered service as the world's largest full-time cruise ship. Her by then secondary role as an Atlantic liner was never taken up, nor has she operated as a two-class ship. Meanwhile *Eugenio C* was built for Giacomo Costa fu Andrea and Lloyd Tirrenico SpA to run a three-class southern Atlantic line service to Argentina. Although essentially structurally unchanged until recently, this ship too has proven successful as a cruise liner. Here thoughtful interior planning has provided for an easy and harmonious amalgamation of her accommodations into a single class.

The design of both ships is based on a nearly identical overall hull form and engine room layout. The machinery is located some 30m farther forward than on *Canberra*. Since these are also express liners requiring powerful and heavy engines, their designers were cautious to avoid a repeat of *Canberra*'s problems of trim. However, the tanker-style arrangement with main boilers aft of the turbines and above the propeller shafts was retained. In this way the boiler uptakes and funnels were kept far enough aft to yield a good run of unbroken passenger space amidships and to convey the desired modern aesthetic appearance. The funnel location of both ships is in fact similar to that of *Rotterdam*.

The hull form of these ships differs considerably from that of *Canberra*. The stern is an inspired combination of a transom below the waterline and conventional cruiser form above. An increased underwater area provided by the transom serves to reduce inherent water resistance and consequently lower the required engine power. The purpose of the cruiser stern, which is entirely above the water line, is primarily aesthetic. However, it does also provide some additional deck space above, and a measure of reserve buoyancy in case the hull were damaged.

The forward body is least dissimilar from *Canberra* in that it generally follows the Yourkevitch principle, with a bulbous forefoot and characteristic hollowness of the waterline form. Amidships there is a 1m tumblehome giving these ships a distinctly pear-shaped midships cross section, more closely resembling that of *Normandie* than the slab-sided *Canberra*.

In her outward appearance *Oceanic* is very much a proportionately smaller relative of *Canberra*. The main body of her superstructure is three decks high, one fewer than on *Canberra*. Above this the massif of her funnel and its supporting structure aft is visually balanced by the forward bridge housing, two rather than four decks high. The lifeboats are half nested at the vertical midpoint of the main superstructure. As a concession to her intended North Atlantic service, the promenade beneath the boats is enclosed. Until the ship's hull was painted bright red after she was purchased by Premier Cruises, it was quite possible to mistake her profile when seen at a distance for that of *Canberra*.

On board, *Oceanic*'s Italian designers took full advantage of her layout to provide superb passenger facilities. The domed swimming pool which had been denied *Canberra* was rendered here on a magnificent scale. The entire midships section of lido deck was covered by a

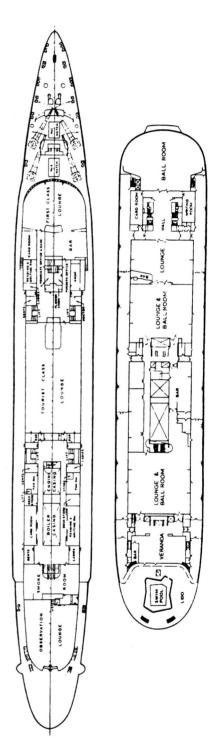

Plans showing the arrangement of the principal public rooms on *Oceanic*'s promenade deck (top) and *Eugenio C*'s lounge deck (bottom). (Builders' drawings, courtesy of Marine Publications International)

fully retractable Magrodome, the first of its kind to be fitted aboard any ship. This sliding roof is in essence a huge glazed motorised hatch cover. The name comes from its manufacturer, MacGregor International, a leading supplier of ships' access equipment. *Oceanic's* Magrodome encloses two swimming pools and a vast lido surrounding them. This area is the focal point of a suite of public rooms extending the full length of the ship's superstructure. The forward rooms were originally intended for First Class, but since the ship has been used exclusively for cruising class barriers were never imposed on her passengers.

This arrangement was the prototype of similar top-deck layouts on a number of noteworthy cruise ships which have followed. One of the best of these is the new Hapag-Lloyd flagship, *Europa*, completed in 1981. Here, the forward observation lounge and its relationship with the pool area amidships can be clearly seen as a luxuriously updated descendant of *Canberra's* Crow's Nest lounge, Bonito Club and pool of exactly twenty years earlier. Naturally it follows that similar arrangements were also featured in Home Lines' two subsequent ships, *Atlantic* and *Homeric*.

Oceanic's designers were not encumbered by the dead-amidships vertical class barrier which somewhat besets *Canberra's* layout. They were able to create a number of other outstanding spaces lower down, taking full advantage of the ship's unbroken centrebody. The most remarkable of these are the promenade deck central lounge and the main dining room on B deck. Both of these large rooms reflect the full fore and aft length of the lido above. The dining room is especially noteworthy for the sense of spaciousness achieved by the absence of supporting columns in its large domed central area.

There are four main stairways, each enclosing three sides of a lift shaft. These are arranged facing each other across the ship's centreline in pairs fore and aft of the central span of public rooms amidships. This allows the passenger circulation pattern in the public rooms to follow a single axis along the ship's centreline. Unfortunately, in this regard *Oceanic's* plan is somewhat spoiled by a central service core forward, reflecting the intrusion of the necessary boiler and engine casings aft. No doubt this was excused in view of the owners' original intention of allocating her forward public rooms on main and lido decks to First Class.

A similar arrangement of stairways and lifts is used to far greater advantage in the layout of *Eugenio C*. Here the First Class public rooms

Costa's handsome *Eugenio C*, seen here in a publicity photo, shows considerable similarity to *Canberra* in several features. Most notable are the twin stacks located aft and the lower location of the lifeboats, albeit carried under conventional davits. (Costa Cruises)

Access to *Eugenio C*'s principal public rooms forward on lounge deck follows the centreline of the ship. Seen from just inside the Opale Lounge (aftmost) is a central vista through the Rubino Lounge to the foyer beyond. (Author's photo)

Another interior view of *Eugenio C*, showing the characteristic Italian shipboard interior styling prevalent in the 1960s. This view shows the Rubino Lounge and Bar with the Opale Lounge in the background. (Author's photo)

occupying the forward half of lounge deck are arranged in open plan along a magnificent wide central axis. These consist of three principal lounges situated one forward and two aft of a wide foyer. There is a lift and stairway at either side of the foyer facing each other as on *Oceanic*. The whole scheme provides a superb vista from the aft end of the third room, ahead through all three rooms and the foyer, to the outside beyond the large forward windows. Here the ship's designers also managed to arrange the service uptakes and crew accesses either side of the centreline, achieving an elegant plan of remarkable simplicity.

The same idea was used on a grandiose scale aboard *Normandie*, whose axial vistas of magnificent public rooms along almost her entire length are legendary. The scheme was later reduced to a more practical scale aboard *Nieuw Amsterdam*, completed in 1938. It seems surprising that similar layouts have not become more popular in subsequently built ships. Perhaps this approach would have flourished had not the alternative rationale of *Queen Elizabeth 2*'s plan with its perimeter circulation pattern ultimately prevailed.

Above decks, *Eugenio C* bears a stronger likeness to *Canberra* than to

The arrangement of *Eugenio C*'s lido deck pool is not unlike that of *Canberra*'s Bonito Club area, especially as seen here with the twin stacks further aft. Perhaps the real origins of the idea belong to *Conte di Savoia*, which emerged from the same Italian yard thirty-three years earlier. (Author's photo)

Oceanic. The relationship of the pool with its adjoining veranda lounge and windscreened open deck above is not unlike that of the P & O ship. The twin side-by-side stacks aft also resemble those of *Canberra*. Likewise, *Eugenio C*'s lifeboats are carried well below her lido deck, although under conventional davits and not nested. While this does limit the width of the upper decks to the dimension between the two rows of lifeboat davits, there is still the same unobstructed view and a similar impression of spaciousness found on those of *Canberra* and *Oceanic*.

This approach to deck layout has since remained as a popular alternative on a great many cruise ships, particularly those designed for Caribbean and other exclusively tropical services. It has since become customary on some of the larger ships for the centre section of the upper decks to be cantilevered outwards above the lifeboats. The enormous *Sovereign of the Seas* represents one of the most dramatic examples of this. The central stretch of her lido, which is over 100m long, spreads outwards to the ship's full beam an entire five decks above the boat deck.

Italia, shown here in Costa colours, represents a miniature adaptation of many design features from *Canberra*, *Oceanic* and *Eugenio C*. (Costa Cruises)

Traditionally Italian deep-sea liners have almost always been tropical ships by virtue of the location of their home ports and their routes of

trade. Even Italy's most prestigious North Atlantic liners stressed the advantage of the more favourable southern route to the sunny Mediterranean. In the 1930s *Rex* and *Conte di Savoia* began to exploit this to the full with their enormous and elaborate lido decks and open-air swimming pools, the likes of which had never before been seen on the New York run. In this regard Italia was far ahead of its British and North European Atlantic rivals. Indeed facilities of this type have remained a key ingredient of Italian passenger ship design ever since.

The Italians, who have a remarkably keen eye for good modern design, were quick to adapt the proven example of *Canberra* to their own ideas on passenger ship styling. Admittedly, it was *Southern Cross* which originally set the pace. However, the topsides deck space freed by moving her funnel fully aft was little more than a flat deckhouse roof buttressed by two files of lifeboats with a couple of deck tennis courts marked out on it. *Canberra*'s elegant equivalent of the same space, raised high above the lifeboats, with its recessed swimming pool, wide open games spaces and unobstructed view was bound to be an inspiration. From this the Italians derived an eminently attractive and functional open-plan suite of indoor/outdoor topsides public spaces typical of many cruise ships which have followed.

In *Oceanic* and *Eugenio C*, other public spaces below were opened up and given a sense of characteristic Mediterranean elegance and informality. To the clean lines and functional forms of *Canberra*'s interiors, the Italian liners of the 1960s added bold and vibrant colour schemes, an imaginative use of materials and an abundance of contemporary art.

These examples represented modern functional design at its best, with that unmistakable Italian chic of Ferrari or a fine Gucci garment. The distinctive character of this work was not imparted by any identifiable nationalist style itself, but rather by an Italian approach to design in general. A key element of Italian industrial design derives from interpretation of outside influences. It is their handling of such interpretation, based on a strong nationalist confidence and clear creative thinking, which stimulates the world-wide appeal of Italian design.

Since the 1950s and 1960s the 'Designed in Italy' label has gained prestige in all manner of consumer goods sold all over the world. These range from sunglasses and fashion shoes, domestic appliances and business machines, to furniture and consumer electronics. Ferrari and Lamborghini are Italian classics which have been household names for many years and have had their share in influencing other automobile

Royal Viking Star was one of the first cruise ships completed long enough after *Queen Elizabeth 2* to incorporate some of the Cunard superliner's design features. (Wärtsilä, Helsinki Shipyard)

Queen Elizabeth 2's funnel which was unique at the time of her building...

...can be seen as the inspiration of those fitted atop the Royal Viking Line's fleet. (Author's photos)

designs. Likewise *Oceanic* and *Eugenio C*, are classic examples of timeless shipboard design whose Italian styling remains and has since continued to flourish in the cruise industry worldwide.

Like *Canberra* and *Oriana*, *Oceanic* and *Eugenio C* have proved eminently successful as cruise ships, although they too are essentially products of the liner era. This fact bespeaks the farsightedness of their owners and builders as well as the soundness of their design. In all four ships the matter of combining their passenger classes and downgrading the machinery for economical operation at lower speeds was accomplished without major structural or engineering work. The inability of many liners from the same era to meet these requirements have heralded their early demise as they were unsuitable for cruising.

Of the two Italian ships, *Eugenio C* is more similar to *Canberra* in character. Like the P & O flagship, she was designed for long tropical voyages rather than North Atlantic crossings and short cruises. While *Canberra* was regularly running to and from Australia *Eugenio C* was plying the route between Genoa and Buenos Aires. As cruising gained precedence in the 1970s, both ships were accommodated in the leisure trade of their original terminal ports during the opposite summer season of each. *Canberra* alternated between Southampton- and Sydney-based cruises while *Eugenio C* became likewise engaged in Genoa and Buenos Aires. For each ship, the original route is followed as positioning voyages are made only once in each direction every year. Accordingly both ships have managed to maintain their original national characters and have avoided the full-scale 'Americanisation' of nearly the whole leisure industry.

The first purpose-built products of the modern cruise ship era began to emerge in the late 1960s. Although the field would quickly become dominated by Scandinavian interests, it is hardly surprising that one of the first of these new ships should be Italian. She was the attractive little motor ship, *Italia*, built in 1967 along the lines of a miniature version of *Oceanic*. At 12,219 tons, she is less than half the larger ship's size, although similar in appearance to *Oceanic*, with her seminested lifeboats and her engines and stack aft. Likewise her plan stresses a central topsides lido and interior open planning amidships. She differs from *Oceanic* and *Eugenio C* as her cabin layout follows the single centreline corridor arrangement used on *Southern Cross* and the forward part of *Canberra*.

What distinguished her as a cruise ship was that all her 500 passengers were accommodated in a single class, and that there was no provision for carrying passengers' cars, hold baggage, revenue cargoes or mails. Her size was between the average 6,000- to 8,000-ton Euro-Scandinavian ferries of her day and that of the larger intermediate-size liners then still in service. With a service speed of 19 knots she was ideally suited to the slower pace of cruising itineraries.

Neither *Italia*'s builders nor her original owners survived, as the venture resulted in bankruptcy for both. The ship herself fared much better. She was chartered by Princess Cruises for Pacific Coast cruising. As *Princess Italia* she cruised the Mexican Riviera in the winter months, and the Alaska coast in the summer. She was a key element of Stanley McDonald's Princess fleet for a number of years prior to the company's acquisition by P & O. Since the end of her charter in 1973 she sailed for many years under the Costa houseflag and her original name.

Two years after *Italia*'s completion, the Norwegian Kloster Rederi took delivery of their first ships designed specifically for Caribbean cruising. Four were originally ordered, two from West Germany's A G Weser yard and two from Cantieri Navale de Tirrenio in Italy. All four were motor ships of around 18,000 tons gross, with service speeds in the 20-knot range. Kloster engaged the Danish firm of Knud E Hansen as consulting naval architects for all four ships. Although they imparted certain unifying influences, the Italian and German pairs were of quite different structural design and layout. The German-built ships, *Starward* and *Skyward*, were essentially based on Euro-Scandinavian ferry layout, with the majority of their public rooms being located on a single deck. However their Italian sisters followed the *Italia* prototype in terms of exterior styling, machinery arrangement and planning of their public rooms and decks. Of this pair, only *Southward* was delivered to Kloster. The remaining ship was later sold to P & O on the stocks following a dispute with the shipyard, and was completed to her new owners' specification as *Spirit of London*.

Southward and *Spirit of London* differ mainly because their cabin arrangement reflects the Scandinavian influence in its layout and high degree of standardisation. The wide diversity of individual cabin plans typical of earlier ships was reduced to three basic types, inside double, outside double and deluxe. *Italia*'s centreline cabin corridors were not repeated since the dead-end side-to-side alleyways required to reach the outer cabins are not permitted. In the interests of safety at sea, the Norwegian regulatory body, Det Norske Veritas, does not permit dead-end corridors of more than 3m in length in a ship's accommodations. This factor has contributed to the straightforward layout of these and subsequent Norwegian cruise ships which emphasise a simple plan giving all cabins direct access from a pair of parallel corridors running the full length of each deck.

Although the overall theme is Scandinavian, the inspiration of Michael Inchbald's Queens Room is apparent here in the ceiling design of *Royal Viking Sea*'s main lounge. (Author's photo)

In the words of S A Bertelsen of Knud E Hansen ApS:

This was actually the very start of today's imposing cruise activity in the Caribbean, and many fine vessels to fly Norwegian and British flags were to come from Knud E Hansen's drawing boards in Copenhagen. We are quite proud to regard the audacious and smart lines and arrangements of vessels like the *Skyward*, the *Southward*, and the *Starward* as the happy result of combined creative inspirations by owners and their consultants.

These ships represented the fusion of diverse influences from a number of the world's leading shipbuilding nations. The rationale of *Canberra*'s integral hotel block from Britain was brought together with Italian styling and Scandinavian modernity in shipboard service and accommodations. In one sense, things came full circle when the last of the quartet, *Spirit of London*, brought a decade of development subsequent to *Canberra*'s lead back to the P & O stable in 1972.

By the time this happened a new leaf had been turned in the history of passenger ship design. In May 1969 the maiden voyage of *Queen Elizabeth 2* brought the eyes of the world to focus once again on another outstanding new British superliner. This was *the* shipbuilding event of the year. The publicity that it created overshadowed other events such as the inauguration of Kloster's three-ship Norwegian Caribbean Line fleet at the end of the year. After all, *Queen Elizabeth 2* was the great Atlantic super ship of the future that everyone had been waiting for. The fact that she was also created as a cruise ship of superlative standards attracted a great deal of attention from owners of the new Norwegian cruise lines as well as their fellow Scandinavian ship designers and builders. The decade to follow would be theirs. In the way that *Canberra* had begun to shape the future through her influence on the Italian ships of the 1960s, so would *Queen Elizabeth 2*'s example inspire the shape of things to come from the modern Vikings of the 1970s.

While there was optimism on Cunard's part that *Queen Elizabeth 2* would spark renewed public enthusiasm for North Atlantic liner service, it was otherwise generally acknowledged that she would be the last ship intended for such a service, certainly in the foreseeable future. Of the twenty or so other passenger ships then under construction, none was destined exclusively for long-range line service of any kind. The last German-flag Atlantic liner, *Hanseatic*, had been completed a few months ahead of *Queen Elizabeth 2*. The only other dual-purpose Atlantic ship to

The Finnish cruise ferry, *Finnjet*, was considered revolutionary for her use of aircraft-type gas turbine machinery. However over the longer run she is credited with bringing about a considerable rationalisation of accommodation layout. (Author's photo)

follow was Norwegian America Line's *Vistafjord*, completed in 1974. Her Atlantic service has amounted to but a few positioning voyages between cruises. A number of these have in fact been made as a stand-in for *Queen Elizabeth 2* since Cunard's subsequent purchase of the vessel.

Compared with *Canberra*, *Queen Elizabeth 2* is of an entirely different appearance and character. Structurally she is more akin to *Oriana*, though her outward appearance bears little evidence of this. Internally the rationale of her layout and the character of her interior decor, inspired conceptually to some degree by *Canberra*'s example, have taken their own distinct direction. *Queen Elizabeth 2* is essentially a modern ship both inside and out, though in character she also bears a strong sense of the tradition bequeathed by her great North Atlantic predecessors.

Generally speaking, the cruise industry continues to favour the style of *Canberra*'s structural design, with its emphasis on open-plan passenger accommodations and topsides deck spaces forward of the engine casings and funnel uptakes. The design influence of *Queen Elizabeth 2* has been more subtle. There have not been *Queen Elizabeth 2* look-alikes in the way that, for instance, *Oceanic* and *Eugenio C* followed *Canberra*'s lines. With the exception of her funnel form, *Queen Elizabeth 2*'s distinctive exterior profile has remained hers alone. Nonetheless, James Gardner's styling of her has provided the impetus for other designers to give distinctive images of their own to later fleets of Scandinavian cruise ships. Likewise the layout and outfitting of *Queen Elizabeth 2*'s public rooms with its emphasis on professional entertainment and services usually found in holiday resorts has since become axiomatic in cruise ship design.

At the time of *Queen Elizabeth 2*'s debut there were several Norwegian-owned cruise ships which were still at an early enough stage of planning or construction for new ideas to be incorporated into their design. Most notable of these were the first of six vessels being built at the Wärtsilä shipyard in Helsinki. They were all three-quarters aft engined motor ships in the 18,000- to 20,000-ton range, based on an overall design concept developed by Knud E Hansen ApS in Copenhagen. Three of these were delivered to Royal Viking Line and three to Royal Caribbean Cruise Line.

Royal Viking Star was the first of these to be built for Royal Viking Line. After studying some forty liners and cruise ships then in service, the line's owners were apparently most impressed with *Oceanic* and *Queen Elizabeth 2*. Of the two it is clearly the Cunard ship which has had the greater influence on this trio of white Nordic cruisers.

Externally, the funnel gives the Royal Viking ships their only readily recognisable link with *Queen Elizabeth 2*. After conducting their own exhaustive series of wind tunnel tests at the Technical High School in Helsinki, *Royal Viking Star*'s designers came to the same conclusions as had James Gardner earlier in England. The outer 'boot' enclosing the stack and the wind scoop at its base together provided the only effective way of keeping exhaust gases and soot away from the decks. This was well illustrated in a series of photographs published in *Shipping World and Shipbuilder* in August 1972. One alternative tried which had the 'boot', but no wind scoop, was shown in these pictures to be little better than the other more conventional shapes tested. The final funnel form is a squat version of the *Queen Elizabeth 2*'s original stack, painted in the same black and white colour scheme. Ironically, the Cunard flagship's own stack has since taken on a similar profile as a side effect of her re-engining in 1986/7.

Queen Elizabeth 2's other influences bear mainly on internal layout. Her quarter deck plan was adopted for the *Royal Viking Star*'s principal suite of public rooms on the Norwegian ship's corresponding Scandinavia deck. The galley is fully forward, the dining room amidships and the main lounge aft. There is also a swimming pool and lido on the open deck still farther aft. At approximately one-third the tonnage and passenger capacity of *Queen Elizabeth 2*, the whole scheme is rendered on a proportionately smaller and thus more intimate scale.

The layout of the two later ships, *Royal Viking Sky* and *Royal Viking Sea*, was refined slightly. A number of small rooms forward of the main lounge on each ship were rearranged to provide the same perimeter circulation pattern as *Queen Elizabeth 2*'s quarter deck. The interior design scheme of all three ships reflects more of the 'international' style used aboard *Queen Elizabeth 2*, than it does the Scandinavian character of their opposite numbers built for Royal Caribbean. The colour scheme is quieter and the expression of form more subdued. The artificially illuminated latticed ceiling of the main lounge on *Royal Viking Sea*, for instance, bears a strong resemblance to Michael Inchbald's treatment of the Queens Room on *Queen Elizabeth 2*.

Here too, the crew day room and cafeteria are beneath the galley, with stores carried still farther down in the forward part of B deck. These areas are all connected by a service lift and crew stairways in the forward part of the ship, providing a similar arrangement of services to those on *Queen Elizabeth 2*. However, similarity to the new Cunarder stops short of the cabin layouts, which on these ships follow the Scandinavian rule of virtual standardisation.

The first of these delivered to Royal Caribbean was *Song of Norway*, followed later by *Nordic Prince* and *Sun Viking*. Their owners opted instead to stay with the Scandinavian layout of the original contract design. They did however engage the remarkable Norwegian designer, Geir Grung to create their own distinctive fleet image. Grung started with the contract plans, as had James Gardner in the days of Q3. He was responsible for the overall exterior styling and the more detailed layout of the open decks and pool areas.

The blue riband encircling the superstructure, an exaggerated rake of the bow, and the words 'Royal Caribbean' displayed on the funnel, together with the company's logo, are the sort of things that were to be expected. The most distinctive image which came from Geir Grung's mind was that of the Viking Crown Lounge incorporated into the funnel of each ship. After the naval architects and other technical people involved recovered from the initial shock of being asked for such a structure on a ship, the idea was enthusiastically adopted. It has since

Royal Caribbean's *Sovereign of the Seas*. The largest cruise ship in the world upon her delivery, she exhibits *Canberra*'s emphasis of open deck spaces atop the superstructure on an unprecedented scale. The interior layout combines features of *Queen Elizabeth 2*'s plan with others from *Finnjet*. (Royal Caribbean Cruise Line)

become the unique trademark of the Royal Caribbean fleet, imparting the same type of unmistakable recognition as does the Mercedes Benz star and front grill. Expressed another way, Geir Grung's Royal Caribbean image is as distinctive in its own right as the profile created for *Queen Elizabeth 2* by James Gardner.

These six ships, along with a number of their contemporaries such as Kloster's Southward-class White Ships and the Fearnley and Eger *Sea Venture* have done a great deal to shape the modern cruise industry's stock in trade. They have done so both in terms of the ships themselves, which continue to be built in unprecedented numbers, as well as in the style of service and accommodation offered aboard. Their clean yacht-like hull lines, steeply raked bows, dominant superstructures, excursion launches, and large windscreened top decks have given the whole cruise business a singular image of contemporary chic. While some, or perhaps all, of these elements may make the traditionalist shiplover cringe with dismay, it is the image that the cruise lines want and what their clientele have come to expect.

As cruising gathered momentum during the 1970s and on into the 1980s, new and larger ships were planned. Along with these come a number of new ideas in operating economics and shipboard layout. 'Economy of scale' became the ship owners' credo as a buoyant market showed confident promise of being able to consistently fill more berths each week. Advances in diesel engineering showed that these larger ships could be powered even more economically.

In 1977 the revolutionary gas turbine Baltic ferry, *Finnjet*, demonstrated the advantages of a vertical rather than horizontal separation of passenger public rooms and cabins. On this trendsetting ship all sleeping accommodations for passengers and crew are located forward, while the public rooms and their associated services are grouped aft. The main rationale of this approach lies in the organisation of ship's services around two vertical cores, one each for the special needs of the public rooms and the cabins.

Finnjet's example was adopted wholeheartedly on the German cruise ships *Berlin* and *Europa*, and has, in a modified form, since influenced the layouts of *Song of America*, *Nieuw Amsterdam*, *Noordam* and *Sovereign of the Seas*. A later conceptual design from Wärtsilä for ships with all outside cabins materialised in 1984 as Princess Cruises' *Royal Princess*. Although she remains the only large ship of this type thus far, other elements of her radical structural design are readily identifiable in recent ships such as *Seaward*, *Nordic Empress* and to a lesser degree on *Royal Viking Sun*.

These ideas have tended to build on rather than supersede the innovativeness of *Canberra* and *Queen Elizabeth 2*. The *Canberra*-style of structural layout, *Queen Elizabeth 2*'s arterial interior promenades and upper deck dining rooms and the Scandinavian approach to cabin design and services planning continue to flourish. The influence of *Finnjet* and *Royal Princess* has served to refine these elements.

The *Song of America* or *Nieuw Amsterdam* style of layout has ultimately proved more popular in cruise ship planning than *Europa*'s plan. This arrangement amalgamates the vertical orientation of catering and hotel services of *Finnjet*, but with the traditional emphasis of a horizontal layout of public rooms. It also offers a satisfactory compromise of the dining room's location.

The wisdom of using valuable space on the upper decks for dining rooms becomes questionable in view of the popularity of informal meal service on deck during the daytime. Many passengers only use the dining room for dinner, usually after nightfall, unless the ship is cruising through Alaska or the Norwegian fjords in summer. Dark or not, passengers have shown a preference for the windows and upper deck location over trudging down to the bowels of the ship for dinner. This is understandable in view of the predominance of accommodation in the superstructures above the main run of public rooms on many large new cruise ships.

The *Finnjet* or *Europa* approach solves the dilemma by locating the dining room aft and beneath the public rooms. Here, sandwiched into the 'tween deck space above the engine room it is not too far out of the way, and is still high enough up in the ship to sport the preferred large windows. In *Europa* the remaining vertical space on the two decks below is occupied by the galley and its related services and stores. *Sovereign of the Seas* stands as one of the best examples of this, with her two large dining rooms arranged one above the other below her main run of public rooms.

The modern cruise ship has now caught up with and surpassed *Canberra* and *Queen Elizabeth 2* in size. *Royal Princess* and the three Carnival Cruises *Holiday*-class ships overtook *Canberra*'s tonnage in the mid 1980s. In early 1988 *Sovereign of the Seas* surpassed *Queen Elizabeth 2* as the first of a spate of huge new ships. She in turn was followed by three more Carnival ships and two follow-up ships to Princess Cruises' *Star Princess*, which were all over 70,000 tons.

The slightly smaller *Star Princess*, which was originally ordered by Sitmar before being taken over by the P & O Group for Princess Cruises, is particularly noteworthy in her resemblance to *Canberra*. Externally her fully nested lifeboats, aft-sited funnel and windscreened upper decks convey the impression of stocky modernised versions of the P & O ship. The overwhelming proportions of the superstructure, minuscule foredeck and complete absence of sheer are features which definitely place *Star Princess* firmly in a later generation than *Canberra*.

The same basic idea is further developed in *Crown Princess*, the first new Italian-built Sitmar vessel to have been transferred to P & O. Here the lifeboat recess is once again two decks high, as opposed to the three decks taken up on *Star Princess*. This alone gives the new ship a sleeker image. Her exterior appearance has unique clean lines designed by the noted Italian architect/designer Renzo Piano. His functional simplicity of form is achieved partly by the treatment of the lifeboat recesses and by the otherwise generally smooth and enclosed expression of the superstructure. This effect is further enhanced by curved lines of the upperworks and the dolphin head shape adopted in the bridge structure.

Still perhaps a little alien in purely traditional terms, her profile has a more seaworthy look than that of some of her contemporaries. It possesses what architects like to call a 'plastic quality of form' which is itself attractive. What this really means is that there is a smooth and uncluttered appearance which looks as though the structure were cast or moulded from plastic or some such substance. It is this quality which gives the lines of *Canberra*, *Eugenio C* and *Queen Elizabeth 2* their enormous appeal.

Internally *Star Princess* resembles *Canberra* in the layout of her public rooms in three strata, above, amid and below the cabins. Here too the main public rooms are on promenade deck, beneath the lifeboats. In line with modern practice, the dining room is situated aft on this deck with its services immediately beneath. The lowest stratum is occupied by the cinema, discotheque and an elaborate health and beauty centre. Above are the informal daytime centres consisting of the observation lounge, café, swimming pools and lido. The intermediate decks are allocated to large and well-equipped passenger cabins.

While the source of certain details of the layout can be traced to *Queen Elizabeth 2*'s original design, the Cunard flagship's renaissance as a motor ship has a stronger technical influence. *Star Princess* is one of the first to follow her diesel-electric machinery arrangement. She is powered by the same combination of MAN medium speed engines and General Electric alternators. However, the lower power requirements of their service speed will demand only four engines as opposed to the nine units fitted on *Queen Elizabeth 2*. Likewise the Carnival *Fantasy*-class ships are to be diesel electric. Although each requiring fewer generating sets than the Cunard ship, they will provide the same flexibility of combining their engines to meet the diverse power requirements in port, while manoeuvring and for running at full speed.

Apart from the various structural, technical and aesthetic influences of *Canberra* and *Queen Elizabeth 2*, the Cunard ship has done much to shape the style of modern cruising itself. Today she is the sole ship in regular North Atlantic service, although she only runs between New York and Southampton for about seven months of the year. She is the world's only liner with the speed to maintain the élite five-day express service. In her cruising role she has served to bring the superlative chic of a crack North Atlantic service to the leisure trade. It is her Atlantic crossings which set the tone of her entire operation. In turn her cruising performance has set the pace for others. She is a ship which retains a trendsetting role. Periodic refits and modernisations have maintained her enviable position as the standard against which other ships are measured.

Even greater ships are being planned for the future – ships which will surpass the elusive 100,000-ton mark. When built, these will be radically different craft with catamaran hulls and oversized cantilevered superstructures. Yet, probably long after *Canberra* and *Queen Elizabeth 2* have been duly disposed of at the end of their illustrious careers, the new breed will continue to owe something of their design heritage to these outstanding British superliners of the 1960s.

A longitudinal section of *Crown Princess*, showing her arrangement of cabins and public rooms. The principal lounges and the dining rooms on 6 and 7 decks are separated from those above on 12 and 14 decks and others below on 2 deck by several strata of sleeping accommodations as was done in *Canberra*. (Builders' drawing)

The last word in cruise ship design at the time of writing – P & O's Italian-designed *Crown Princess*. Her advanced rationalist styling bears a strong impression of *Canberra*, designed about thirty years earlier. (P & O)

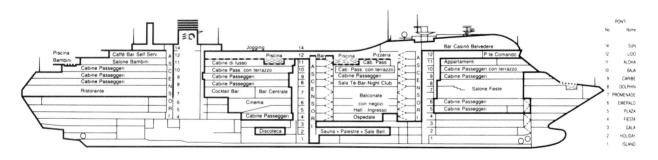

Appendix A

Technical Specifications

Canberra

Length, overall	249.93m (820ft)
Length between perpendiculars	225.55m (740ft)
Beam, moulded	31.08m (102ft)
Draught, maximum	9.90m (32ft 6in)
Height, keel to base of funnel	32.46m (106ft 6in)
Gross Register Tonnage	44,807 tons
Maximum trial speed	29.27 knots
Service speed	27.50 knots
Propulsion	Turbo-electric – twin-screw
Propulsion power, maximum	Two 31,705kw (42,500shp)
Propellers	Two four-bladed fixed pitch, diameter 6.24m (20ft 6in)
Propeller speed	147rpm, Maximum
Turbines	Two BTH single cylinder 17 stage
Drive motors	Two double 42 pole synchronous
Boilers	Four Foster Wheeler type ESD
Steam conditions	53kg/scm @ 515 °C (750 psi @ 960 °F)
Transverse thrusters	One 597kw (800hp) bow unit 9 tons thrust
Stabilisers	Two pairs Denny-Brown fin type
Auxiliary power	Four 1.500kw AEI turbo alternators
Fresh water distilling capacity	750 tons/day
Fuel consumption	NA
Number of decks	14
Passenger capacity	2238
Crew	960
Cargo capacity	4245cu m (150,000cu ft)
Builders	Harland & Wolff Ltd, Musgrave Yard, Queen's Island, Belfast
Keel laid	23 September 1957
Launch	16 March 1960
Completion	28 April 1961

Oriana

Length, overall	245.05m (804ft)
Length between perpendiculars	225.55m (740ft)
Beam, moulded	30.48m (100ft 0in)
Draught, maximum	9.63m (31ft 6in)
Height, keel to base of funnel	NA (NA)
Gross Register Tonnage	41,923 tons
Maximum trial speed	30.64 knots
Service speed	27.50 knots
Propulsion	Steam Turbine – twin-screw
Propulsion power, maximum	Two 29,840kw (40,000shp)
Propellers	Two four-bladed fixed pitch, diameter 6.09m (20ft)
Propeller speed	157.5rpm, Maximum
Turbines	Two Vickers/PAMETRADA triple expansion geared sets
Boilers	Four Foster Wheeler type ESD
Steam conditions	53kg/s cm @ 515 °C (750psi @ 960 °F)
Transverse thrusters	Four 410kw (550hp) units, Two forward and two aft, 20 tons thrust combined
Stabilisers	One pair Denny-Brown fin type
Auxiliary power	Four 1.750kw turbo alternators
Fresh water distilling capacity	650 tons/day
Fuel consumption	300 tons/day @ 27.5 knots
Number of decks	15
Passenger capacity	2184
Crew	899
Cargo/mail capacity	5190cu m (183,378cu ft)
Builders	Vickers Armstrong, Barrow
Keel laid	18 September 1957
Launch	3 November 1959
Completion	15 November 1960

Queen Elizabeth 2 (as built)

Length, overall	293.57m (936ft)
Length between perpendiculars	269.75m (885ft)
Beam, moulded	32.00m (105ft)
Draught, maximum	9.91m (32ft 6in)
Height, keel to base of funnel	40.84m (134ft)
Gross Register Tonnage	65,862 tons
Maximum trial speed	32.66 knots
Service speed	28.50 knots
Propulsion	Steam turbine – twin-screw
Propulsion power, maximum	Two 41,030kw (2 × 55,000shp)
Propellers	Two six-bladed fixed pitch, diameter 5.79m (19ft)
Propeller speed	174rpm, maximum
Turbines	Two Brown/PAMETRADA double expansion geared sets
Boilers	Three Foster Wheeler type ESD
Steam conditions	60 kg/s cm @ 510 °C (850psi @ 950 °F)
Stabilisers	Two pairs Denny-Brown AEG fin type
Transverse thrusters	Two 746kw (2 × 1000hp) bow units, 22 tons thrust combined
Auxiliary power	Three 5.500kw AEI turbo alternators
Fresh water distilling capacity	1200 tons/day
Fuel consumption	520 tons/day (Atlantic service)
Number of decks	13
Passenger capacity	2025
Crew	906
Roll on/roll off facilities	80 cars, side port loading
Builders	Upper Clyde Shipbuilders (formerly John Brown and Company)
Keel laid	5 July 1965
Launch	20 September 1967
Completion	8 April 1969

Queen Elizabeth 2 (following re-engining and conversion 1986–7)

Length, overall	unchanged
Length between perpendiculars	unchanged
Beam, moulded	unchanged
Draught, maximum	unchanged
Height, keel to base of funnel	unchanged
Gross Register Tonnage	66,451 tons
Maximum trial speed	34.60 knots
Service speed	unchanged
Propulsion	diesel-electric – twin-screw
Propulsion power, maximum	Two 44,000kw (2 × 65,000shp)
Propellers	Two five-bladed controllable pitch
diameter 5.79 m (19 ft)	Two seven-bladed Grim wheels, diameter 6.7m (22ft)
Propeller speed	144rpm, maximum
Engines	Nine MAN-B & W type 9L58/64 diesels
Drive motors	Two GEC synchronous
Alternators	Nine GEC 10,500kw @ 10kv/60hz
Boilers (auxiliary)	Nine Sunrod exhaust gas units / Two Sunrod donkey units
Stabilisers	unchanged
Transverse thrusters	unchanged
Fresh water distilling capacity	1450 tons/day
Fuel consumption 270 tons/day	(Atlantic service)
Number of decks	14*
Passenger capacity	1850
Crew	900
Roll on/roll off facilities	unchanged
Conversion	Lloyd Werft GmbH, Bremerhaven, W Germany
Conversion period	27 October 1986 to 25 April 1987
Commercial service resumed	29 April 1987

* 'Penthouses' added above Signal Deck in earlier refit.

Appendix B

Register of Other Ships

The following assembly of vital statistics, from a somewhat eclectic assembly of tonnage, represents those ships which have received more than a mere passing mention in the text. The reason for inclusion is given in the note accompanying most entries. The three superliners, *Oriana*, *Canberra* and *Queen Elizabeth 2* are excluded here as their full technical specifications are given in the preceding appendix.

There may be some inconsistency in the tonnages quoted, as the rules of measurement can vary from country to country and from time to time. Wherever possible, Lloyd's Register of Shipping has been used as the standard reference source.

For the sake of consistency, all other measurements are given in metric. Service speeds are quoted rather than maximums. The nationality shown is that of the owners, and not necessarily of the ship's registry.

Arcadia　　　　P & O, United Kingdom.
　　Built　　　John Brown & Co, Clydebank, 1954.
　　Specifications
　　GRT, 29,734; Length, 219.66m; Beam, 27.58m;
　　Draught, 9.28m Geared steam turbine, 25,350kw;
　　Speed, 23.50kn; Screws, two;
　　Passengers, 1414 in two classes; crew, 704.
　　Note　　One of the last traditional British tropical liners. P & O's *Arcadia* and *Iberia* were *Canberra*'s immediate predecessors.

Assiniboia　　Canadian Pacific, Canada.
　　Built　　　Fairfield Co. Ltd, Glasgow, 1907.
　　Specifications
　　GRT, 3880; Length, 102.54m; Beam, 13.31m;
　　Draught, 4.6m; Compound steam, 390kw; Speed
　　15.00kn; Screws, one;
　　Passengers, 300.
　　Note　　*Assiniboia* and *Keewatin* were perhaps two of the best examples of Great Lakes passenger ships with engines aft. No doubt it was they which most inspired the design of Matson's *Maui*.

Carmania　　Cunard Line, United Kingdom.
　　Built　　　John Brown & Co, Clydebank, 1905.
　　Specifications
　　GRT, 19,524; Length, 205.74m; Beam, 22.10m;
　　Geared steam turbine, 15,658kw; Speed, 19.00kn;
　　Screws, three;
　　Passengers, 2650 in four classes (incl steerage);
　　Crew, 700.
　　Note　　Although short by a few tons in size and about a knot in speed, this ship was the first Cunarder in the 20/20 class (*see* Chapter 1).

Crown Princess　P & O Group (Princess Cruises), United Kingdom.
　　Built　　　Fincantieri Cantieri Navali Italiani (formerly Cantieri Riuniti dell'Adriatico), Monfalcone, 1990.
　　Specifications
　　GRT, 70,000; Length, 245.05m; Beam, 32,25m;
　　Draught, 7.82m; Diesel electric; Speed, 19.50kn;
　　Screws two;
　　Passengers, 1562 in one class; Crew 678.
　　Note　　An outstanding example of modern cruise ship design incorporating some of *Canberra*'s most prominent design features.

El Djezair　　Cie de Navigation Mixte, France.
　　Built　　　Forges et Chantiers de la Médit, La Seyne, 1952.
　　Specifications
　　GRT, 7608; Length, 132.03m; Beam, 18.07m;
　　Draught, 5.79m; Geared steam turbine, 6,940kw;
　　Speed, 21.50kn; Screws two;
　　Passengers, 344 in two classes plus 650 deck.
　　Note　　The first modern passenger ship to use a tanker-style arrangement of her machinery fully aft.

Empress of Britain Canadian Pacific, Canada.
　　Built　　　John Brown & Co, Clydebank, 1931.
　　Specifications
　　GRT, 42,348; Length, 231.80m; Beam, 29.72m;
　　Draught, 9.75m; Geared steam turbine, 46,600kw;
　　Speed, 24.00kn; Screws, four;
　　Passengers, 1165 in three classes; Crew, 714.
　　Note　　The last ship in the 40,000 GRT range to be built in the United Kingdom prior to *Oriana* and *Canberra*.

Eugenio C Costa Armatori SpA, Italy.
   Built   Cantieri Riuniti dell'Adriatico, Monfalcone, 1966.
   Specifications
GRT, 30,567; Length, 217.39m; Beam, 29.30m; Draught, 8.60m; Geared steam turbine, 40,975kw; Speed, 27.96kn; Screws, two; Passengers, 1636 in three classes; Crew, 424.
   Note   One of the fine Italian ships to adopt many of *Canberra*'s design features.

France CGT (French Line), France.
   Built   Chantiers de l'Atlantique, St Nazaire, 1961.
   Specifications
GRT, 66,348; Length, 315.50m; Beam, 33.70m; Draught, 10.50m; Geared steam turbine, 119,360kw; Speed, 29.00kn; Screws, four; Passengers, 2044 in two classes.
   Note   The last elite North Atlantic express liner, she represents the type of ship Q3 might have been if built.

Marmora P & O, United Kingdom.
   Built   Harland & Wolff, Belfast, 1903.
   Specifications
GRT, 10,509; Length, 166.15m; Beam, 18.29m; Draught, 8.05m; Compound steam, 7,829kw; Speed, 17.00kn; Screws, one; Passengers, 564 in two classes; Crew, 365.
   Note   Sir William Currie used the example of this ship in comparison with *Arcadia* to illustrate the development in passenger shipping during the first half of the twentieth century (*see* Chapter 1).

Maui Matson Navigation Co, United States.
   Built   Union Iron Works, San Francisco, 1917.
   Specifications
GRT, 9,801; Length, 147.52m; Beam, 17.68m; Draught, 12.0m; Geared steam turbine, 1,765kw; Speed, 15.00kn; Screws, two; Passengers, 240 in one class; Crew 140.
   Note   One of the first ocean-going ships with engines aft. Her unusually deep draught bears evidence of her dual role as a passenger and cargo ship.

Normandie CGT (French Line), France.
   Built   Chantiers de l'Atlantique, St Nazaire, 1935.
   Specifications
GRT, 79,280; Length, 313.75m; Beam, 35.90m; Draught, 11.16m; Turbo electric, 160,000kw; Speed, 29.00kn; Screws, four; Passengers, 1972 in three classes; Crew, 1345.
   Note   Her powerful turbo-electric machinery and sophisticated hull form were to some extent the prototype of *Canberra*'s design.

Oceanic Home Lines, Panama.
   Built   Cantieri Riuniti dell'Adriatico, Monfalcone, 1965.
   Specifications
GRT, 27,644; Length, 238.45m; Beam, 29.40m; Draught, 8.58m; Geared steam turbine, 45,073kw; Speed, 26.52kn, Screws, two; Passengers, 1600 in two classes; Crew, 560.
   Note   Another of the Italian ships to adopt many of *Canberra*'s design features.

Queen Elizabeth Cunard Line, United Kingdom.
   Built   John Brown & Co, Clydebank, 1940.
   Specifications
GRT, 83,673; Length, 313.50m; Beam, 36.10m, Draught, 12.04m; Geared steam turbine, 119,296kw; Speed, 28.50kn, Screws, four; Passengers, 2082 in three classes; Crew, 1280.
   Note   Both she and *Queen Mary* were the starting point from which *Queen Elizabeth 2*'s design originated.

Queen Mary Cunard Line, United Kingdom.
   Built   John Brown & Co, Clydebank, 1936.
   Specifications
GRT, 81,235; Length, 310.59m; Beam, 36.10m, Draught, 12.00m; Geared steam turbine, 119,296kw; Speed, 28.50kn, Screws, four; Passengers, 1948 in three classes; Crew, 1260.

Q3 Cunard Line, United Kingdom.
(unbuilt)
   Specifications
GRT 75,000; Length, 301.75m; Beam, 34.75m; Draught, 9,14m; Geared steam turbine; Speed, 29.50kn, Screws four; Passengers, 2270 in three classes.
   Note   What might have turned out to be a larger version of *France* if built.

Royal Viking Sea   Royal Viking Line, Norway.
      Built   Oy Wärtsilä Ab, Helsinki, 1973.
      Specifications
      GRT, 21,897; Length, 177.70m; Beam, 25.20m;
      Draught, 7.45m; Diesel, 13,420kw; Speed,
      21,50kn; Screws two;
      Passengers, 582 in one class; Crew, 323.
      Note   A fine example of one of the modern
                  twenty/twenty-class cruise ships. Her
                  design clearly shows the influence of
                  Queen Elizabeth 2.

Rotterdam   Holland America Line, Netherlands.
      Built   Rotterdamsche Droogdok Mij, 1959.
      Specifications
      GRT, 38,645; Length, 228.10m; Beam, 28.60m;
      Draught, 9.10m; Geared steam turbine, 28,320kw;
      Speed, 20.50kn; Screws two;
      Passengers, 1556 in two classes; Crew 776.
      Note   One of *Canberra*'s most notable con-
                  temporaries, although slightly smal-
                  ler.

Southern Cross   Shaw Savill, United Kingdom.
      Built   Harland & Wolff, Belfast, 1955.
      Specifications
      GRT, 20,204; Length, 184.10m; Beam, 24.40m;
      Draught, 8.00m; Geared steam turbine, 14,711kw;
      Speed 20.00kn; Screws two;
      Passengers, 1160 in one class; Crew 490.
      Note   The first modern British liner with
                  engines aft, she had a significant in-
                  fluence over *Canberra*'s design, hav-
                  ing also been built by Harland &
                  Wolff.

Appendix C

Canberra Route Analysis

Day	Port	Arrive	Depart	To next port Speed	Power	Note
01 Tue	Southampton	–	Midnight			1
				25.42kn	43.04mw (57,000hp)	
05 Sat	Marseilles	0600hrs	1700hrs			2
				26.53	50.88 (68,200)	
08 Tue	Port Said	0500hrs	1100hrs			3
				26.53	50.88 (68,200)	
09 Wed	Suez	0400hrs				
				26.14	48.19 (64,600)	
11 Fri	Aden	0800hrs	1800hrs			4
				26.38	49.83 (66,800)	
15 Tue	Colombo	0600hrs	midnight			5
				25.80	45.73 (61,300)	
21 Mon	Fremantle	0600hrs	1300hrs			
				26.85	53.34 (71,500)	
24 Thu	Melbourne	0900hrs	1700hrs			
				26.50	50.73 (68,000)	
25 Fri	Sydney	1800hrs	–			
28 Mon		–	2100hrs			
				23.37	28.35 (38,000)	
31 Thu	Auckland	0800hrs	midnight			
				25.90	46.48 (62,300)	
38 Wed	Honolulu	0800hrs	1800hrs			
				26.44	50.43 (67,600)	
42 Sun	Vancouver	2000hrs	–			
43 Mon		–	2100hrs			
				25.14	41.03 (55,000)	

Day	Port	Arrive	Depart	To next port Speed	Power	Note
45 Wed	San Francisco	0800hrs	midnight			
				26.31	49.24 (66,000)	
49 Sun	Honolulu	0800hrs	midnight			
				25.22	41.63 (55,800)	
56 Mon	Auckland	0800hrs	1600hrs			
				26.27	48.94 (65,600)	
58 Wed	Sydney	1700hrs	–			
61 Sat		–	1700hrs			
				25.25	41.78 (56,000)	
62 Sun	Melbourne	1900hrs	–			
63 Mon		–	1300hrs			
				26.45	50.43 (67,600)	
66 Thu	Fremantle	0600hrs	1300hrs			
				26.90	53.71 (72,000)	
71 Tue	Colombo	0900hrs	1900hrs			5
				25.70	45.06 (60,400)	
75 Sat	Aden	0400hrs	1400hrs			4
					(70,000)	
77 Mon	Suez	1500hrs	1900hrs			
				26.70	52.22 (70,000)	
78 Tue	Port Said	1000hrs	1500hrs			
				26.80	52.97 (71,000)	
80 Thu	Naples	1000hrs	1900hrs			6
					(71,000)	
84 Mon	Southampton	1000hrs	–			

Notes

1. Embarkation Tuesday. Afternoon trains approx 1320hrs, 1420hrs, 1438hrs and 1643hrs from Waterloo Station to Southampton Docks.
2. Southampton-Marseilles speed must allow adequate margin for winter weather conditions when encountered.
3. Arrival at Port Said must be early enough to join canal convoy.
4. Ten hours is allowed at Aden for bunkering. However, the discharge of water ballast from oil tanks may require additional time here.
5. Aden–Colombo leg, speed makes allowance for adverse weather conditions of the southwest monsoons, subject to the actual speed possible.
6. Naples is substituted for Marseilles on the homeward voyage to avoid an overnight call at the French port.

Acknowledgements

As the author of *British Superliners of the Sixties*, I have often thought of my work as being chiefly that of assembling what has been imparted to me one way or another by others. They are those connected with the designing and building of *Oriana*, *Canberra* and *Queen Elizabeth 2*. Others are involved with running these ships, both at sea and in the offices of their respective owners. There are also the custodians of various printed and graphic marine, technical and architectural records from learned institutions on both sides of the Atlantic. Fellow authors, friends and family members have also contributed their enthusiastic support in a variety of ways. Without all of them, and the many kindnesses that they have shown, this book quite simply could not have been possible.

Canberra was the starting point for this project back in the early 1980s, when I sailed aboard her for the first time. It was the enormous hospitality of her master, Captain Michael V N Bradford CBE, RD and of Commodore Chief Engineer Officer David H Smith which helped to get things rolling in the beginning. Both men gave me the great privilege thoroughly to acquaint myself with their ship and her workings to an extent seldom granted to any passenger. The many hours spent in the engine room and on the bridge afforded me an insight into *Canberra* which was as unique as the ship herself. Later, Captain Bradford, now Director, opened a number of doors for me in P & O head office. I am particularly grateful to him for arranging my unforgettable interview with the line's inimitable Commodore John F Wacher CBE, RD. The Commodore's frank and straightforward remarks about *Canberra* and his own practical comparisons, having actually handled both *Canberra* and *Oriana*, has helped me to keep things in proper perspective. I am inclined to get a bit carried away with my special love of *Canberra*.

Among the other P & O people who have helped in various ways, I am especially indebted to Christina Marsh (née Masser), who is now Commercial Manager for Princess Voyages in London. She has been my primary contact with P & O. Among the many valuable contacts which she helped me to make at P & O are their naval architect David W McKee and group librarian Stephen Rabson. Mr McKee kindly read a large part of the book's technical content, and offered a number of most valuable suggestions, while Mr Rabson has been very helpful with photographs and illustrations. I shall always be most grateful to Christina for making arrangements for me to travel to Gibraltar aboard *Canberra* on her first voyage following the ship's Falklands engagement.

I have also been very lucky to enjoy the enthusiastic and wholehearted support of *Canberra* and *Queen Elizabeth 2*'s principal designers. They have provided me with copies of their own working papers, information from their diaries, lecture notes and various other unpublished items. I had a number of long and most informative discussions with John West BSC, PHD, CENG, FRINA at his office in 1982. My thanks also to Dr West for putting me in touch with his friend and associate, James Davis, who also worked on the planning of *Oriana* and *Canberra*. Sir Hugh Casson KCVO, PRA, RDI, RIBA was kind enough to share with me the only half day that he was in London during my stay in England. His ongoing friendship and interest in the project are most appreciated as are the contacts with his firm, The Casson Conder Partnership. Also to be thanked there are Neville Conder RIBA AA Dip Hons FSIA, Anthony Tugwell RIBA and Pamela Robinson for their help in providing me with information on *Canberra*.

I am also grateful to J Rankin, Publicity Officer of Harland & Wolff, who has answered a number of my technical questions and has offered suggestions on *Canberra*'s coverage from her builders' standpoint.

Unfortunately my research on *Queen Elizabeth 2* did not afford me the opportunity for another visit to England, although I had sailed aboard her in 1979. Nonetheless, her designers, James Gardner CBE, RDI, Dennis Lennon CBE, MC and Michael Inchbald FSIAD have all leant their enthusiastic support via correspondence. Mr Gardner, in particular, has provided a wealth of material from his diary, along with various other notes written especially for me.

My primary contact with Cunard has been through Mrs Susan Alpert, public relations representative of the line's New York office. She has been a long-standing source of information, illustrations and valuable referrals. She managed to dig up some early anonymous handwritten notes on how various things were accomplished in designing the ship.

A great deal of help has come from various notable museums and libraries. I am particularly indebted to Mr Fred M Walker, Curator of Naval Architecture at the National Maritime Museum in Greenwich. He has read the manuscript, and been kind enough to set me straight on a number of the finer points of, for example, transverse stability, as well as some of the background of *Queen Elizabeth 2*'s builders. Mr Walker, along with John Falconer of the museum's Historic Photographs Division have helped greatly with my quest for illustrations, both directly and by referral. My thanks also to Mr J Leather, Assistant Secretary (Technical) of the Royal Institution of Naval Architects for having initiated these contacts and for providing copies of materials from the Institution's own records.

From The University of Glasgow, Mrs Alma Topen provided me with copies of several outstanding construction photos of *Queen Elizabeth 2*. She is to be congratulated for managing to get this done while the archives were being moved to new premises – indeed services rendered beyond the call of duty! Mrs Topen's efforts were matched by Mr Michael Cook and Mrs Andrea Owens from the University of Liverpool, who expeditiously furnished a number of photos and other material despite pressing demands on their resources from within the University itself. I am also most grateful to J Gordon Read, Curator of Archives at the Merseyside Maritime Museum, who has made a number of fine photos from the Stewart Bale Collection available to me.

Although this is a British publication about British liners, it has considerable Canadian content by way of its authorship and the fine facilities available here. Much of the research was done in Montréal at the Blackader-Lauterman Library of McGill University's School of Architecture and at the Canadian Institute for Scientific and Technical Information in Ottawa. I would consider these to be among the finest facilities in the world. It is their rich and extensive collections, which are readily available to the public, modern facilities and courteous staffs that make these institutions so outstanding.

There are numerous others who have helped bring *British Superliners of the Sixties* together. My work colleague Sandra Cassalman has helped out with various aspects of the artwork, including touch-up, mounting of illustrations, etc. Dean Miller from Vancouver has helped keep me up to date with the latest developments at Princess Cruises, for which he is the Canadian public relations representative. My thanks as well to Frank O Braynard, William H

Miller Jr, George C Devol III, Göran Damström, Jan Hedegaard, Peter C Kohler and Klas Brogren. To those whose names I may have inadvertently omitted, my sincere thanks also.

Finally there are two very special people who deserve a great deal of credit. My good friend, neighbour and fellow author, Gordon Turner has been most generous with his own vast collection and his time. His home is a veritable mini National Maritime Museum, holding one of the most extensive private collections known to me. His enthusiasm for this project has led us in many directions such as Strombos funnels and the origins of ships with engines sited aft on the Great Lakes. Ranging from the profound to the occasionally humorous, these exchanges of ideas have been of great benefit. Turner's critical editorial eye, thoroughness and attention to detail, enlightening and indispensable, exasperating at times, have also been of enormous value.

Last, and by no means least, there has been the staunch support of my loving wife, Ingrid. She came on board, so to speak, after we got married in 1986, when I had only about a third of the work done. Apart from her own editorial eye, trained at the Freie Universität, Berlin, and her many practical suggestions on style and content, she has contributed the vital element of some much-needed moral and practical support. I must admit that there have been some very black hours indeed during this project, and it is her support, understanding and patience at these times that made it all work out in the end. Not to be overlooked either are the countless other things such as helping out with German translations, filling in government forms, phoning around for various things, lugging bundles of mail to and from the post office in blistering summer heat. Certainly there is a good wife behind this man's success!

Bibliography

Articles

'A Dual-Purpose Cunarder?', *The Shipping World*, London, 25 October 1961.

'A Ship is an Island', Sir Hugh Casson, *The Architectural Review*, London, June 1969.

'Acoustical Problems in Passenger Ship Design', John West & D G Smart, *Quarterly Transactions of The Institution of Naval Architects'*, London, 1960.

'Britain's Bid for Supremacy on the Pacific', Gardner Soule, *Ships and the Sea*, Milwaukee, USA, 1957.

'Amid Ships', Stephen Garrett, *The Architectural Review*, London, September 1961.

'Architecture Afloat – The *Orion* Sets a New Course', William Tatton Brown, *The Architectural Review*, London, October 1935.

'Canberra – Souvenir number', *Shipping World and*

Shipbuilder, London, June 1961.

'*Canberra* – Souvenir number', *The Shipbuilder and Marine Engine Builder*, London, June 1961.

'Concept to Cunarder', Kenneth Agnew, *The Architectural Review*, London, June 1969.

Design in Ships of Contrasting Function', Robert Spark, *Shipping World and Shipbuilder*, London, October 1969.

'Designed In Italy', Richard Gwyn, *The Toronto Star*, Toronto, 24 April 1988.

Details of the 40,000-ton Orient Liner', *Shipbuilding and Shipping Record*, London, 31 May 1956.

'Don't Spoil the Ship', *Shipbuilding and Shipping Record*, London, 9 June 1960.

'Eugenio C – New Passenger Liner for Italian Owners', *Shipping World and Shipbuilder*, London, November 1966.

'Fahrgastschiff *Canberra*', *Hansa*, Hamburg, 17 November 1961.

'Further Details of 27-knot Orient Liner', *Shipbuilding and Shipping Record*, London, January 17, 1957.

'Holland-America Line's New Flagship', *Sea Breezes*, Liverpool, January, 1960.

'ID – *Canberra*', *The Architectural Review*, London, September 1961, and October 1961.

'Liners of the Past Present and Future on Service East of Suez', Sir William Currie, *Quarterly Transactions of The Institution of Naval Architects*, London, July 1955.

'Oceanic – New Cruise Ship for Home Lines', *Shipping World and Shipbuilder*, London, May 6, 1965.

'Passenger Accommodation Arrangements in the Design of Modern Ships', George G Sharp, *Marine Engineering and Shipping Review*, New York, December, 1947.

'Plastics in Ships' Hull and Accommodation Spaces', John West, *Quarterly Transactions of The Institution of Naval Architects*, London, 1958.

'QE2: Design for Future Trends in World Travel', Kenneth Agnew, *The Architects' Journal*, London, April 9, 1969.

'QE2 interiors', *The Architectural Review*, London, June 1969.

'Queen Elizabeth 2', *The Motor Ship*, London, January 1969

'Queen Elizabeth 2 – A Ship With a Past and a Future', *Shipbuilding and Shipping Record'*, London, 31 January 1969.

'Queen Elizabeth 2 – Some Design Considerations',

Dan Wallace, *Shipping World and Shipbuilder*, London, January 1969.

'Ship Interiors', Ian McCallum, *The Architectural Review*, London, February 1956.

'Some Aspects of Passenger Liner Design', R V Turner, M Harper, D I Moore, *Quarterly Transactions of The Institution of Naval Architects*, London, October 1963.

'Some Thoughts About *Canberra*', C M Squarey, *Shipbuilding and Shipping Record*, London, 1 June 1961.

'Some Thoughts About SS *France*, C M Squarey, *Shipbuilding and Shipping Record*, London, 8 February 1962.

'SS *Canberra*', *The Architects' Journal*, London, 22 June 1961.

'The Interior Design of Passenger Ships', Sir Colin Anderson, *Journal of the Royal Society of Arts*, London, May 1966.

'The P & O-Orient Liner *Oriana*, *Shipbuilding and Shipping Record*, London, December 1, 1960.

'The Passenger Ship – Backward or Forward', *The Architectural Review*, London, November 1960.

'The *Southern Cross* At Work', A C Hardy, *Shipbuilding and Shipping Record*, London, 6 October 1955.

'The Wind Blows Free', J B Boothroyd, *Punch*, London, 31 May 1961.

'Umbau *Queen Elizabeth 2* Auf der Lloyd Werft in nur 179 Tagen', Hansa, Hamburg, Nr 12 1987.

'Whither Cunard?', *Sea Breezes*, Liverpool, September 1960.

'Why Machinery Aft', A C Hardy, *The Shipping World*, London, 7 March 1951.

'534 and All That', *The Architects' Journal*, London, 25 January 1934

Books

Casson, Sir Hugh, *Sir Hugh Casson's Diary*, MacMillan, London, 1982.

Dunn, Laurence, *Passenger Liners*, Adlard Coles Ltd, London, 1961.

Gardner, James, *Elephants in the Attic*, Orbis, London, 1983.

Heskett, John, *Industrial Design*, Thames and Hudson, London, 1980.

Howarth, David and Howarth, Stephen, *The Story of P & O*, Weidenfield & Nicolson, London, 1986.

Hughes, Tom, *The Blue Riband of the Atlantic*, Patrick Stephens Ltd, Cambridge, 1973

Kludas, Arnold, *Die Grossen Passagierschiffe der Welt*, Gerhard Stalling Verlag, Hamburg, 1974.

Landstrom, Bjorn, *The Ship, An Illustrated History*, Doubleday & Co. Inc; New York, 1961.

Maxtone-Graham, John, *The Only Way to Cross*, The Macmillan Company, New York, 1972.

Miller, William H Jr, *The Fabulous Interiors of the Great Ocean Liners*, Dover Publications Inc, New York, 1985.

Morris, Charles F. *Origins, Orient and Oriana*, Teredo Books, Brighton, 1980.

Munro-Smith, R, *Ships and Naval Architecture*, The Institute of Marine Engineers, London, 1973.

Padfield, Peter, *Beneath the House Flag of the P & O*, Hutchinson & Company, London, 1981.

Potter, Neil and Frost, Jack, *QE2, The Authorised Story*, George G. Harrap & Co Ltd, London, 1969.

Robertson, Howard, *Modern Architectural Design*, The Architectural Press, London, 1955.

Rowland, K T, *Steam at Sea*, Praeger Publishers, New York, 1970.

Stevens, Leonard A, *The Elizabeth, Passage of a Queen*, George Allen & Unwin Ltd, London, 1969.

Stirling, James, *James Stirling*, RIBA Drawings Collection (exhibition catalogue), RIBA Publications Ltd, London, 1976.

Talbot, F A, *Steamship Conquest of the World*, William Heinemann, London 1912.

Walker, Fred M, *Song of the Clyde*, Patrick Stephens Limited, Cambridge, 1984.

Warwick, Ronald and Flayhart III, William, *QE2*, W W Norton & Co, London, 1985.

Index

air-light system 72
airconditioning 15, 26,
aircraft 4, 13, 20, 48, 85, 86
alleyways/passageways 46, 63, 72, 74, 75, 78, 84, 116, 136, 137
aluminium structures 24-28, 30, 55, 97, 100,
Apollo 1 112, 129
Arcadia 4, 5, 12, 146
Architects' Journal 79, 81
Architectural Review 21, 22, 79, 81, 82, 87, 88, 118, 122, 125, 128
Assiniboia 42, 146
automobiles 12, 53, 85, 135, 136
axial layouts 84, 133

Bannenberg, Jon 120, 121, 126, 127
Beloe, Elizabeth 124
Bergensfjord 26, 28, 114
Bertelsen, S A 138
Bibby cabins 71, 72
bi-metallic joints 29
Black, Misha 83, 87, 121
Bremen 24, 81, 82
Britannia (royal yacht) 64
Brocklebank, Lady 119
Brocklebank, Sir John 85, 89, 120
bulbous forefoot 48, 51,
bunkering 16, 17, 27
buoyancy 19, 48, 49, 131
Buzas, Stefan 121

cabin layouts 9-10, 71,76, 117-119, 137, 141
camber 89, 103, 104
Campania 9, 10, 106
Canberra 1-3, 12, 13, 16-21, 24, 25, 30, 32, 40-79, 84, 87, 88, 93, 95, 100, 104, 105, 112, 118, 121, 125, 130-136, 138, 139, 141-143, 144
Cantacuzino, Sherban 118, 129
Carmania 10, 12, 105, 146
Caronia 10, 12, 87, 105
Casson Conder Partnership 62, 87
Casson, Sir Hugh 21, 22, 62- 66, 73, 88, 121, 124,
centre of gravity 19, 30, 115
City of Berlin 9, 80
class divisions 114, 116, 132
Conte di Savoia 24, 135
convertible cabins 76
conveyors 54, 55
Council of Industrial Design 119, 120
court cabins 69, 71, 72, 74-76, 118, 135
Cowdrey, Colin 69
Crosby, Fletcher, Forbes 121
Crown Princess 142, 146
Currie, Sir William 4, 12, 13

Davis, Arthur 10, 21, 79-81
davits 31-33, 103, 108, 137
Design Centre 122
Design Research Unit 83, 87
draught 17, 25, 92-94, 96
Dreyfuss, Henry 85, 86
dummy funnels 39, 46
Dunn, Lawrence 111

Eide, Njal 121
El Djezair 2, 42, 44-47, 52, 53, 106, 146
electric propulsion 20, 42, 52-53, 78, 145-146
Empress of Britain 24, 25, 146
engine room casings 34, 35, 62
Eugenio C 130-136, 139, 142, 147
Europa (1930) 24, 81
Europa (1982) 132, 141, 142
Excalibur class 72
expansion joints 26, 27, 55

fairings 39, 60
fibreglass 67, 122, 125, 128, 129
Finnjet 53, 141, 142
fire prevention 20, 43
France 56, 62, 69, 91, 93, 95, 96, 104, 106, 147
Franconia 12
funnel uptakes 39, 45, 84, 97, 139
funnels 3, 35, 39, 46, 55, 84, 89-91, 94-95, 97, 101, 104-111, 131, 135, 139, 140, 142
furniture 21, 81, 83, 87, 126, 129, 135

Gardner, James 22, 62, 89-92, 94, 96, 104-107, 120, 122, 139-141
goal post funnels 46, 56
Grand Hotel style 79-83
grid plan 98
Grung, Gier 140, 141

Hansen, Knud E 136, 138, 139
Harland & Wolff 20, 22, 45, 46, 144, 147, 148
Heaton, Tony 124
Hicks, David 121
Hockney, David 63, 70
holds 34, 35, 48, 53, 54, 136
hull form 2, 10, 19-20, 24, 47, 50-51, 131
hydrodynamics 48-49

Iberia 4, 13
Imperator 24, 30, 74, 80
Inchbald, Michael 121, 124-126, 129, 140
Italia 84, 131, 135-137

John Brown Shipbuilders 20, 96, 145, 146, 147

Kameen, Tom 92
Keewatin 42
Kipling, Rudyard 88
Kloster, Knut 75, 91, 136-138, 141
Kronprinsesse Ingrid 83
Kungsholm (1928) 81, 82
Kungsholm (1966) 117
lateral transporters 53

lavatories 9, 12, 45, 76, 78, 83, 84, 117
Lennon, Dennis 119-122, 124, 127, 128
lifeboats 14-15, 30-32, 56, 100, 105, 131, 134, 142
lifts 41, 54, 62, 76, 103, 132, 133, 140
lighting 9, 10, 63, 65-67, 69, 117, 122, 125, 128, 129
Loewy, Raymond 85, 86
longitudinal strength 19

machinery layout 2, 18-20, 25, 41-49, 51-53, 93, 98, 101, 103, 131, 137, 142
machinery weight 46, 51-53, 93, 96, 101
Magrodomes 66, 132
Marmora 4, 5, 12, 147
Maui 42, 147
Mauretania 10, 46, 89, 112,
McCallum, Ian 82-84, 122
McCarthy, John 63, 65
Mèwes, Charles 10, 21, 80, 81
Michelangelo 106, 130
mock-ups 73, 85, 122
Morris, Charles F 24, 35, 39

National Physical Laboratory 20, 50
nested lifeboats 30-32, 56, 131, 136, 142
noise 41, 42, 45, 52, 76, 77
Normandie 48, 49, 51, 81, 84, 93, 95, 112, 131, 133, 147
nursery cabins 76

O'Rorke, Brian 81, 83
Oakley, Barbara 63, 73, 74
Oceanic 66, 130-136, 139
open plan layouts 34, 64, 65, 133, 136
Orcades 2, 23, 79, 104
Oriana 1-3, 12, 13, 17-20, 23-39, 55, 56, 69, 74, 76, 79, 83, 84, 87, 93, 96-98, 100, 101, 104, 106, 118, 121, 130, 136, 139, 144

PAMETRADA 92, 93, 96, 101
Patrick, Jo 121
perimeter circulation 2, 117, 133, 140
Piano, Renzo 142
portholes (see sidelights)
promenade decks 10, 32-33, 56, 60, 61, 84, 94, 94, 113, 116-117, 123, 125-127, 131, 132, 141, 142
public rooms 10-12, 32-34, 61- 69, 115-117, 121-129, 132- 133, 137, 139, 141, 142

Q3 1, 23, 87, 91, 92, 94-96, 106, 113, 114, 120, 140, 147
Q4 1, 88, 91-95, 114, 115, 117
Queen Elizabeth 12, 13, 40, 79, 84, 87, 96, 100, 103, 104, 147
Queen Elizabeth 2 1-3, 10, 13, 18-20, 22-24, 52, 79, 85, 88, 89-129, 130, 133, 138-143, 145
Queen Mary 12, 34, 49, 79, 81, 84, 89-91, 96, 104, 112, 147

Raffaello 130, 131
railways 6, 12, 9, 62, 73, 76, 86, 89
Rannie, John 22
rationalisation of QE2's layout 115, 117, 126
Rendle, Timothy 62
Rex 24, 135
Rotterdam 27, 46-48, 56, 62, 69, 93, 95, 104, 111, 131, 148
Royal Caribbean Cruise Line 139-141
Royal College of Art 22, 70, 12
Royal Princess 2, 141, 142
Royal Viking Star/Sea/Sky 139- 141, 148
rudders 6, 19, 35, 39

Ryndam   106, 131
safety of life at sea   14, 19-21, 103, 137
Schreiber, Gaby   121
Seaward   141
seaworthiness   4, 5, 103
service trolleys   78
shaft bossings   19
Sharp, George G.   19, 72, 123
sheer   89, 103-104, 142
shell plating   28, 39, 51, 100, 104
sidelights   28, 66, 72, 74, 75, 104, 118
Smallpiece, Sir Basil   107, 110, 120
Spender, Humphrey   63, 65
Southern Cross   20, 22, 45-47, 52, 55, 84, 135, 136, 148
Southward   137, 138, 141
Sovereign of the Seas   134, 141, 142
spiral staircase   62, 64, 65
Spirit of London   137, 138
Squarey, C M   78
stability   16, 18, 19, 21, 30, 48
staircases   10, 47, 62, 63, 64, 65, 89, 127
Star Princess   2, 142
Starward   137, 138
stevedoring   17, 54
Strathaird/Strathnaver   39, 51
strength deck   27, 28, 30, 51, 55, 97, 100

stress-bearing structures   28, 97, 100
Strombos funnels   106
structural webs   20, 27, 30, 97, 100-101, 123, 127
superstructure design   19-21, 26-28, 30, 34, 35, 39, 55- 56, 60, 89, 94-98, 100, 103-105, 131, 132, 142, 143
swimming pools   60, 65, 121, 131-132, 134, 135, 140, 142
Sylvania   4, 12, 87, 94, 101

tankers   40, 42, 44, 52, 131
Tanner, Audrey   63
Teague, Walter   85
Tillberg, Robert   121
toilets (see lavatories)
tonnage   7, 16, 96, 140, 142
transverse thrusters   15, 35, 144, 145
trim 19, 49, 52, 69, 131
Tweedsmuir, Lady   119

Umbria   10, 80
United States   26, 28, 83, 92, 93

Vaterland   30
ventilation   12, 15, 35, 39, 69, 76, 78, 101
VertiVeyor   54

vibration   7, 20, 45, 51, 52, 76
Viceroy of India   51
Vickers Armstrong   15, 24-26, 28, 92, 96, 103
visual illusions   27, 28, 46, 55, 56, 81, 87, 94, 95, 104-107, 122, 127, 129, 132, 142

walk-in cupboards   118
Wallace, Dan   92, 94, 101, 119, 120
Wärtsilä   139, 141
watertight subdivision of hulls   19, 101, 103
weight economy   20, 24, 26, 39, 55, 94, 96
welded hull construction   26
West, John   40-41, 49
Willem Ruys   30, 33
wind tunnel testing   39, 60, 106, 139
windscreens   33, 56, 60, 104
Windsor Castle   87, 121
Wright, John   63, 69, 73

Yarrow-Admiralty Research Department   51
Yourkevitch, Vladimir   10, 48, 49, 131